BOCA *by* MOONLIGHT

BRAD GRABER

ISBN:

Paperback: 978-0-9976042-6-9
eBook: 978-0-9976042-7-6

DEDICATION

To my dad, who taught me everything
I know about Boca Raton.

ACKNOWLEDGEMENTS

To Jules Hucke of Red Pen Refinery who was my editor on this book. I'm grateful for her attention to detail and guidance with storytelling. Every insight made the novel better. To Megan McCullough who created the design and layout for the paperback and ebook. A very humble thank you. To Lance Buckley for his wonderful cover design. And to my friend Ed Marley who was kind enough to read the sections that take place on a golf course. And to Yucel, the photographer who snapped the photo of me on the back cover. Ah, the wonders of Photoshop.

PROLOGUE

December 2018

GEORGE'S EYES FOCUSED on the doctor's lips. The man was talking, but what was he saying? Something about end of life?

Three days had passed since Jeanette, George's wife, had been admitted to the intensive care unit at Boca Raton Regional Hospital. Three days that seemed an eternity as George struggled to come to grips with the reality of Jeanette's condition. She'd been diagnosed a year earlier with non-Hodgkin's lymphoma. At the time, a course of chemotherapy and radiation had promised a remission. But George had learned cancer didn't play by the rules. It had metastasized.

"There are no good options," the doctor said, as if George was consulting on the case. "You should consider removing the ventilator and let nature take its course."

George struggled to remain calm. He was certain Jeanette would rebound. That she'd soon be sitting up, alert, and smiling. He searched the doctor's face for another answer. There had to be more that could be done.

The doctor placed a hand on George's arm. It was a kind gesture. "I'm sorry, Mr. Elden. I know it's a hard decision. But more time won't change the outcome or make it any easier."

George reluctantly agreed to remove the ventilator. But once the doctor stepped away, he had second thoughts. He tried to reassure himself. *This isn't what she'd want. Hooked up to monitors. Unable to breathe on her own.* He examined his wife's ashen face. Was Jeanette in pain? Was she even aware he was there? How had this progressed so quickly?

It'd been a difficult year. Their lives had been consumed by cancer. Between the doctor appointments and multiple hospitalizations, it had been a whirlwind. George was certain Jeanette would pull through. The survival rate was in her favor. He'd done his best to be strong. He'd become her fierce advocate. Her main emotional support. But now, at her bedside, exhaustion overwhelmed him. And still, despite the doctor's words, he wasn't prepared to give up.

George gripped Jeanette's bed rail as he steadied himself. Lately, he'd been suffering from an odd dizziness. Moments of lightheadedness followed by a terrible sense of claustrophobia. He assumed he was run down. Needed a good night's sleep. But after giving the doctor the go-ahead to remove the ventilator, the dizziness was returning with a vengeance. And now, there was a new symptom. A tingling running up and down his arms.

He prayed the moment would pass. *Get a hold of yourself. Take a breath. You'll be okay.*

But he wasn't okay.

A wave of adrenaline surged through George's body. From the top of his head to the bottoms of his feet, he felt suddenly amplified. He needed to move. Run. Jump. Anything to expel the energy.

His heart raced as he pressed a hand to his chest; the pounding was so intense George feared his heart might shatter into a million pieces.

He struggled to breathe as he rushed past the nurses' station. *I need air,* he thought as the panic heightened. Perspiration gathered on his brow and upper lip; his body was in full revolt.

He picked up his pace, footsteps echoing loudly.

A voice called out. "Mr. Elden, please wait. I need to talk to you."

George's stomach clenched as he burst through the doors of the intensive care unit and into the hallway. He spotted an exit sign.

I've got to get out of here.

He leaned forward, willing himself to defy gravity. *One foot in front of the other...*

And then a hard tug on his arm. "Mr. Elden, please don't make me chase after you."

He turned and made eye contact.

A mistake.

A stout woman, clipboard in hand, glared at him. She'd been a warm and engaging presence at the nurses' station. Answering his questions with a smile. George's head throbbed. He read the nurse's name tag. "Whatever you need, Ruby, I'll do it later."

Ruby held out the clipboard and pulled a pen from a coat pocket. Her tone was firm. "I've spoken with the doctor. I'm sorry. But we need your signature before shift change."

"No," George said emphatically, denial kicking in. "She can still..."

Ruby's eyes widened. "Has she squeezed your hand?"

There was a quiver in George's voice. "Not exactly."

Ruby cocked her head. "Mr. Elden, if you'd like, there's a private room where we can talk. I'd be glad to sit with you."

George forced a smile and lied. "Thank you. But, I'm managing."

"Well then, this will only take a moment. These are the consent forms the doctor discussed. We need a signature here, here, and here," she said officiously as she provided small crosses next to the spots where George should sign.

George could no longer contain the emotion. Nervous energy erupted like Mount Vesuvius, hot and destructive as he pushed the clipboard away. His voice was the pleading, angry wail of a wounded animal caught in a trap. "I can't do this now. Don't ask me. Can't you see I need to be alone?"

A family huddled nearby turned and stared.

George caught the eye of the matriarch. "I'm sorry," he mouthed, horrified by the woman's shocked expression.

A few more steps and George's hand connected with the red metal bar marked *Emergency Exit.* With a push, there was a shrill, high-pitched, deafening blare. George covered his ears, afraid his head might explode.

Outside, he took a deep breath. He leaned against the building and shivered in the chilly night air. He wiped away the moisture from his forehead with the back of a hand as the clouds shifted. A bright December moon lit up the Boca night.

Jeanette always loved a moonlit sky. *George, make a wish. It just might come true.*

He'd thought it so silly. "Oh, Jeanette..." he whispered as he finally succumbed. "I wish for one more year. One more month. One more week."

But the moon held no mystical powers. Its presence only marked the end of another long day at the hospital; a foreshadowing of Jeanette's death. She'd soon be gone and he'd be alone. What would come next? How could he move forward? The future—impossible to grasp.

He heard Jeanette's voice. *Living is hard, George. Dying... that's easy.*

– 1 –

Seven Months Later

THE SUNSHINE CHAPEL at The Golden Funeral Home was standing room only. The July crowd packed the pews. "Thanks for saving me a spot," George said to his friend Herbie as he slipped into the aisle seat in the eighth row.

Dressed in a freshly pressed black suit, shoes polished to a high luster, George thought he looked the ideal mourner. The Cary Grant of the Sunshine Chapel, if Cary Grant had been born in New York City, the only child of a mixed marriage between a Sephardic and Ashkenazi Jew.

George stared at the pine box up front that held their friend Willy. "Only the good die young."

"That's why we're still here," Herbie meekly answered, sparse gray curls barely concealing his thinning crown. "God doesn't want us."

George forced a smile as he tugged on his belt. He'd become accustomed to the elastic waistbands of retirement, and the dress pants were uncomfortably tight. He imagined a cobra, struggling to swallow him whole. "God, I hate this place."

Herbie arched a brow. His cherubic face retained the glow of hours spent outdoors, mostly on the golf course. "Who doesn't? Did you see the welcoming committee?"

George shuddered. Two pasty-faced greeters sporting white carnations had stood at the front door directing mourners. "You couldn't miss them. They look like they died last month."

"And no one bothered to tell them," Herbie deadpanned. "If that's their idea of marketing, forget it. I'm never dying."

George understood Herbie. When anything got too emotional, he'd make a joke to cover the pain. And though George played along, he would've preferred to just stay home. Hide from reality. But some things couldn't be avoided. And being back at The Golden Funeral Home, this time for Willy, was one of them.

George glanced about the oak-paneled space with its high ceiling and row upon row of wooden pews, mostly filled by women, younger than George had expected. But then young was a relative term. There was so much plastic surgery in Boca Raton, it was impossible to guess anyone's age. *Let's just say I'm over fifty*, one Boca matron had offered when the topic of age came up. Amused, George had pondered whether seventy had become the new fifty.

George craned his neck. The front row reserved for the family was empty. Typically, family was sequestered with the rabbi for a private viewing. Once the casket was out front, the future was about memory: trying to recall a loved one's voice, the glint in their eye, the warmth of their touch.

George rubbed the soft silk of his black tie. He wished he'd thrown the tie away. Burnt the suit. Why hadn't he?

He remembered when Jeanette had first broached the topic of downsizing. He'd been in the master bath of their Long Island home, shaving, the water running, a towel wrapped around his waist. "Hold on. I can't hear you," he'd shouted, poking his head out the bathroom door with dabs of shaving cream clinging to his cheeks. She'd looked lovely, even with no makeup, her light brown hair in a short bob. She wore a blue robe he'd given her five birthdays earlier.

She was still his girl. The girl he'd met and married when he was twenty-two. The same petite frame. The same hauntingly lovely green eyes.

She stood in front of the open closet taking inventory. She held a notepad and pencil as she looked at him over the top of her reading glasses. She suggested he keep a few sport coats. Not the heavy ones, only the light-colored ones. And a dark suit. The very one he was wearing. The rest would have to go. There'd be limited closet space when George retired from his job as a healthcare administrator and they moved from the four-bedroom house in Garden City, New York, to a Florida condo. She caressed the sleeve of one of his white button-down dress shirts, talking about his clothes as if they were hers.

Herbie nudged George back to reality. "When do you think they'll get this show on the road? And where the hell is Benny?"

George had last seen Benny the day before at breakfast. "He must be in the back. You know he hates funerals."

Red velvet curtains framed Willy's casket, hiding the private reception area where Willy's family would be congregating. George knew it well. He spotted the podium off to the side of the casket where the rabbi would deliver the eulogy. Though it had been seven months, the timbre of the rabbi's high-pitched voice still haunted him.

Jeanette was a loving wife and mother. She adored her family. They were the center of her universe.

George closed his eyes. Time had not diminished the pain. How surprised he'd been by Jeanette's diagnosis. He took a fast breath. *Men always go first,* he thought as he looked about the chapel. *How could she leave me alone?*

Herbie checked his watch. "We're really running late."

George shrugged. "It's not like we're in any rush."

"The family should've been seated by now," Herbie said, rather indignantly. "It's not right to keep everyone waiting."

It was odd. In all that time together on the golf course, Willy must have talked about his family. But George couldn't recall the details.

Herbie's blue eyes sparkled. "Did I tell you about the Realtor I met last month at a Boca open house? She's sitting in the back. A tall redhead. A real knockout." Herbie crossed his legs wide, bumping George's knee. A yellow Nike bobbed on the end of Herbie's ankle.

George's eyes traveled from Herbie's foot to the green Izod collar sticking out of Herbie's blue sport coat. "What the hell are you wearing?"

"Clothes," Herbie snapped.

George raised an eyebrow. "Love the sneakers."

"I have bad feet. You've been on the golf course with me. You know that."

George nodded. Herbie had bad feet, a strained back, and aching knees. Earlier in the week, he'd added a sore shoulder to the lineup. Anything to excuse a poor golf score.

Herbie rubbed his left shoulder as if reading George's mind.

"Maybe you should see a doctor," George suggested.

"I don't need a doctor. Do you know what an orthopedic surgeon charges?"

George shook his head in disbelief. Herbie was a successful pediatrician with junior partners. He had plenty of money. "How about a chiropractor?"

"No thank you. The last time I went, the guy wrapped his arms around me. Then, he pulled me in for a hug."

"That was to adjust your spine," George said dismissively.

Herbie offered a sour expression. "It was like we were on a first date."

George stifled a yawn. He'd heard it all before. Herbie's discomfort at being touched by other men. He'd known Herbie for over forty years, and in all that time, Herbie had loved the ladies. George remembered the night Jeanette's sister had brought Herbie over to introduce him to the family. Jeanette had been so excited. "Judy thinks he's the one," Jeanette enthused as she rushed about the living room of their small Queens apartment, straightening up. "You have to be on your best behavior, George," she warned as she repositioned the sofa pillows. "No teasing Judy. Promise?"

George smiled at the memory.

It had been Jeanette's idea to buy a condo on the grounds of the exclusive Boca Raton Resort & Club. George believed their money would go farther in Weston or Plantation, but Jeanette insisted on the setting. And so George had purchased a two-bedroom unit on the second floor of the first building, right off of the East Palmetto Park Road entrance. The Realtor had promised it was one of the best deals in south Florida. *It'll go fast. You'd better grab it.* George succumbed to the pressure and bought the condo sight unseen. Unfortunately, the balcony overlooked the parking lot of an Intracoastal boat launch. "If you lean over the railing and twist your head to the right, you can see the Intracoastal," George explained to Jeanette as they stood on the balcony the day they'd taken possession.

The disappointment on Jeanette's face still haunted him.

Herbie bumped George's elbow. "Willy would be so happy with the turnout. The place is packed."

George doubted Willy would be happy to be dead.

"You'd think they were serving food or giving away money," Herbie said sarcastically. "Where were all these people when Willy needed them?"

George blushed. He'd rarely visited Willy in the hospital. After Jeanette had died, he'd developed an aversion to hospitals. He nervously jerked a leg forward, kicking the seat in front. A blonde, hair teased to a full fluff, turned around.

"Excuse me," George mumbled.

The blonde held his glance long enough for George to decipher the half-smile as flirting.

Herbie's eyes popped as he caught the blonde's intent. He offered George a toothy grin. "We may not have longevity. But we do have fun."

George ignored Herbie as his eyes settled back on the casket. He tried to imagine Willy lying inside, but all he could see was Jeanette in her final repose. The frozen half-smile. The unnatural makeup with its heavy foundation. Her hair brushed up and away from her face, revealing a forehead she'd always covered with bangs.

"I can't afford to lose another friend," Herbie suddenly said. "We've been friends a long time, George. Promise me you'll never die. You just might be my dearest friend."

"Who are you kidding?" George answered without a moment's thought. "Besides Benny, I'm your only friend."

Sylvia Haddit, seated in the fifteenth row, gasped. Her stacked bracelets jingled as a hand covered her mouth. She'd spotted a familiar face. Well, not exactly a face. It was more the back of a head.

"Oh my God. There he is," Sylvia said, pointing with her chin, feeling the skin under her neck pull taut from the lift she'd undergone the previous summer when the snowbirds left town. Her bright red hair was swept up and off the face to emphasize her high cheekbones. "That's the guy I've been telling you about. Over there."

Eleanor Rifkin tucked a strand of silver-gray hair behind an ear. She stretched her neck. "Where, where? Who?"

Sylvia broke into a smile. "The guy with the curly hair."

"The one with the green collar sticking up?"

Sylvia nodded, blinking hard as a contact lens suctioned.

"Gosh, I hate that look," Eleanor said. "Whoever told men they could do that with a collar?"

"Right," Sylvia agreed as she waited for her tears to lubricate the dry eye. With the next blink, the contact lens shifted. "They might as well wear their underwear over their pants."

The two giggled.

Eleanor tilted her head. "So how do you know him?"

"I showed him a property. He pretended to be interested. Then he made a pass." Sylvia pulled down the hem of her skirt, which barely reached mid-thigh. "You'd think in this day and age of Me Too, he'd know better." She lifted her head as if posing for a photo.

Eleanor crinkled her nose as if catching a whiff of something awful. "Why are we always talking about men? There must be something else to discuss."

"Like the economy or global warming?"

Eleanor sighed. "So, is he cute?"

Sylvia considered. "He's a dust bunny with legs."

"Oh, he's turning around," Eleanor said as the gentleman in the eighth row scanned the room. "Who is he looking for?" she whispered.

The man's eyes flashed back and forth across the chapel and then zeroed in on Eleanor. At once, his baby blues lit up.

"He's bad news. Just bad news," Sylvia warned.

"I think he's adorable," Eleanor said in a soft voice. "He looks like Billy Crystal in *When Harry Met Sally*. But older."

"Much older." Sylvia tugged on a stiff cuff. The dry cleaner had added too much starch.

"So you're not interested in him?"

"I'd rather be drawn and quartered," Sylvia flatly answered as she focused on the sparseness of the hair on the back of the man's head. Why hadn't Herbie acknowledged her? Wasn't she far more attractive than Eleanor? "He's all yours," she said with a flutter of a hand, pretending disgust, yet determined to undermine any adventure Eleanor might have with the eligible suitor.

George winced. The hardness of the wooden bench was beginning to flare his sciatica.

Herbie pulled out a roll of peppermint Life Savers. "It's just like Willy to run late for his own funeral." He popped a mint in his mouth. "How many times have we waited around for that guy? Always late. And such a slow eater. It used to drive me crazy the way he picked at his food. A bite here. A bite there."

After golf, they'd usually eat lunch together. Willy would be the last to order. The friends would exchange impatient glances as the waitress flicked her pen back and forth against the order pad. As soon as Willy opened his mouth, they'd all say in unison, "A tuna on rye, chips, and a sour pickle on the side."

Willy always seemed surprised they knew his order.

There was a sudden rustling from behind the red velvet curtain. A search for an opening. The murmur in the chapel softened as others noticed the movement. Then, a loud thud sounded as the curtain bounced. Someone had fallen. A number of ladies raised their voices in concern.

"What the hell is going on back there?" Herbie asked. "A wrestling match?"

George offered a blank look.

The side door to the right of the velvet curtain flung open. A huge man with a gray beard and wire-rimmed glasses, face bright red, burst forth like a baby chick from its cracked shell. He looked about the chapel. His expression reminded George of his Uncle Morty the day the toilet had overflowed in their Queens apartment. "Morty!" Aunt Clara had yelled. "I told you not to use so much toilet paper."

"It's Benny," Herbie said with a chuckle. "What a dope. He must have come in through the back entrance."

Benny made a beeline to where they were sitting.

"There's no room here," George said as he strained to look up. "You'll have to go to the back."

Benny knelt on one knee in the aisle next to George. His size-thirteen shoes impinged on George's space. "I need to talk with you, George. You too, Herbie."

"What were you doing back there, you clumsy ox?" Herbie said with an impish grin.

"Talking to the rabbi," Benny answered, his tone serious. "He wants to speak to the three of us. Together. Now."

George squinted. "Us? About what?"

Benny placed a hand on George's knee. "I can't talk about it here."

"Are you kidding?" Herbie checked his watch. "He should be doing the service."

"Come on, guys." Benny stood to his full height, his huge mitt using George's knee for leverage.

"Benny!" George cried in pain as he furiously rubbed the joint. "What are you trying to do, kill me?"

The eyes of the chapel occupants followed the three friends as they passed by the casket and through the side door leading to the area behind the velvet curtains.

"What's going on?" George asked as he spotted the rabbi waiting for them.

Rabbi Sherman had the kind of face that firmly held a frown. A gnome in an ill-fitted sport coat, his hair was a kinky gray mess. "So these are the friends," he said, a hand extended in greeting to George and Herbie. "Now you, young man," he addressed George, "look familiar. That's a very handsome face. Like a Jewish movie star. We've met. Am I right?"

"Yes." George nodded, hoping to skip any discussion about Jeanette.

"How do we know each other?" the rabbi asked.

"Jeanette. Jeanette Elden. My wife."

"Oh!" The rabbi's eyes lit up. "She runs the auxiliary at the temple."

"No. You presided over her funeral."

The rabbi scratched his head. "Elden?"

"Yes."

The rabbi searched the floor before looking up with an expression of clarity. "Yes," he said, this time with determination. "She passed of a heart attack."

"No. Cancer."

"Of course. A tragic case."

George nodded, keenly aware that the rabbi had no clue who Jeanette was.

The rabbi rubbed the bridge of his nose. "Now to the sad business at hand." He looked over at Benny. "Have you told them?"

"I didn't think it was appropriate to discuss it in the chapel," Benny confessed.

Rabbi Sherman clasped his hands together. "Well, gentlemen, we have a problem."

George looked at Benny, who then looked at Herbie.

The rabbi cleared his throat. "I've been asked to speak to the family. You see, the check provided to the funeral home has failed to clear. I've assured the Goldenblatts, who own the mortuary, this was just a mistake. I promised, once the family arrived today, we'd clear up this entire matter."

George shrugged. "And the problem is?"

The rabbi waved a hand at the empty reception room. "There's no family. No one showed."

Herbie looked at Benny. "Is this a joke?"

Benny's expression indicated it wasn't.

Herbie's Izod collar seemed to sag. "But you must have met the family. How else could you do the eulogy?"

Rabbi Sherman shook his head. "I'd hoped to meet them today." He pulled on an earlobe. "This is very unusual."

"Now wait," George said. "How can there be no family? Who claimed the body? How did Willy get here? Someone made the arrangements."

Rabbi Sherman knitted his brow. "They were at the hospital, but they seem to be gone now. For some unknown reason, they've skipped the funeral."

"So what does that have to do with us?" Herbie asked.

"We've spoken, your friend and I." The rabbi nodded at Benny. "Before the body will be released for burial, someone needs to pay the bill."

Benny stared at the floor.

"Oh no," Herbie burst forth. "I'm not paying to bury Willy. He's not my responsibility."

Benny put a hand on Herbie's shoulder. "Herbie, come on; there's no other choice. We were his buddies."

"Heck no. Tell them to put him on ice. I'm not doing it."

Benny turned to George. "What do you say?"

George couldn't believe it. How had it come to this? How could Willy's family abandon him? The whole thing seemed crazy. "I don't know what to say," he stammered as he thought about Jeanette's past-due medical bills stacked up on his desk. He'd known health insurance wouldn't cover it all, but he hadn't anticipated the enormity of the out-of-pocket expenses when someone was dying. If only he hadn't taken early retirement. If only he hadn't purchased that cheap policy. If only Jeanette had been old enough for Medicare. He'd already passed many sleepless nights worrying about bill collectors. "I've never known this to happen," George said, blushing as if he'd just admitted he was seriously strapped for cash.

The rabbi agreed. "It's highly unusual. But something needs to be done."

"Okay," George relented, a sinking feeling in his gut. Had he reached his credit limit? Was he about to be publicly humiliated? "But only if we split the cost three ways." He pointed at Herbie.

Benny pulled Herbie in close. A huge hand tightly grasped Herbie's right shoulder.

Herbie squirmed. "Jesus, that's my bad shoulder. Take it easy."

George could have sworn the left shoulder was the problem.

"Are we all set?" the rabbi asked.

George nodded.

Herbie nodded.

Benny smiled.

"Good then," the rabbi said. "I'll be back in a moment. Get those credit cards ready, boys," he called out as he disappeared through a door leading to the funeral home's back hallway. "We have a funeral today!"

– 2 –

ELEANOR RIFKIN HAD no idea what she was doing at Willy Krause's funeral. *This is crazy,* she thought as she looked about the crowded chapel. Why had she allowed Sylvia to drag her to a funeral on a perfectly lovely July morning? What was it about Sylvia? Why did she always seem to get her way?

Eleanor remembered the first day they'd met. It was the beginning of February, and Sylvia, acting as Eleanor's Realtor, was showing her a condo. Eleanor had been referred to Sylvia by a friend of a friend. Someone she'd barely known back in New York City. And as she and Sylvia admired the view from the fourth-floor terrace, Eleanor struggled to remember the name of the person who had actually referred Sylvia. "This place has one of the best views in Boca Raton," Sylvia had said when she'd described the 4,000-square-foot condo on the grounds of the exclusive Boca Raton Resort & Club. "Completely redone. All you need to do is move in."

Joel, her late husband, had hoped one day to retire to Boca Raton. He loved the Boca Raton Resort & Club. And so Eleanor booked a room at the hotel as she did her condo shopping. But it all seemed so grand. Maybe, too grand.

"The building is very private," Sylvia emphasized. "Very discriminating," she said with a wink as her voice dropped an octave. "Only the best people. People with money. Very conservative."

Eleanor cringed. She'd always been a fierce liberal. Donating to democratic causes. Supporting fundraisers for organizations that helped children in third-world countries. Marching for Planned Parenthood. Being described as discriminating was oddly offensive—yet the view from the terrace *was* breathtaking, the interior of the condo divine. But did she want to be part of an exclusive club? Would she fit in? And what did that mean in terms of the other members?

Eleanor's silver bangs flapped in the breeze as she struggled with Sylvia's inference. She opted to ignore the comment. "I should be able to see the sunrise from this east-facing terrace."

"Absolutely," Sylvia assured her. "It's gorgeous for enjoying a cup of coffee in the morning or a glass of wine at dusk."

Eleanor thought Joel would have loved it.

"Are you okay?" Sylvia asked as if reading Eleanor's mind. "You seem sad. There's another unit on the other side of the building, but there's no water view."

A boy walking his dog along the Intracoastal captured Eleanor's attention. The white dog crisscrossed the path as if searching for the best smell. *Innocent and peaceful,* Eleanor thought as she took in the view below.

"Whatever's wrong, we can fix it," Sylvia said with clear determination to close the deal.

Eleanor refocused. Did she really want to buy the condo? She wasn't quite sure.

Sylvia looped a finger around a pearl necklace. "I always say, 'Whatever you don't like is ten percent off the asking price.'"

Eleanor scrunched her face. "I'm concerned it's too big."

Sylvia gasped. "Too big?"

"It's just me," Eleanor whispered, suddenly ashamed of the excess the condo represented.

Sylvia reacted as if Eleanor had blasphemed. She reached for Eleanor's hand, giving it a gentle tug. "Just you? Well, you matter. You deserve this."

Eleanor took a deep breath. The ocean air was invigorating. The breeze refreshing.

"Just remember," Sylvia added, "the square footage is really a reflection of the size of the rooms and that huge master bath. And the walk-in closet. You could die from that closet!"

Eleanor wondered if she had enough clothes to even fill a corner of it.

"And the grand entryway." Sylvia's green eyes lit up like she'd just won the lottery. "So very impressive. And with three bedrooms, you have plenty of space for company and an extra room just for you. You told me that you paint. Then one bedroom will be your craft room. You can set up an easel. And with the morning light, it'll be breathtaking."

Eleanor did like the idea of getting back to painting.

"And that library is just perfect for reading or watching television. I think the light maple paneling is simply gorgeous. Did you see the ceiling with those beams?"

Eleanor nodded.

"And besides," Sylvia rambled on, "you're not buying a condo. You're buying a lifestyle. A community. You do golf."

"My husband did." Eleanor gripped the terrace handrail and leaned forward to take in the full view of the Intracoastal. A white vessel passed by. The captain looked up and waved. Eleanor waved back. "Joel would have loved all this. But no. I don't golf. Will that make it difficult to meet people?"

Sylvia's right eye twitched. "Not for the ladies. There's always mahjong."

Eleanor didn't play mahjong. She found it too complicated.

"Cards? You play bridge."

Eleanor nodded, even though she didn't. Card games always seemed like such a waste of time. Besides, she found cards too stressful. In truth, she'd never considered herself much of a woman's woman. Women's talk bored her. Mostly because it required her to pay attention to the details of the lives of other women. It all seemed so silly when she had Joel, her husband and best friend.

"You'll join the club," Sylvia suggested. "That'll give you access to the amenities of the hotel and the beach club. And there's afternoon tea every day at the hotel. You'll informally mingle with the other residents in a private room. Of course, not everyone is here unless we're in season. But your grandchildren will love the little cakes they serve. And it's all very informal. But tasteful. You can come in jeans or shorts, but not a bathing suit."

Eleanor nodded. She saw no reason to explain that grandchildren would not be visiting. "I love the wraparound terrace." She walked to the south side of the terrace with its long view of the Intracoastal and ocean.

"Yes, it's lovely," Sylvia agreed, close behind. "Shall we make an offer?"

Eleanor had always relied on Joel to handle the business side of life. Now, she was on her own. But there was a certain thrill in taking control. Making her own decisions. "Yes," she said, proud to have secured the Realtor and found the property. "Let's do that."

"Wonderful." Sylvia checked her iPhone. "How about we lunch at the hotel? It's getting close to noon."

Eleanor's hand found its way to her stomach. Earlier that morning, before a full-length mirror, she'd decided she was too plump. She'd vowed to drop five pounds, the most reasonable amount for her tiny frame. She'd hoped to skip lunch, fasting a full twelve hours from breakfast until dinner.

She'd heard fasting could kick the body's metabolism into gear. "I'm afraid I'm going to have to pass." Eleanor focused on Sylvia's trim figure. "Tell me. How do you stay so slim? Just one cookie and the fat settles into my thighs for the duration. And please don't tell me it's genetics."

"Oh, but it is," Sylvia insisted as a strong breeze kicked up. Her meticulously coiffed red mane remained frozen in place. "I eat whatever I want."

Eleanor had always wanted to be tall and thin like Sylvia. Clothes looked so much better on a tall woman, she'd surmised from her college days at Columbia University. And like some things from youth she'd held onto for far too long, Eleanor remained convinced her body was of disappointing proportions. No one wants to be five foot one when they can be five seven. Of that, she was absolutely certain.

"At the very least, let me show you the private beach club," Sylvia insisted.

Eleanor regretted giving in. As they walked toward the boat dock that shuttled guests from the hotel to the resort's private beach, Eleanor's hair blew freely in the wind, and she wished she'd worn a hat. Compared to Sylvia's bright yellow form-fitted dress and high heels, Eleanor felt like a disheveled hobo in jeans, a white peasant blouse, and red Keds. She should've dressed more fashionably.

"So, you're a widow. How long were you married?" Sylvia asked as they sat together on a bench waiting for the shuttle.

Any discussion of marriage was painful. She'd given up hopes of a medical career to work as a secretary, supporting Joel through law school. Eventually, she'd stay home to raise a family. But now her sons were adults and she was alone. "Thirty-six years."

"Well, good for you," Sylvia said, astonishment on her face. "He must have been quite something."

Eleanor wondered if Sylvia was being condescending. She looked down at the chipped polish on her bare ring finger. "He was."

Sylvia removed her sunglasses and squinted. "And you've only been married once?"

"Only once." A sudden gust came up. Eleanor pressed her blouse down, certain she looked like a waif in a storm.

Sylvia assumed a girlish grin as she leaned in, seemingly eager for details about Eleanor's life. "It must have been nice to be with one man for all those years."

"It was." Eleanor studied Sylvia's face, wondering if she'd had work done. There wasn't a line anywhere. And Sylvia had to be Eleanor's age or older. Definitely older. Probably in her late sixties.

Sylvia pulled back as if reading Eleanor's glance. "Where is that darn boat?" she complained as she turned away.

The moment for Eleanor to share the deep, dark secrets of her life had thankfully passed. The two women sat in silence until Sylvia picked up the slack.

"We have a lot of second and third marriages here. Lots of widows. And quite a few unmarried couples." Sylvia lifted her head and stuck out her chin. "Those are the women I worry about the most. You can live with a man for years, but when he dies, if you're not married, the estate always goes to the family. I've known some occasions when a man's children have kicked the girlfriend out. What protection does a woman have? Of course, some women have their own money. The men don't tend to outlive us, but believe me, when it comes to money, families can be merciless."

Eleanor pondered what to say. "Well, I think if you love someone, you should take care of them."

Sylvia smirked. "You'd think so. But it doesn't always happen. You have to protect yourself. Especially if you're the one without money. But then, that doesn't apply to you."

Eleanor didn't like being classified based on her financial holdings. "Well, I have no intention of remarrying," she blithely answered.

"That's refreshing. Most women in Boca think it's never too early to start hunting for their next husband." The shuttle approached. The loud motor drowned out any further conversation.

A blond youth in white sailor pants and a fitted blue T-shirt waved hello as he stepped off the boat and tied a thick rope about the dock's cleat.

"This a private shuttle?" Eleanor asked.

"It's for residents who join the club and hotel guests. They can rent cabanas, but only if they're available."

The youth took Sylvia's hand, helping to steady her as she stepped onto the motorboat.

"He's awfully sweet," Eleanor said once seated next to Sylvia. The young man reminded her of a nephew back in New York City. She wondered what had become of him. It'd been years since she'd been in touch with her family.

"Isn't he?" Sylvia answered with a coquettish grin. "I could eat him up."

"He's awfully young," Eleanor said, unsettled by Sylvia's bold manner.

Sylvia stared at the young man's rear end as he untied the rope anchoring the motorboat to the dock. "Maybe for you, but I don't like to focus on age."

Eleanor was certain the young man had no idea Sylvia was ogling him. What might he think? Would he jump overboard? The very thought made Eleanor cringe. She held tight to the bottom of the seat as the motorboat made a short trip up the Intracoastal to the private beach club. Eleanor's stomach fluttered with each jerking motion while Sylvia chatted away.

"The beach club serves a lovely lunch. If I see some of the regulars, I'll introduce you."

Eleanor bit her lip. "Please don't." She didn't want to meet anyone the way she was dressed. "And I'm really not hungry."

"Well, at least let me buy you a cup of coffee."

Eleanor realized that once at the beach club, there'd be no escaping Sylvia. She'd be trapped. "I'm really not feeling well," she said as Sylvia stepped off the motorboat and onto the club's dock. "I should get back to the hotel and lie down."

Sylvia's mouth hung open as the young man untied the boat and stepped back in.

"Please proceed with the offer and let me know how it goes," Eleanor called out as Sylvia and the dock receded in the distance.

Eleanor moved into the condo the second week in April. All seemed fine at first, until the night she awoke in a cold sweat. She instinctively reached over, running a hand across Joel's side of the bed. It had been a year since Joel had died. She still couldn't get the image out of her head. Joel slumped in the shower, water running over his naked form. He'd said that morning he didn't feel well. She should have insisted he go to the emergency room. But then, how could she possibly have known it wasn't indigestion? Joel always had indigestion.

"It wasn't just his heart," the doctor explained. "When he fell, he hit his head, causing a brain bleed."

Eleanor rolled over. She didn't want to think about it anymore. Isn't that why she'd left New York City? Bought the new condo? Stayed at the hotel until the condo's closing date? She'd hoped a change of scenery might help her forget.

And it had for a while.

Unpacking, decorating, doing all the things to make the condo her own. Her home. And yet, could it ever truly be a home? A home without Joel.

Eleanor sat up in bed. Why, after all their years together, did the morning of Joel's death have to be her final memory of him? What about the life they'd shared? The love, travel, fabulous meals. And the laughter. How sad that those memories had been replaced by the events of that horrible last morning.

I should have…

Her thoughts lingered on how she might have intervened to change the outcome. Controlled the situation. Managed it all so that Joel would still be with her. Lying in bed. Snoring gently so she could nudge him to turn over.

The clock read three a.m. She lay back down and pulled the covers under her chin as she tried to relax. All she could hear was the silence. The indisputable emptiness of a life without Joel.

She couldn't go on like this. But she was uncertain how to change any of it. Perhaps this was how it would end. All alone. No reason to get up in the morning. No purpose.

A sadness hugged her tightly as she began to cry. Tears shed not over her last memory of Joel, but for the prospect of her future. Whatever that might be.

Boca mornings proved irresistible. Eleanor nestled into a lounge chair on the terrace in faded sweats. The days of April might be a bit warm, but the mornings were perfect. She sipped coffee as the sun broke on the horizon. The cry of the seagulls, lonely and sad, were her only company in the crisp morning air. She held the mug tightly, clinging to the warmth of the hot liquid, as her thoughts drifted to the first time she'd seen Joel.

A crowded, off-campus bar. They'd brushed up against each other in passing. He'd looked down at her, smiled, and stepped aside. The next day, she spotted him at the library. She'd pretended to be reading. She could still conjure the expression on Joel's face when their eyes met that second time. The dark-haired boy, tall and lean in his worn denim shirt opened at the neck, revealing a tuft of black hair. His smile, slightly crooked, evoked a confidence that he could have anything he wanted, anytime. When he walked up to Eleanor, she held her breath.

Then his gaze.

"What are you reading?" he'd asked with a smirk as he slid into the seat next to her, an elbow on the table as he slouched sideways, long legs stretched out by her feet.

"Nothing." She blushed at her petulant response to such a simple question.

He lifted the scientific journal. "This is an article about the blood-brain barrier," he read aloud with surprise. "You're a biology major?"

"Yes." She examined his angular face. Admired the cleft in his strong chin. Her heart beat rapidly.

"Wow. A pretty girl like you? Intelligent too. Do you want to be a doctor?"

She looked down. She hadn't quite decided yet.

He sensed her discomfort. He extended a hand. "I'm Jam."

She burst out laughing. "Jam!"

"I know," he admitted, hand still extended. "It's strange."

She placed her hand in his. It was warm. "How did you get that name?" A smile on her lips.

"I play the sax."

She shook her head, still unclear as to the origin of the nickname.

"I have trouble sticking to the sheet music," he confided, brows raised. "So the fellas gave me the name." A strand of hair fell across his brow.

She nodded. "Do you always do things your own way?"

"Not always," he admitted. "When I meet a pretty girl, I'm very flexible."

She rolled her eyes. "Does that line ever work?"

"You tell me," he said with a laugh. "Sorry. I couldn't help myself. Still, I think we should get to know each other."

Oddly, she felt as if she already knew him. As if she could anticipate what he was about to say. "Why?" she asked, teasingly.

His eyes narrowed. He hesitated. "Because…"

"Oh," she answered. "There's a good reason."

He picked up her journal and started to read aloud. "'The blood-brain barrier is a semi-permeable border that protects the brain from—'"

She pushed the journal away. "What are you doing?"

"I wasn't being clear. So, I thought maybe I should try communicating in a language you were certain to understand. Something medical."

She took the journal back. "You think you're pretty cute, don't you?"

He offered a self-effacing grin. "I, myself, prefer the sports section. Could I convince you of my worth by reading game scores?"

"No. But you can take me to a basketball game Friday night at the gym."

He rubbed the stubble on his chin. "Are you asking me out on a date?"

She suddenly felt foolish. "I just thought it could be a scientific experiment."

"Something like the blood-brain barrier?"

"Yes." She smiled, admiring the flecks in his hazel eyes. "But I'm never going to call you Jam."

He stood up. "Friday then. I'll meet you in front of the library at five. We can grab a bite."

She giggled. "Don't you want to know my name?"

He blushed. "I don't know your name."

"Eleanor. Eleanor Hart."

"Eleanor." A cocky smirk graced his lips. "Nice to meet you. I'm Joel Rifkin."

By the end of April, Sylvia began to reach out with regular phone calls, encouraging Eleanor to tap into the social side of Boca Raton.

"I'm really a homebody," Eleanor explained as she put her phone on speaker. "I appreciate the invite, but I'd prefer to pass."

"Now don't be silly," Sylvia had pressed. "It'll be good for you. You're not going to meet anyone sitting at home."

Of course, Sylvia was right. But did Eleanor really want to meet anyone? What was the point? There could never be another Joel.

"We'll just have one drink," Sylvia promised. "Catch up. Share a little gossip. And besides, you haven't been to the hotel bar yet. You might even have a nice time."

"I don't know. You want to meet men. I'm really not interested."

"Do you honestly think the bar will be full of men waiting for our arrival? Like we're God's gift of womanhood. You can't plan these things. It's not like shopping at Saks and finding the perfect dress. It's just a drink in a public place. You're making too much out of it."

Eleanor hemmed and hawed.

"You're still an attractive woman," Sylvia had said with all the coded intent such statements are meant to convey. And yet Eleanor wasn't so sure. Some women, like Sylvia, carried their age with elegance and style. Perfect posture and beautifully dressed. Eleanor thought of herself as earthy. Less fuss and bother. More intellectual than physical.

Eleanor was no match for Sylvia's persistence. She finally relented, concluding that perhaps Sylvia was right. What harm could it do?

That afternoon, before leaving to meet Sylvia, Eleanor turned the bathroom dimmer to bright and checked her makeup. Was her lipstick too red? Did her foundation blend? She swiveled her head back and forth, stretching her neck to reveal every angle.

Eleanor forced a smile at her reflection, and still, she looked frightened. Unsettled. Was it the expression in her eyes? The fierce gaze? Or the way her mouth seemed frozen in a permanent grimace? She wasn't quite sure, but knew it wasn't her best look. At least she hoped not. And as she tried to shift expressions, soften her mouth and eyes, each successive mask seemed forced and unnatural.

Eleanor's mind jumped to sex as she ran a hand over her waist. What if she did eventually meet a man? Who the hell wanted to get undressed in front of a stranger? She shuddered at the mere thought. To calm her nerves, she switched gears: *Now don't get ahead of yourself. It's just a drink in a bar with a girlfriend.*

But was Sylvia a girlfriend?

Eleanor had no illusions. Sylvia had been kind, but she remained very much the Realtor. A relationship based on commerce. Mostly, Sylvia's commission. Eleanor wondered if Sylvia thought she'd be a source of future business referrals. But then, Eleanor dismissed the thought. Since leaving New York City, she'd been alone. Perhaps Sylvia simply felt sorry for her.

Eleanor was suddenly uncomfortable. She didn't like the thought of anyone pitying her. But there was no reason to focus on all that. She gave her hair a final pat. She'd done what she had to do. One life traded for another.

She straightened her shoulders.

Well, dear, you're no spring chicken.

It was her mother's favorite expression. And now, it had come true. When had life caught up with her? Only yesterday she was a young mother. Now, she hardly recognized herself. When had she become the grandmotherly type? A younger, smarter version of her own grandmother, but a grandmother, nonetheless.

Eleanor caught sight of Sylvia at the hotel's Palm Court Bar. *Just one drink*, she told herself. And if she didn't want to stay, she could always leave.

"Hey, you," Sylvia said with enormous frivolity, cocktail in hand as Eleanor approached. She was smartly dressed in a white spaghetti-strap dress that showed off her tanned shoulders. "Now isn't this nice?"

Designed in the style of an Italian piazza, the brightly colored indoor courtyard bar covered by a glass ceiling, provided the natural beauty of a garden escape amid the hotel's elegant ambiance. As Eleanor slipped onto a barstool next to Sylvia, she wondered if Sylvia was already tipsy. After all, there wasn't much to celebrate. It was just another day. Nothing special. And the Palm Court was practically empty, except for a corner table of three men in shorts and baseball hats. What was all the fuss about? And why had she been so nervous to meet Sylvia?

"It's early yet," Sylvia said as if reading Eleanor's mind. "In another thirty minutes, the place will be crawling with men."

"Really? That's hard to imagine."

"It's Wednesday afternoon. The men will be back from eighteen holes and need a little libation." Sylvia offered a mischievous smile.

Eleanor ordered a vodka tonic. "It's silly, sitting here, dressed up like a man trap." She noticed the three hairy-legged gentlemen across the room sipping beers. "You'd think those guys could have at least put on pants."

Sylvia stole a glance over her shoulder. "Those three? They're wearing collared shirts and dress shorts. No jeans. Besides, who cares what they're wearing?" Sylvia purred. "They have money."

"Money?" Eleanor thought they looked like bums. "How could you know that?"

"Darling, this is an exclusive hotel in an exclusive town. They don't just let anyone in. Have you seen the prices of the drinks? Besides, there are plenty of public golf courses. You don't pay for membership here unless you can afford it. And like it or not, those men can afford it."

"I've told you, Sylvia. I don't need a man to support me."

Sylvia was aghast. "Of course not. But you don't want someone living off of you. You need to meet a man who can take care of himself financially."

"Really, Sylvia." Eleanor reached for the salted nuts. "You've given this way too much thought. There must be an easier way to meet someone."

"Oh, there is. The Internet. But God only knows who you'll dig up. No, you have to meet a man where he lives. Where he drinks. Where he golfs!"

Eleanor doubted a bar was the right setting. "I don't know. It's so…" she stammered, uncertain how to complete the thought. "Awful."

"Or, you have to have friends. And dear, forgive me, but you seem to have none." Sylvia straightened up as if excellent posture proved her point.

Eleanor brought a hand to her throat. "Honestly, Sylvia," was all she could manage as the blood rushed to her face.

Sylvia softened her tone. "I'm not saying this to hurt you. But really. How can you have a social life without friends? You can't."

"I've just never been great at making friends," Eleanor admitted.

"Well, it's high time that changed. All you need to do is put forth a bit of effort. And in the meantime, you need to be seen. No one wants to be friends with someone who is alone."

Sylvia's very assertion was illogical. If Eleanor was alone, there'd be no one to object.

Sylvia persisted. "People are going to assume something is terribly wrong with you. You need to project an aura of confidence. Fun. You can't do that unless there are other people around."

Eleanor sighed. She'd much prefer to read a good Ken Follett novel than bother with all this nonsense. Hadn't she earned the right to spend her time any way she chose? And yet, there was a persistent voice nagging at her. Being alone was like living in purgatory. Joel may be gone, but her life wasn't over. At least, not yet. There had to be a reason why she was still here.

"Trust me, dear." Sylvia raised a martini glass in the air. "I know what I'm talking about. But then, I always know what I'm talking about."

Eleanor wasn't so sure. What made Sylvia such an expert? She, too, was alone.

"So tell me about your life, Sylvia," Eleanor said between sips of her cocktail. "You seem to know all about what I need. But I know nothing about you. What's your story?"

"Story," Sylvia repeated. "Like there's a story."

"Yes," Eleanor pressed. "I'm all ears."

Sylvia tilted her head. Her expression shifted from ebullient to thoughtful. "Well, there isn't much to tell. I'm not much different than you, except I've never been married."

"Really." Eleanor leaned in. "That's a big difference. And yet, you profess to know everything about men."

Sylvia offered an imperious look. "Not just men. Clients. Remember, I'm a Realtor. We specialize in customer service. Knowing what our clients need."

Eleanor didn't care for Sylvia's air of superiority. "So you think you know what's best for me. Someone you hardly know."

"I try." Sylvia took another sip of her drink. "Remember, it's my job to anticipate. To stay ahead of the curve."

Eleanor picked up a nut from a side dish on the bar and rolled it between her fingertips. "What if I told you that you have no clue about me? That I enjoy my alone time. I'm happy, alone."

"Well then," Sylvia smirked, "I wouldn't believe you. I'd think you were lying. Darling, there's no shame in needing help. We all do from time to time."

Eleanor locked eyes with Sylvia. "Do we? And who helps you?"

"Who indeed?" Sylvia smiled as she dabbed the corners of her mouth with a cocktail napkin. "My friends. The ladies who have used me as a Realtor. I have gads of friends. Rooms and rooms of friends. Women in South Florida who have shared their deepest secrets and relied on me to hide their intrigues."

Eleanor understood. "So you collect people."

Sylvia nonchalantly waved a hand. "Well, I wouldn't put it that way."

"Then how would you put it?"

"I befriend them. Counsel them. I'm there when they need me."

Eleanor suddenly felt queasy. "Gathering up their secrets."

Sylvia's eyes glowed. "A few here and there."

Eleanor took a final sip of her drink. "Well, I hate to disappoint you, Sylvia, but I won't be one of your collectibles.

I don't tell tales. If we were friends, I'd expect to know as much about you as you'd know about me."

Sylvia's posture softened. "I see."

Eleanor stood up and straightened her skirt. "So, when you decide to open up about your life, please feel free to call me," she said with a smile.

"You know," Sylvia said, "you're not the first woman to think me contemptible."

Eleanor imagined not.

"But this is a different world, our Boca Raton. This town is about who you know and what you know."

"It sounds lonely. Very lonely," Eleanor answered with sudden empathy. Perhaps she and Sylvia had more in common than she'd realized. "It must be difficult to always feel as if you can't let your guard down."

Loneliness has a way of changing one's perspective, and given time, Eleanor accepted other invitations from Sylvia. The month of May passed easily as the two connected over lunch, cocktails, and shopping. And then, Sylvia invited Eleanor to attend a symposium of some sort in early June at the hotel. Sylvia had promised Eleanor would find it informative.

A tall woman in a wide-brimmed hat with a red sash stood at the front of the conference room. Behind her, a sign recognized June as National Cancer Survivor Month. "Ladies, please," she said in a commanding voice, a gavel in one hand, a piece of paper in the other. "Let's call this meeting to order."

It was a warm Tuesday morning and the air conditioning was cranked up so high, Eleanor regretted not wearing a sweater. Women of all ages, dressed in red to support the CancerOne mission, filled the large ballroom. Eleanor looked about the sea of tables covered in white linen with centerpieces of red roses. Women engaged in chitchat, oblivious to the speaker.

"This is a wonderful organization," Sylvia whispered in Eleanor's ear. "A great cause to get involved with to meet other women. Serious women."

From the look of the crowd, everyone in Boca Raton had a connection to the disease. Eleanor tried to focus but was overcome with emotion. She stifled a nervous yawn as she wondered if her time might be better spent volunteering elsewhere. "I'm not sure, Sylvia. I don't know anything about cancer," Eleanor lied.

"You don't need to. Many of us just want to give our time and attention to a worthy charity. And to network. This is one of the best places to meet the right people."

Eleanor clasped her hands in her lap. Her fingers bound tightly together as she focused on the speaker.

The gavel banged twice. "Ladies, ladies...please."

Slowly the room came to order as heads turned to face the front. Eleanor too shifted her view, trying not to focus on the women with headscarves.

"For those of you who don't know me, my story is much like yours." The speaker paused for dramatic effect. "When I was forty, a mammogram revealed an irregularity in my left breast. My doctor told me it was probably nothing to worry about. But when a man tells you not to worry, *you know trouble is brewing*."

There was a nervous titter in the audience.

"And so, I took matters into my own hands. I found the best darn surgeon in the country. She happened to be a woman." There was a long pause as the speaker looked about the room. "This physician understood what was at stake with my health and well-being. She respected me and was someone I respected. She's a brilliant oncologist, a trusted friend, and someone I know you'll all enjoy hearing from today."

The woman sitting on the other side of Eleanor leaned in close and pointed to the center of the table. "Could you please pass that pamphlet?" She'd arrived late and Eleanor had only momentarily acknowledged her presence. As the woman scanned the pamphlet, Eleanor noticed the sallowness of her skin. The absence of eyebrows and eyelashes. She could see the perspiration on her brow. The woman looked up and caught Eleanor staring. She smiled. A defiant smile. The eyes of a brave warrior.

"Cancer has nothing to do with courage," Eleanor's mother had announced during her fifth week of chemotherapy for ovarian cancer. It had been ten years since she'd passed, and still Eleanor could hear her mother's voice. Clear and decisive. "No one wants to be sick. But it happens. And what choice do you have? You can't curl up into a ball and roll away. Not if you want to live. You have to fight the urge to give up. It's a survival instinct. It's anger at the indignity we suffer at the mercy of this goddamn disease."

Jessie Hart had been one tough cookie.

Sitting beside Jessie's hospital bed, Eleanor had teared up as she reached for her mother's hand.

"I'm not dead yet," Jessie scolded her daughter as she pulled her hand away. "Today is a good day. I'm alive and I'm here with you. Save those tears for the funeral. Which by the way," Jessie said with a howl of laughter, "has been canceled due to sunshine."

Jessie had never been the kind of mother for soft hugs and adorations. She'd demanded respect and obedience, even from her adult daughter. With the clock running down, Eleanor itched for a real connection. For an intimacy that perhaps Jessie's illness might allow them to share. "Mom, I just want you to know I love you."

But Jessie wouldn't abide sentimentality. "Honestly, Eleanor. The look in your eyes is scaring the shit out of me. How about if we don't focus on the cancer? It's already occupying too much of my life."

"I don't know what I'll do..." Eleanor started to say, but she couldn't finish.

Jessie's eyes moistened as she took a deep breath. "What's there to do? We're born, we die. Hopefully in between we have a good life. Now," she said, straightening up in bed, "I didn't raise you to fall apart. You're a smart college girl. Behave like one."

Eleanor objected. "What does being a college graduate have to do with this?"

"You should know better. And when I'm gone, you won't be alone. There's Joel and the boys."

Eleanor nodded. A tear escaped.

"Now stop it," Jessie warned. "No crying. There's nothing to be sad about. I've had my life. I've enjoyed every moment. And to be honest, ever since Dad died, I've been terribly lonely. Oh, there have been friends and family, but when you climb into bed at night, you're alone." Jessie looked away for a moment as she gathered her thoughts. "It's just no fun. And I've been thinking. This could be a great adventure. It could be just what the doctor ordered!"

Eleanor stifled a laugh. Leave it to her mother to say the most absurd thing at such a serious moment.

"You listen to me, young lady. I don't want all this drama." Jessie flashed a smile. "I want my big, strong daughter to show me she's going to be just fine."

Eleanor nodded.

"No. You have to say it."

Eleanor resisted.

"Do as I say," Jessie pressed. "Otherwise, I'll have to tell the staff to bar you from my room."

"You wouldn't dare," Eleanor said incredulously.

Jessie's eyes signaled she was serious as she scootched over and patted the bed, motioning for her daughter to sit next to her.

"There's not enough room," Eleanor said.

"Of course there is," Jessie insisted. "Now get over here before you make your mother mad."

Eleanor abided.

"My darling daughter. Ever since you were a child, you've preferred a world of whimsical fantasy."

Eleanor attempted to interrupt.

Jessie would have none of it. "Not everything in life is pretty. You already know that. And not every man is good for you. And when you discover that, there's nothing wrong with making a change. Don't ever delude yourself by staying with someone who may not love you."

"Mother," Eleanor chided. "I don't know what you're getting at."

"I think you do," Jessie said with a serious expression. "A mother knows."

Loud applause interrupted Eleanor's reverie.

"Isn't the speaker marvelous?" Sylvia added with a knowing glance.

Eleanor mindlessly nodded as she remembered the last day of Jessie's life. Her pale, shrunken form, hooked up to oxygen. The eyes Eleanor loved, forever dulled.

Eleanor longed for her private terrace. Her beautiful ocean view. "I've got to go," she whispered to Sylvia as she pushed her chair away from the table.

Sylvia offered a confused look. "What are you talking about?"

"I just remembered; I have an appointment."

"Appointment?"

"Yes. Something important. I don't know how I forgot. Excuse me. I'm sorry."

"Darling, is that you?" Sylvia's voice crackled. "Have you heard the news?" Her voice was so high-pitched, Eleanor pulled the phone from her ear. "Willy Krause is dead!"

Eleanor wasn't sure how to react. "Oh my," she said sympathetically. "That's terrible." She had no idea who Willy Krause was.

"And tomorrow is the funeral. We must go. Mona will be a mess."

"Sylvia," Eleanor deferred, "I don't know Willy or Mona."

"Of course you do," Sylvia insisted. "Mona Krause. She's slightly overweight. She had a facelift last year. You remember. We were at lunch and she waved at me. Where were we? What's the name of that Italian restaurant in Mizner Park? Anyway, she came over. Her brows way up on her forehead. It looked like she was about to ask a question. Remember?"

Eleanor didn't. Though she recalled being at the restaurant with Sylvia for one of their many lunches together.

"We should stop by. We both know what it's like to be alone."

Eleanor ran a finger across the wall-mounted Wolf microwave. There was a bit of grit. The girl really needed to do a better job cleaning. "Sylvia, I won't be going."

"That's not very neighborly."

"Neighborly?" Eleanor laughed. "Sylvia, she's not my neighbor."

There was a silence on the line as Eleanor walked into the living room, phone in hand. She spotted the Lalique bowl on the coffee table. It was a treasured wedding present from Joel's maiden aunt. She shifted it a quarter of an inch. *There. Better.*

"Reconsider," Sylvia pleaded. "I'd like my best friend to be with me. And if you agree to come, lunch will be my treat."

Eleanor was stunned. Best friend? How could that be? She hardly knew Sylvia. And yet, hearing those words made a difference. As if Sylvia declaring Eleanor her best friend magically made it true, elevating Eleanor to an esteemed position. And with such a position came new responsibilities.

Eleanor softened. "I'll go to lunch with you. We can certainly meet afterward. But I'm not going to a funeral."

"Okay, so you don't really know Mona," Sylvia conceded. "But here's a perfect opportunity to meet her. She's absolutely delightful. And it's not like you have so many friends you can't afford another."

Eleanor thought Sylvia absurd. "I'm not going to a funeral to make a friend. That doesn't even seem possible."

"Well, you're wrong. She'll see you and be touched that a stranger bothered to reach out. And then, well, you know how it is. She'll need cheering up and we'll be right there. You being a widow, it's a natural."

"I hate being part of the welcoming committee."

"Oh honey, don't be silly. It'll be good for you."

Eleanor had no idea what Sylvia meant. How could a funeral be good for anyone?

"And it will be a blessing to Mona. She'll need all the friends she can get. And it'll get you out of the house. When was the last time you went anywhere?"

Eleanor stuck her tongue in her cheek as she thought about it. "Yesterday. I was at the supermarket."

"Food shopping for one."

"Well, I have to eat and I'm only one person."

"You need to get out."

"To a funeral?"

"Trust me," Sylvia said. "You won't want to miss it."

Eleanor couldn't imagine why Sylvia seemed so intent on her going. Maybe Sylvia was the one who was truly lonely. Whatever the reason, Sylvia had worn her down.

"Now I'll pick you up at ten o'clock tomorrow morning. Wear something pretty."

"Pretty? Aren't you wearing black?"

"Don't be silly, dear," Sylvia enthused. "This is Boca!"

"I CAN'T BELIEVE WILLY stuck us with the cost of the funeral," George said as the three friends settled into the empty front row of the crowded chapel. George sat in the middle, Benny and Herbie flanking him. Heads bobbed back and forth as they discussed the sudden turn of events.

"Actually," Herbie said, "it wasn't Willy. It was Willy's family."

Benny corrected him. "You mean, Willy's nonexistent family."

George bit his lip. Would his credit card even clear? He cringed at the thought of coming up short. Jeanette had always handled the day-to-day finances. Now, it seemed as if their finances had gotten away from him. How could he ever explain it to Herbie and Benny? "There has to be an estate," he said, trying to reassure himself. "We just need to submit the invoice to the executor. We'll get our money back in a week, tops. No big deal."

"It's a big deal to me," Herbie said as he leaned in, crowding George. "I have four ex-wives. I'm living on a fixed income."

Benny rolled his eyes. "You're living on a fixed income in Boca? You play golf three times a week. You're a member of two country clubs. How often do you go out to lunch and dinner? And if I recall correctly, last month you bought a Jag."

"That doesn't mean anything," Herbie groused. "It's leased. Besides, that's all self-care."

"Self-care?" George asked. "What the hell is that?"

Herbie's mouth hung open for a moment. "It's when you nurture your wounded inner child."

Benny smirked. The weight of his shoulder pressed against George. "Oh, brother. You've got to be kidding."

George shoulder-bumped his friends apart. "Gentlemen, we're at a funeral. Not a Three Stooges revival. Everyone breathe."

George, Herbie, and Benny each took a deep breath, exhaling in unison.

"This kind of reminds me of Yom Kippur." Benny chuckled at his own joke. "Each year, we buy tickets to atone for our sins. Maybe this is our down payment on the Book of Life."

Herbie leaned across George's lap, directing his contempt at Benny. "Oy vey. How could you be so dumb? We're not in Temple and this isn't Yom Kippur."

Benny's eyes narrowed. "You don't get to be Boca's premier dental implant specialist by being dumb."

"Well then, Mr. Big Shot, you should have paid for the funeral. You were his best friend."

George elbowed Herbie. "We were all Willy's friends. And that's what friends do. They help each other."

Herbie gave George a twisted look. "It isn't considered helping a friend if the friend *is dead*."

"You're not angry about the money," George said. The debt from Jeanette's medical bills was never far from his thoughts. Like a yoke he couldn't shake off. In plain sight, waiting for his next expenditure to tighten the binding. "You're upset Willy's dead. That's why you're angry."

Herbie eyes moistened. "After he had that first heart attack, I thought he'd be fine. And then, to drop dead on the golf course. I'll never get that image out of my head. I may never play golf again."

George could still see Herbie frantically pumping on Willy's chest as he performed CPR.

Herbie sighed. "He shouldn't have been exerting himself."

George hesitated, and then put an arm about Herbie's shoulder. He'd never seen Herbie so distraught, his emotions so raw. "You're not responsible for Willy's death."

Herbie bolted straight up, pulling away, a surprised look on his face. "Of course not. I didn't put that golf club in his hand. That damned cardiologist said he was fine."

Benny shook his head. "It was just Willy's time."

"I guess we all have a ticking clock," Herbie said.

"Like a bomb ready to go off," George added.

"Look on the bright side," Benny pointed out. "At least he was outdoors in the fresh air with friends, playing a game he loved."

Herbie cheered up. "You're right. He had a good death."

"Sure," Benny said as he looked about. "But tell me. Who are all these women?"

"Friends," George answered.

Benny cracked his knuckles. "No one has this many women friends. For a quiet guy who didn't say much, this is quite the tribute."

Herbie agreed. "He must have known every lady in Boca."

Benny leaned in. "My grandmother used to say, 'Still waters run deep.' He must have been quite *the man*."

"Come on," Herbie said. "That little guy weighed less than a toothpick."

"A toothpick can still do the job in a pinch," George said.

Herbie chuckled. "You actually think Willy slept with all these women?"

George had no idea. "For his sake, I hope not."

Benny laughed. "Maybe that's what killed him."

"No freaking way," Herbie insisted. "He didn't have the stamina."

Benny held a finger in the air. "My grandmother used to say, 'The proof is in the pudding.'"

Herbie cocked his head. "I think your grandmother's pudding was 100 proof."

George checked his watch as the rabbi, in a crumpled blue sport coat with his wiry gray hair in a tangle, stepped up to the podium. He looked as if he'd awoken from a nap. "Ladies and gentlemen, thank you for your patience today. For those who don't know me, I'm Rabbi Sherman."

George was relieved. His credit card must have cleared.

"Someone should buy that guy an iron and a comb," Herbie whispered. "I'd bet he got that jacket at Stein Mart."

George nodded, hoping if he agreed, Herbie would shut up.

The rabbi recited a passage about life and death and those who believe in an eternal God. George zoned out, eyes focused on the pine box up front. He remembered selecting Jeanette's casket. The showroom of colorful, highly polished coffins, lids ajar to offer a peek at interior options. A pine box had been in the catalogue but not on display. No matter. George couldn't have purchased a pine box. *We're not orthodox,* he'd thought at the time. *And I'm not that cheap.*

George made a mental note. He couldn't trust his kids. He'd better make his own arrangements.

"He's so somber," Herbie muttered, mocking the rabbi. "Like he's about to reveal the meaning of life."

George squirmed. He thought it best to ignore Herbie. Benny, however, leaned across George's lap and pointed a thick index finger at Herbie. He then raised it to his lips in a shush.

Herbie crossed his arms and legs, a yellow sneaker bobbing up and down. "Oh, be quiet yourself."

George was reminded of a train set he'd had as a boy. It had been one of the few gifts he'd received as a child. With increased speed, the locomotive eventually jumped the tracks. He reluctantly placed a hand on Herbie's jostling thigh. "Herbie, please stop."

Rabbi Sherman, in the middle of a psalm, looked down at the front row with an expression of disapproval.

"Guys," Benny whispered. "Let's listen to the rabbi."

"Why should we listen to him? He didn't know Willy," Herbie grumbled.

George stiffened. There was no telling how far Herbie might go. "Maybe they met. You never know."

"Willy never met with a rabbi in his life."

"Now that's just anti-Semitic," Benny said in a hushed tone as he leaned across George's lap. "No one knows what's in the heart of another man."

Herbie dug in his heels, turning to face Benny. "If he'd been Catholic, Protestant, or Muslim...he'd never have gone along with any of this. Willy didn't believe in organized religion."

George was losing his patience. "If you know so much about Willy, what happened to the family? Where are they?"

The rabbi stopped the eulogy. "Excuse me, gentlemen."

The three friends straightened up as the rabbi directed his gaze at George.

"I'd appreciate it if we could have your full attention, and then, if you'd like to have the floor, you certainly can. I'm sure everyone would welcome hearing your remarks."

George and Benny nodded, but Herbie was not so easily cowed. He stood up. "We were just discussing the life of Willy Krause. He was our dear friend."

George tried to pull Herbie back into his seat, but Herbie swatted George's hand away.

"Rabbi," Herbie continued, "Willy didn't believe in God."

There was a murmur among the crowd. George heard "Who's that?" mixed in with "Oh, my," and even "Sit down and let the rabbi speak."

The rabbi blinked twice as he considered Herbie's declaration. "Well, not everyone has to believe in God. Some of us are merely culturally affiliated. That's fine, too."

"No." Herbie waved a hand as he turned to face the rest of the room. "Willy thought this was all bullshit. Total bullshit. And if he could, I guarantee you, he'd jump out of that box and tell you so in his own words."

There was a muffled cry from the back. "Why, God, why?" a female voice moaned. "He was a good man. He never harmed anyone. Why take him in the prime of life?"

"Who the hell is that?" Herbie turned in the direction of the voice.

George pulled hard on Herbie's jacket, wrestling him to the seat. "Sit down; you're making a fool of yourself."

Herbie plopped back down. "The prime of life? How long does that woman think we're supposed to live?"

Herbie waited in line as George and Benny ogled the glass display at TooJay's Delicatessen counter. Lox, whitefish, and herring. Chopped liver and knishes. Potato pancakes and blintzes. Black and white cookies. George's stomach rumbled. It was just about one o'clock. Willy's funeral had lasted well past George's lunchtime. He could already feel himself bloating with gas, an unfortunate side effect of a late meal.

"Hey guys," Herbie called. "We're up."

A blonde hostess in a short skirt led them to a booth. "Is this okay?"

Herbie offered the hostess a lecherous grin. "Perfect."

"She's young enough to be your daughter," George said as the hostess withdrew.

Benny slid into the booth next to George. "Try granddaughter."

Herbie had a faraway look. "I don't feel a day over thirty."

Benny reached for a menu. "Well, you sure as hell look it."

Herbie stretched his arms over his head, as if doing so proved a youthful flexibility. "I can still do whatever I did at thirty."

George laughed. Herbie sounded foolish. "No, you can't."

"Yes," Herbie insisted. "I can."

"We golf with you," Benny interjected. "Don't even try."

Herbie leaned forward, elbows on the table, face cradled in his palms. George was reminded of a little boy waiting to hear the end of a bedtime story. "Sure, I have aches and pains. But inside, I'm still the same guy."

George wondered if that was true because Herbie hadn't grown up. But surely after four marriages, he must have learned something. The guy couldn't possibly go through life and still be so darn clueless. George eyed Herbie suspiciously. "C'mon. I'm nothing like I was when I was young. For one, I never thought about death. And now here I am, mired in it. First Jeanette, and today Willy. God knows who'll be next."

Benny turned his menu over. "How can you worry about what you have no control over?"

George had recently become obsessed with warding off the perils of aging. He'd changed his diet, cut out snacks, and had even started a daily stretching routine. All recommended remedies for a healthier life in the latest issue of *AARP*. "I just think we'd all kill ourselves if we knew how it was all going to end."

Herbie laughed. "That's so you, George. Always worrying. Am I making enough money? Do I need to change jobs? How am I going to die?"

"I am a worrier," George agreed. "My dad died when I was six years old of a heart attack. I don't even remember him. My mother worked all sorts of hours to make ends meet. I barely saw the woman. I was the original latchkey kid. We lived on the edge of a dollar."

"Maybe that's why you were so focused on that damn career. You had a lovely wife and terrific kids, but your mind was always on the next step up the ladder. Well, look around, George. Guess what? You've worried yourself right to the edge of the cemetery. Jeanette's gone. Willy's gone. Really, it's kind of pathetic, if it weren't so absurd."

George sat back. Herbie had cut him to the quick. A solid jab to the gut. "Nice," he managed to say as he gathered his wits.

Benny pulled on his beard. "Hey, Herbie, take it easy on old George. It's a tough day. No need to get nasty."

"I'm not being nasty. I'm being real. I'm telling the truth."

"Your truth," Benny said.

Herbie sighed. "George, can you really say I've changed that much from when I was young?"

George was unsure how to answer. "There's nothing wrong with change."

"I wish I was young again," Benny admitted. "For one, I wouldn't play college ball. My back and knees are all screwed up. And then, what did I choose as a career? I became a dentist, standing all day with my fingers in people's mouths. Please, tell me." Benny looked at George. "What was I thinking?"

George imagined Benny must have cut quite an impressive figure as a young man. Someone every kid would have wanted as a friend. "That you were helping others. That you'd be young forever. That you were invincible."

"I am invincible," Herbie cried out in a deep baritone as he pounded his chest like a wild ape. "Kong, the eighth wonder of the world!"

Benny winced. "Joke all you want; I'm in real physical pain. My doctor prescribed Percocet. And when it gets bad, even that doesn't help."

"Have you tried hot baths?" George asked, keenly aware that athletes had a harder challenge with aging.

Benny glared at him. "I can barely get my little toe in a tub. I have to squeeze in like a pretzel."

"Hey, maybe," Herbie said, "that's why your back is hurting. What I don't understand is how did you get those thick fingers in someone's mouth without them choking to death?"

Benny shook his head as if he'd expected the insult. "So what are you guys going to eat? After that funeral, I'm not even hungry."

"Maybe something light." George was too rattled for a big meal. Besides, dining out had become a big expense. He needed to pace himself. So far, he managed the minimum payments on his Visa. But the balance with interest due was steadily growing. He didn't want to hit his credit limit. Thank goodness he had other credit cards.

Benny inspected the rim of his water glass. "I could manage a small something. Is this glass cracked?"

"My stomach's upset," Herbie admitted as he rubbed his gut. "I just can't get past the fact that no one in the family showed. And who was that woman in the back of the chapel who cried out?"

"I was wondering about that too." George's eyes landed at the bottom of the menu. "Hey, what about an all-day breakfast entrée?"

"I asked around," Herbie said. "I didn't find out, but I got a phone number."

George was stunned. It was too creepy. Too low-life. Too desperate. "A woman gave you her number at the cemetery?"

"I didn't ask for it. She just shoved it into my hand."

Benny seemed to take it all in stride. "But then, who was the woman who called out? Why would she come to the service, create a spectacle, and not identify herself?"

Herbie ran a hand through his curls. "Identify herself to whom? There was no family."

George thought for a moment. "We sat in the front row. We shoveled dirt on the casket."

Herbie crinkled his brow. "Maybe she didn't go to the cemetery. Maybe she had a pressing engagement. Like those two in the back of the chapel in their tennis whites. Did you see them in the last row? Who attends a funeral in tennis attire?"

"Only in Boca." George stared at the photographs in the menu. The pastrami looked good. His mouth watered. "They probably had tennis lessons scheduled. Or were playing in some sort of tournament. God only knows."

"I still don't understand," Herbie said. "Who were all those women?"

Benny tipped a saltshaker over and salt sprinkled onto the table. He wiped it away with the back of his hand. "Mourners."

"The usual crowd," George said. "People who love to go to funerals. I've read about them. Professional mourners."

"No way," Herbie disagreed. "Not in Boca. People are too busy for that."

George had to admit that the turnout was surprising. "So how would Willy know all those women? It doesn't make any sense."

Benny pulled at his beard. "Do you guys think I need to get this thing trimmed?"

George and Herbie looked at Benny, but neither answered.

"Did he have siblings? Nieces or nephews?" Herbie asked.

George had no clue, and by the look on Benny's face, he didn't know either. He was suddenly alarmed. "Wait a second. We don't know whether Willy had brothers or sisters?"

Benny shrugged. Herbie offered a blank stare.

"How can that be possible?" George asked. "We're his friends. We should know."

"Okay, then," Herbie said. "Tell us about Willy's family."

George leaned back and crossed his arms. "I have no clue. We never talked about family."

"And do I have brothers or sisters?" Herbie asked.

George arched his back. "Well, I should know that."

"But you don't." Herbie seemed certain of his point. "We were once family, and you still don't know."

"You have a sister," George blurted. "Pam."

Herbie looked at George in disbelief. "Pam was my second wife."

"There was a Beth," Benny interjected.

"Nope. Never. Christ," Herbie moaned. "If we don't know anything about Willy's family, how are we going to find the executor of the estate?"

George winced. He *had* to be reimbursed for the funeral. He couldn't carry a large credit card balance in addition to the stack of Jeanette's unpaid medical bills. How had he gotten himself into this mess? And how much longer could he stall his creditors?

The crowd at TooJay's Delicatessen had thinned. George leaned back in the booth and tugged on his belt buckle. If eating was a sport, he'd just been through the post-funeral Olympics. He pushed aside an empty plate. The five potato pancakes that had arrived twenty minutes earlier now rested in his stomach. The sweet taste of applesauce lingered on his tongue. "I swear, I wasn't even hungry. I probably should have skipped the chopped liver appetizer. Whose idea was that?"

Benny belched. "Mine. My grandmother used to say: 'Feed a cold, starve a fever. If a Jew dies, overeat.'" He lifted the empty breadbasket. "Chopped liver. Real comfort food. But I think it was the rye bread that put us over. We probably didn't need a second basket."

"You guys are such lightweights. There's still rugelach left." Herbie nudged the plate with two strawberry pieces toward Benny.

Benny waved it away.

George moaned. "I can't eat another bite."

Herbie offered a dour expression. "Your mothers would be ashamed."

"I think this is what they mean by eating your feelings." Egg salad clung to Benny's beard.

George pointed to Benny's chin. Benny wiped it with a napkin, sticking his chin out for George's inspection. George signaled okay.

Herbie took a deep breath and exhaled. "So, what are we going to do? We need to get ahold of the executor of Willy's estate. How are we going to figure this out?"

"How about one of us meets with Rabbi Sherman?" Benny suggested.

"The rabbi? Are you kidding?" Herbie said. "That guy doesn't know anything."

"You're right," George agreed. "But the funeral home does. Someone made the arrangements. They have the bounced check. They have the paperwork and family contact. That's where we start."

Herbie nodded. "Okay. We go back to the funeral home."

"When?" Benny asked.

Herbie held a hand in the air. "How about now?"

Benny frowned. "It's nearly two thirty. I'd like to get out of these shoes. I left my arch supports in my sneakers."

"We're not walking there." Herbie turned to George. "And you think I complain."

"You do," Benny and George said in unison.

Herbie took a last sip of coffee. "We should get out of here. The sooner we figure this all out, the better."

"I'm sure there's nothing to worry about." George held up a finger to attract the waitress's attention. "Willy was a wealthy man."

"Sure," Herbie agreed. "He was an original investor in Donna Karan."

Benny laughed. "Dumb luck. She was his next-door neighbor in Manhattan. It wasn't that he was a financial genius. He just wanted to help her out."

George wished he'd been so lucky. His neighbors in Garden City had all been doctors and lawyers. Not a creative bone among them. "Well, whatever it was, he made a fortune on that initial ten thousand dollars. So we know there's plenty of money somewhere."

"Sure," Benny said. "But exactly where?"

The three friends exchanged concerned glances. George hoped if they put their heads together, they could figure it out. It wasn't impossible. He considered them all fairly sharp.

"It'll just be easier if we ride together," Herbie insisted as the waitress dropped off the check. "We arrive together. We take care of business together."

"Herbie doesn't trust us," Benny said as he reviewed the tab. "He thinks we'll skip out. Like we're afraid to go back to a funeral home." He squinted as he checked out the tab. "Holy crap. This can't be right. Check out this total." He passed the tab to Herbie.

"Now why would three men in their sixties be afraid of a funeral home?" Herbie joked, his voice full of play as his eyes popped. "Did we eat all this?"

George didn't want to think about the medical bills, but every time a discussion of money came up, or a tab presented, there it was again. Weighing on his mind. "All you guys care about is money."

Herbie passed the tab to George. "It makes me mad the family didn't bother to show."

"He didn't deserve that." The veins in Benny's forehead stood out.

George had rarely seen Benny so upset. During the Super Bowl, sure. World Series, absolutely. But in a normal conversation? No.

Herbie crushed a napkin. "Does anyone deserve to be treated that way?"

Holy crap, George thought as he studied the tab. *When did deli get so damn expensive*?

"No one does," Benny answered.

"Maybe we should wait before we do anything." George dug out his wallet from his back pocket. "This has already been a tough day. Maybe we should just let it lay. Take care of it tomorrow. When we're fresh. In the morning. And clear headed." He put his Mastercard on top of the tab and slid it to the edge of the table. He thought about using his Visa card, but he'd just used Visa to pay for Willy's funeral expenses. He didn't want to push his good luck and risk the card being rejected.

Herbie shook his head. "Oh, no. We need to do this now while we're together. Together we stand. Divided we fail."

"You mean *fall*," George corrected.

Herbie flashed his big blue eyes. "Whatever!"

Benny stepped out of the booth and stood to his full height. With two bolts in his neck and painted green, he could pass for a bearded Frankenstein. "I'd like to find those no-show relatives. Imagine stiffing Willy like that."

"Stiffing the stiff," Herbie muttered as he too stepped out of the booth. "It would be funny if it wasn't so sad."

The waitress picked up the tab with George's credit card and rushed off. "Hey, wait a minute," George called out as she disappeared around a corner. "What's wrong with you two?"

he said to Herbie and Benny. "You didn't put your credit cards down. We were supposed to be splitting that tab three ways!"

The parking lot of The Golden Funeral Home was deserted as George maneuvered the car into a spot by the front door. "I don't know about this, fellas. The place looks dead," he said before realizing the irony of that description. Out on the street, George jiggled the front door before he spotted a sign referring after-hours visitors to the rear of the building. He waved Herbie and Benny to follow him around to the back.

George rang the after-hours bell. He spotted a camera angled at the top of the doorway, the eye pointing downward. George wondered if they looked like an unsavory trio. Coats long discarded in Boca's late-afternoon sun. Shirt sleeves rolled up. Dark perspiration stains showing through the front of unbuttoned dress shirts. George wiped his face with a handkerchief. Gosh, July in Florida was humid.

When the security buzzer sounded, George pushed the door open. He wished he and his friends didn't look like such a motley crew as they stepped into a dimly lit anteroom, the only light coming from the frosted glass of the reception window that separated the public space from the administrative offices. In the gloom, George spotted a black leather sofa and a glass coffee table with a large vase of flowers. A distinctive scent of lilacs filled the air. George coughed. He remembered sitting on that exact sofa trying to compose himself. *That was the worst day of my life,* he thought as he released a sneeze so fierce, he bit his tongue.

Herbie supplied a cheery "gesundheit!" as he touched one of the flowers in the vase. "Fake," he announced.

"Creepy." Benny looked about. "You'd think they could at least turn on a light."

"It reminds me of your waiting room," Herbie teased. "Without all the dental art."

"That isn't art. Those are photographs of satisfied customers with their before and after smiles."

George laughed, and then unexpectedly sneezed. His head wretched sharply forward. "Yow!" He pressed a hand to the back of his neck, rubbing vigorously.

Benny pointed at George. "Did you know sneezing was once considered a form of death? People thought that when you sneezed, the heart stopped. Of course, it was an old wives' tale."

"Actually," Herbie said as he plopped onto the sofa, "when you sneeze, your blood vessels momentarily constrict, which affects the rhythm of your heart. But your heart keeps beating. Now, they also once believed that if you sneezed, your eyeballs might pop out."

"Wow," George smirked. "You two are a wealth of information."

The reception window screeched open. The three men jumped as the window quickly slammed shut, before opening again, barely an inch. A female voice beckoned. "May I help you, gentlemen?"

"Yes." George moved toward the smoky glass. "We'd like to meet with the funeral director." He spotted the name of the funeral home on a wall plaque. "Mr. Golden."

"There is no Mr. Golden," the voice answered. "Mr. Goldenblatt is the funeral director."

"Fine," George said, hands in his pockets. "Goldenblatt."

There was the sound of a buzzer, followed by a click, and the security door to the administrative offices popped open.

George let out another sneeze, followed by two more.

"Better hold on to your eyeballs, George," Herbie said with a sinister Jack Nicholson sneer as they stepped through the doorway. "We're entering the inner sanctum."

She wore her auburn hair pulled back in a French twist and was dressed in a black pencil skirt and simple white blouse. George guessed her to be in her mid-forties.

"I'm sorry about the locked door," the woman said as George, Herbie, and Benny followed her through a long, narrow hallway. "I'm the only one here at this time of the afternoon. I don't usually let anyone in. But you three looked harmless enough."

George didn't like being thought of as harmless.

The hallway was lined with photographs of pasty-faced undertakers in black suits and dark ties sporting empathetic smiles. George thought their bright expressions a bit too enthusiastic.

They stopped outside a door labeled *Family Reflection*. Ms. Auburn flipped a light switch, but the room remained dim as she welcomed them inside. George caught the scent of lilacs. Once again, he sneezed. This time, his ears popped. He desperately needed an antihistamine. He took a seat on the sofa next to Benny and Herbie. Ms. Auburn settled into a nearby chair as George exploded with two more sneezes. She offered a box of Kleenex, which George gratefully took.

"Are you okay?" Ms. Auburn asked, but she didn't bother to wait for an answer. "Now, gentlemen. How can I help you?"

George looked at his two companions. Neither said a word. "Thank you for seeing us," he began. "My name is George Elden. These are my friends, Herbie Marshall and Benny King." George wiped his nose with a tissue.

"Right," she said, nodding. "I processed your credit card payments."

"Oh," George said, his tone indicating that should make things easier.

She tucked her feet under the chair, crossing them at the ankles. George's eyes settled on her full bosom. She caught his eye and he blushed, wondering why such an attractive woman would ever consider working at a funeral home.

She leaned forward. "It's very nice to meet you in person."

There was a genuine kindness to her voice. George wondered if that was part of the job description. "Well, thank you," he answered, unsure of what to say next. The woman was staring at him, and he was suddenly uncomfortable.

"And your name is?" Herbie asked, breaking the silence.

"Oh, I'm sorry," she said. "My name is Jill. Jill Winters. I'm the head bookkeeper."

Benny scooted forward on the sofa, knees projecting upward. "Is the funeral director able to meet with us?"

"Mr. Goldenblatt is out on a run."

"A run?" Herbie repeated. "He's jogging?"

"Oh, no," she giggled as she shifted in her chair. George thought her adorable. "He's picking up a client. It could be another hour or so."

Benny scratched at his beard as if he had a rash. "Well, Ms. Winters, maybe you can help us. We want to contact the family of our friend, Willy."

Ms. Winters nodded. "Willy Krause."

Three heads bobbed.

"Was there something wrong with the arrangements? The casket? The plot?"

"No, no," George assured her. "The funeral was lovely." He glanced at Benny and Herbie. "Gentlemen."

"Yes, lovely," Benny chimed in so enthusiastically George nearly laughed.

Herbie merely nodded.

"Then what's the problem?"

"We don't have the contact information for the family."

"Oh." Ms. Winter straightened up. "That's odd. Where's the shiva being held?"

George turned to Herbie and Benny. In all the confusion, they hadn't realized there'd been no shiva announcement. But then, how could there be? There was no family. "Oh my God. There's no shiva." George crumpled the tissue in his fist.

Ms. Winters offered a confused expression. "Really?"

"I know. This whole thing is odd." George reached for another tissue. "Frankly, we're as surprised as you. I—I—I—" he let go of another sneeze. "Oh God," he moaned, the nerve in his neck twinging.

Herbie laughed. "That was a real eyeball popper."

Benny chortled. "Poor George. He just can't help himself."

"Excuse me," George apologized. "I can't understand it. I know the flowers are fake."

"It's the fresh scent," Ms. Winters explained. "It's pumped throughout the public areas."

George's eyes watered. "I didn't have a problem earlier."

"It's not as intense in the chapel," Herbie guessed as he glanced up at the low ceiling in the family room.

Benny took over. "Can we please just have the contact information for the family?"

Ms. Winters was quick to respond. "Well, that's a matter for the funeral director to handle."

"But why?" Herbie asked.

"It's private. Confidential."

"You're telling me," Herbie argued, "that you can't just give us that information?"

Ms. Winters shook her head.

Benny rebounded. "But we wanted to make a donation in Willy's name. We were thinking of setting up a scholarship at Florida Atlantic University in his honor. Surely the family would want to know about that."

Ms. Winters smiled. "That's a lovely idea. My daughter attends there."

– 4 –

IT WAS UNUSUALLY cold the week George Elden buried his wife. The sudden December chill, courtesy of a front that had slipped in from the north, threatened a hard freeze. Forecasters promised Florida would warm up in a day or two, but George had his doubts.

The traffic on I-95 slowed to a halt just in sight of the 103rd Street exit. "Your mother would have appreciated this," he said to his daughter, Carole, seated in the passenger seat of the Ford Escape. "It's like Mom took the warmth of the world with her."

Carole had always looked so much like Jeanette, but now, with spiky black hair, a snake tattoo wrapped about her neck, and a tiny metal ring through a nostril, George wasn't so sure anymore. He couldn't imagine doing all that to his body, and though he'd initially objected, Jeanette had warned him: "She doesn't do drugs. She's not promiscuous. Make a big deal and watch her continue to defile herself."

George suppressed a laugh at the memory. He'd always associated the word *defile* with a sexual ritual. The Huns defiled virgins. But what Carole had done had nothing to do with sex. And if it did, he didn't want to know about it. For goodness sake, Carole was his daughter. His little girl.

"She's twenty-one. It's her body to do with as she pleases," Jeanette had stressed. He only hoped that now, at twenty-five, Carole was finished. Self-expression could only go so far.

Carole stared out the passenger window. "I hate to think of her lying out there."

Peter, seated in the back, scooted forward, a hand grasping George's headrest. "Mom's not there," he said. "She's in a better place."

Carole wiped away a tear. "If only we could be sure that was true."

George gripped the steering wheel, eager to change the subject. "There must be an accident ahead. Or construction. They're always working on this damn road. And nothing ever changes. It's still a mess."

"Will I miss my flight?" Peter asked.

"Not to worry." The car inched forward, the exit to Miami International Airport still a mile and a half away. "We have plenty of time. I'm familiar with this parking lot. Did I ever tell you kids about the time your mother and I almost missed our flight to Aruba?"

Carole rolled her eyes. "Only a million times."

"Well, as long as I'm not boring you," George answered sarcastically before realizing Peter was out of his seat. "Peter, sit back and put on that seatbelt."

"Dad, we're almost there."

"*Seatbelt*," George repeated in a tone he'd used with Puff, the family's long-dead bichon that had refused to be housebroken.

Peter slipped backward, securing the belt with a click. "Dad, I hate to leave you like this. Are you sure you'll be okay?"

George looked at his son via the rearview mirror. Peter had Jeanette's eyes. A warm cast of green peeking out from below a shaggy, bedhead mess of black hair. He'd been quiet as a child, but as an adolescent, a hellion. A girl in high school had accused him of coming on too strong. Jeanette had been frantic when the girl's parents threatened to press charges. But in the end, it was all dropped with an apology. George had talked with Peter about respecting a woman's boundaries. "A no means no. Even a yes might turn out to be a no," George had explained. "We expect you to treat every woman like you'd hope some man would treat your sister."

There'd been no more problems after that discussion. Certainly none that George had heard about. And now, after a week of shiva, Peter needed to get back to his IT job in Chicago, doing something George couldn't quite explain. Something with computers.

Peter had once teased him, "Dad, you have no idea what I do for a living, do you?"

George had been annoyed. *Little shit*, he'd thought. *I bet he couldn't describe what I did for a living.* But instead of challenging Peter, George blew the comment off. It was easier.

"Now don't worry about your old dad," George said as the car finally exited the highway. He wished he felt as brave as he sounded. "You have your life to live. I have mine."

"I know," Peter said, "but Carole will be leaving tomorrow to head back to San Francisco. You'll be alone."

George was touched. "I'll be fine. We'll speak every weekend. Nothing will change. We'll be just as we were. A loving and close family." Jeanette's voice echoed in George's head. *Peter will be the man he was meant to be. We can only hope for the best.* "You need to get back to your life," George said as he pulled up curbside at departures. "That's what your mother would have wanted."

Peter opened the car door. "Okay, Dad. I love you."

George watched Peter in the rearview mirror retrieve his luggage from the back of the SUV. "We love you too," George called out, keenly aware that he was no longer a *we*. "Safe travels," he said just before Peter slammed the hatchback shut.

"Let's go to Atlantic Avenue for brunch," Carole suggested as George entered I-95 heading north.

"Are you really hungry?" George hoped to sidestep Atlantic Avenue. It had been one of Jeanette's favorite haunts.

"We have to eat. And it'll be fun."

Atlantic Avenue, a hip, happening neighborhood in downtown Delray Beach, was relatively quiet that chilly Thursday. The open-air restaurants, so popular during warm weather, had closed up their sidewalk patios. Carole, all smiles, led the hostess to a table on the enclosed patio with a view of the sidewalk. George acquiesced when he spotted an overhead heater, but still grumbled when he ran a finger across the dirty plastic tablecloth. He made a mental note to check the silverware.

Two Lance Armstrong wannabees cycled by in fitted black-and-yellow outfits. George spotted gray ponytails peeking out from under psychedelic helmets. A lady in a Santa hat strolled by with an Irish setter sporting a set of antlers. A Hispanic kid on a skateboard cut across Atlantic Avenue mid-block. George marveled at the young man's speed and agility.

Carole leaned forward, an elbow on the table. She rested her face in her palm. "You look exhausted. Maybe I should stay another week."

"I'm tired," he admitted as he slumped in the chair. "Really tired."

"Do you want me to stay?"

George most certainly didn't. "Carole, you need to get back to your routine. You have a job."

"It's more than a job. I'm a manager, Daddy. Two art galleries in Union Square. Another in Berkeley. One in Sausalito."

"Right," George said. "Standing around, procuring other people's work instead of expressing the special gifts God has given you. Carole, why did you give it up?"

Carole's expression darkened. "We've discussed this before. I wasn't good enough."

"That's crazy," George said. "You're so young. How do you know? It takes time to develop a talent. You have to work for it."

Her eyes shot daggers. "Maybe you should get away. Take a trip."

George sighed. "I don't know. All I need to do is sleep. Crawl into bed. But the odd thing is that whenever I lay down, I see your mother's face. That pained expression."

Carole nodded. "Did she know what was happening?"

"Your mother didn't want to admit it, but we both knew she was dying." George rubbed his chin. He needed a shave. "I guess we thought if we didn't talk about it, it might not come true." George saw Jeanette's sad expression in the corners of Carole's downturned mouth. His eyes moistened. "How can it be possible to love someone, stand by and watch them die, and never talk about it?"

"She was scared."

"We both were. And now I have to sell the condo. I can't stay there. Not without your mother."

Carole crinkled her forehead. "We just buried Mom. Losing a spouse is a major life crisis. Give yourself time to grieve. Don't make any decisions when you're in an emotional state."

George nodded, though he hadn't a clue what Carole was saying. For days, he'd been slipping in and out. Physically present, but mentally unprepared for the flood of emotions that had come with Jeanette's passing. He'd never been an emotional guy, or so he'd thought. That had always been Jeanette's department.

"There must be something I can eat that won't send my cholesterol through the roof," George said as he scanned the menu.

"Daddy, did you hear me?"

"Loud and clear," George lied, wishing his tone wasn't so abrupt. "Honey, I know it's scary, but Mom is gone and there's nothing we can do or say that will bring her back."

Carole looked away. "Just give yourself time. Selling the condo seems so rushed."

"Carole, look at me." George searched his daughter's face. How could he explain this to her? "Is it too soon for you or for me?"

The waitress interrupted. Petite with bony fingers, she sported bright red polish on curled fingernails that reminded George of Barbra Streisand. Her hair, the same jet-black shade as Carole's, was surprising on a woman George guessed to be in her late seventies. "Are you folks ready?"

Carole nodded.

"My name is Gladys," the waitress said in a raspy voice. "What can I get for you, doll?" Her accent was unmistakable.

George leaned back and gave Gladys his full attention. "Brooklyn. Canarsie."

The woman smiled, revealing a smudge of red lipstick on a front tooth. "Sure," she said in a singsong way. "How could you tell?"

"I was born in the Bronx," George said. "But I went to college with a lot of guys from Brooklyn. I had a roommate from Canarsie."

Gladys's eyes brightened.

George caught the look on Carole's face. She was embarrassed by his familiarity.

"So tell me, Gladys, what do you recommend?"

Gladys gave George a dismissive glance. "How would I know? I'm not your mother. It's all good."

George laughed. He ordered the Spanish omelet. Carole ordered coffee and the salmon plate with a pumpernickel bagel.

"We'll have that right up," Gladys said as she turned to Carole. "Honey, are you okay? I know it's none of my business, but you look like you've lost your best friend."

Carole straightened up. "Oh no, I'm fine," she said, handing the menu over.

"A pretty girl like you should be happy. You have this nice man in your life. Everyone needs someone to take care of them." She smiled at George before turning to put in the order.

"Daddy!" Carole shrieked with horror, to George's amusement. "She thinks we're together."

Florida had more than its share of May-December romances. Jeanette had thought it horrid. *How can these young women sleep with these old farts?* she'd say whenever they crossed paths with such couples. *Money has a way of making strange bedfellows*, George would answer, astonished at Jeanette's naïveté.

"Well, at least Gladys thinks I'm still alive and kicking," George joked.

"Daddy, you'd have a better shot at dating Gladys. She's closer to your age."

George smiled at Carole's honesty as he heard Jeanette's voice. *A son is yours until there's a wife. A daughter is yours for all her life.*

The days following Jeanette's death came and went as George sat alone in a daze, staring at the television.

By the end of January, Jeanette's medical bills started to arrive.

George wished he'd paid more attention to the insurance plan. He'd opted for an inexpensive policy, thinking of it as short-term gap coverage before they'd qualify for Medicare. He hadn't realized the plan provided minimal coverage. Disallowed so many procedures. Had a limited cap and a limited network of providers. He should have known better. He was a healthcare administrator. But the expense of living on the grounds of the Boca Raton Resort

& Club had clouded his judgment, requiring some fancy budgeting on Jeanette's part. And when Jeanette got sick, it was too late to make any changes. His sole focus was on Jeanette. Managing her care. Her very well-being in hopes of a quick recovery.

Golf with Willy, Herbie, and Benny seemed the only escape from the stress and loneliness. And George very much needed an escape.

The temperature hovered in the low forties, unusually cold for a January morning, as George prepared to tee off on the fifteenth hole of the Broken Sound Club. It was a long view down the fairway, bending to the right. A sand trap lay directly ahead. George had spent many an unhappy afternoon trying to hack his way out of that trap.

"Just take your time," Willy said as he and Benny walked to their golf cart. Herbie was within a few feet of George.

"So you want to unload the condo?" Herbie asked as George set the tee and motioned for Herbie to step back. Ever since Jeanette's death, George's swing had been off. He'd already lost a ball on the sixth hole.

"Hey Herbie," Willy called out. "Leave him alone. Let him concentrate."

George placed the Titleist logo up, taking a moment to swipe the grass with his index finger. A good-luck ritual that, so far, wasn't working. *Breathe,* George thought as he gripped the club.

Herbie cleared his throat. "You shouldn't sell the condo now. Real estate isn't strong."

George closed his eyes to block out the distraction. He bent a knee slightly and relaxed his grip. *Head down.*

"I know it's not for me to tell you what to do," Herbie continued. "Jeanette's only been gone a few weeks."

"Herbie, please!" George lifted his chin slightly, trying to maintain form. "Can this wait?"

"Sure." Herbie took a step back. "I just hate to see you make a mistake."

George straightened up, temporarily abandoning the shot. How could he explain he needed cash? That Jeanette's medical bills had to be paid? That his money was tied up in the market and the tax implications of selling stock made it a no-win scenario? He took a deep breath. "What do you mean?"

"You just bought the unit."

"Not exactly." George leaned on the club. "The year before Jeanette got sick."

"And so it hasn't really appreciated in value," Herbie pointed out. "All I'm saying is, selling now isn't the smartest move."

George rested the club against his stomach as he rubbed his hands together to generate some warmth. Herbie might be an excellent pediatrician, but he was no financial wizard. It would take both hands to count the bad advice Herbie had offered through the years: *Sell Netflix. They'll never be able to compete against Blockbuster. Don't bother with Starbucks. Who in their right mind is going to spend that kind of money on a cup of coffee? Don't buy Amazon. They're too dependent on the United States Postal Service to ever make a go of it.*

George licked his lips as he assumed his stance. There was water in the cart, but he wanted to take the shot first. As he started the swing, his mind raced: *I should have held on to that Netflix stock.*

"Christ," he moaned when he sliced the ball, sending it sharply to the right of the fairway, far short of Herbie's, Benny's, and Willy's positions.

George's friends circled. "It's your knees." Benny demonstrated the proper stance with a driver.

"You've got to keep your head down," Willy added.

"It's your grip," Herbie argued, fingers interlaced. "See where I'm placing my thumb?"

George glared at the three. "Or it could be that you guys are breathing down my neck."

Herbie, Benny, and Willy exchanged surprised looks.

"No, that's not it." Benny gently swung a club. "You need a session with Doug, the club's golf instructor. He's a miracle worker. Last year after two sessions, I got that kink out of my swing. You remember, Willy. My swing was really off."

Willy nodded. "It was your footing."

"No," Herbie interjected. "It was the position of the shoulders."

"Anyway," Benny said, "that's the whole point of having access to a golf pro. Doug will know what's wrong."

George doubted Doug could pay off Jeanette's medical bills or bring her back to life.

"It's all in your head," Herbie explained as he guided the golf cart down the fairway, Willy and Benny trailing behind in another golf cart. "You're distracted. And the last thing a golfer needs is distraction." He stopped the cart near a massive oak tree.

"I was just telling George he needs to relax," Herbie said as the four gathered.

Benny stretched his long arms overhead. "Nothing bothers me when I'm out here. It's so peaceful. Have you tried meditation, George?"

George thought meditation was a lot of hooey.

Benny took a deep breath and exhaled. "You use the breath to clear your mind. When I discovered meditation, my world changed. It calms me."

"Oh, please," Herbie laughed.

"George, you should listen to Benny," Willy said. "Meditation can change everything."

"Can it make you eat any faster, Willy?" Herbie snapped as George located his ball. "Hey George. How about meditating your way back onto the fairway?"

A quick swing and George's Titleist landed in the sand trap.

"It's your stance," Benny said.

"It's your head. You've got to keep it down," Willy advised.

"It's your grip," Herbie asserted.

George shook his head in disgust. "I think it's this damn game."

"Now don't get upset," Willy said as he passed George a bottle of water. "We all have an off day every now and then."

"Sure," Benny agreed. "It's just an off day."

"It's more than that," George said as he twisted the cap off the water bottle and took a long swig.

"Can we be honest?" Herbie said with a chuckle. "George needs more than a lesson or two. Maybe ten or twenty. He really stinks. Now, who's willing to chip in for that?"

George listened to Herbie's advice and held on to the Boca condo. Unable to sleep in the master bedroom without his wife, he watched cable news into the early morning hours, falling asleep on the living room sofa. He dreamed of Jeanette, only to wake to the essence of gardenias and the sobering reality that she was gone, and that no matter how hard he grieved, or how long he held onto the condo, Jeanette was not coming back. Meanwhile, the medical bills continued to arrive. Overdue notices that George shuffled into a neat pile and placed off to the side of his desk. Hundreds of thousands of dollars of out-of-pocket expenses.

Peter, who used to speak to his mother frequently throughout the week, now called George every other day. "Hey Dad, how are you doing?" he'd ask without waiting for an answer.

George had gotten used to Peter's one-sided soliloquy.

"Remember that woman I was telling you about?" he said during one conversation. "Last night we went out. To tell you the truth, I'm not sure she's that into me. She was on her phone throughout dinner."

George was uncertain what to say. "Give it time, son. It's just a first date. She'll come around."

"I don't know, Dad. I'm spending a lot of time alone. I thought by now, I'd have hooked up. I probably shouldn't have dropped Peggy. What do you think, Dad? Do you think there's something wrong with me? Should I give Peggy a call?"

George couldn't remember there ever being a Peggy. Did he and Jeanette meet her? Was she the pretty brunette Peter brought around the Thanksgiving before Jeanette was diagnosed? George was at a loss. "Maybe you should stop pushing so hard. Sometimes, good things present when we least expect them. Have you spoken to your sister? Maybe she can offer better insight."

"Carole? She won't talk to me."

"She won't? Why not?"

Peter's voice became defensive. "You know how younger sisters can be."

George chuckled. "She can be tough."

"But Dad, how are you doing?" Peter asked again, almost as an afterthought.

"Fine. Everything's fine," George lied as he walked into the bedroom, iPhone pressed to his ear. A dressing table displayed a bottle of Estée Lauder perfume along with a tiered jewelry box. Nearby, gold earrings nestled in a dish as if waiting for Jeanette's return. Strolling back to the living room, he looked at all the tchotchkes arranged as Jeanette had placed them. With the blinds open, George could see a layer of dust. A hand imprint on a glass table where he'd leaned. *I should get someone in here to clean,* he thought before deciding against it. *I can do it myself.* So far, he'd failed to do anything.

"So what have you been up to, Dad?"

"Not much," George admitted. "Golf with the guys."

"Are you alone the rest of the time?"

"I'm okay," George deflected, though he could barely manage being with Herbie, Benny, and Willy. It was a struggle to keep up with the conversation. Herbie, sarcastic as ever, commented on every woman. Benny loved sports and could talk for hours about the minutia of any game, stats rolling off his tongue with the ease of a weather report. Willy, the quietest of the three, puppy dog eyes and shock of white hair shooting in all directions, listened too intently, dissecting every word George uttered as if searching for a hidden meaning.

It was with Willy that George felt the most uncomfortable.

"I'm managing," George said to Peter. "So, are you seeing anyone now?" he innocently asked.

"Dad. I just told you about my date last night."

George caught himself. "Sorry, Peter. My mind's elsewhere. Yes, you did." He contemplated the enormous task of living without Jeanette as Peter rambled on. *I'm still young,* he thought. *I may have another fifteen or twenty years. Some men even live into their nineties. I could be one of those. Especially if I take care of myself.*

"…you'd like her, Dad."

George perked up. "I'm sure," he said. Who was Peter talking about now?

"And Dad, I was thinking…"

George walked back into the bedroom. He opened the closet door and stared at Jeanette's things. Rows and rows of shoes lined up in the original boxes. Dresses, skirts, blouses. Handbags hanging on pegs. He pulled open the dresser drawers. Scarves, hosiery, undergarments. It all felt so hopeless. So overwhelming.

"Well, I've got to go," George said, interrupting Peter in mid-sentence before adding, "Is the weather okay there?"

"I told you; it's been snowing like crazy. Chicago's buried."

"Right, right," George muttered.

"I love you, Dad. Take care of yourself."

"Sure," George said. "And say hello to your new friend from me."

"New friend?" Peter's voice cracked.

"Yes, that new lady friend," George clarified.

"Were you listening at all?"

George's eyes fell upon Jeanette's favorite outfit. A yellow summer dress. "Did I miss something?"

"I want to come visit, Dad."

George sighed. "Peter, this isn't a good time."

"It doesn't have to be this month. Maybe later. Maybe, April."

"We'll see. Let's play it by ear."

There was a silence on the other end. And then, "Sure, Dad."

On Valentine's Day weekend, TooJay's Delicatessen in Boca was packed with the typical Sunday lunch crowd. Large families with infants, grown children, and grandparents crowded around rows of tables that had been pushed together. Fragile seniors, accompanied by a family member and a caregiver, sat hunched over in the leather booths that lined the walls. Wheelchairs and walkers stood parked in a nearby alcove as waitresses buzzed about taking orders, refilling drinks, and delivering the finest of Kosher-style food. Patrons munched on free sour pickles served on silver trays amid the din of constant conversation.

"I can't take it anymore. I really can't," George said, a half-eaten hot dog covered in sauerkraut and mustard on the plate in front of him. "This is just the worst."

Herbie, seated next to George, was engrossed in the Sunday *New York Times*. "We don't have to always eat here, George." He folded back a page of the Arts section. "I wouldn't mind Italian. A chicken Parmesan hero might be nice. A cannoli." He reached for his half-eaten pastrami on rye and took a bite.

Benny gazed over George's head at a widescreen television mounted across the way. The Miami Dolphins were playing the Bengals in Cincinnati. "Italian sounds good."

Willy, tucked in next to Benny, had barely taken a bite of his tuna sandwich. "Gosh, it was chilly this morning when I went for a walk. I should have kept my winter coat from New York." He poked at the sour pickle on the plate.

George sighed as he looked around the table. If he lay on the floor and refused to get up, would his friends notice? Would Herbie stop reading the paper? Benny stop watching the game? Would Willy stop playing with his goddamn tuna fish sandwich? Perhaps if he stood up and screamed at the top of his lungs, he might get their attention. But he didn't have the energy. Instead, he ran two fingers over his lips. His face was numb, as if he'd gone to the dentist and the Novocain had yet to wear off. "I'm not talking about the food," he meekly said.

"Then what's going on?" Willy asked in a squeaky voice that reminded George of a cross between an elf in Santa's workshop and the late actor Wally Cox, with whom Willy shared a remarkable likeness.

George sank back into the booth. He closed his eyes. "I wish I knew." When he opened his eyes, the three friends were staring at him.

"Well if you don't know, who does?" Benny's broad forehead was lined with concern. He shifted his gaze back up to the television and released a groan. "Come on, Miami."

George looked down, the same way he'd seen Peter do as a little boy. "It's been two months since Jeanette died. I'm living in that damn place by myself. The loneliness is overwhelming. How do you guys do it?" George could feel the color rising in his face.

"Who's alone?" Herbie said indignantly as he closed the newspaper. "I'm always busy."

"Doing what?" George asked.

"Out and about," Herbie said. "I have my lady friends. I have the gym. I have golf." He shrugged as he looked about. "I have you guys."

"You should get a dog," Benny suggested, eyes glued on the Dolphins. He pulled at the hairs on his beard as if he were picking petals off a flower. "They provide great companionship."

George shrugged. "I don't think a dog is going to solve my problem."

"How will you know unless you try?" Willy rotated his plate 90 degrees so the pickle was positioned at twelve o'clock. "When I was a kid, I had this mutt that followed me everywhere. A terrific dog."

Herbie scrutinized Willy's plate. "What was the dog's name?"

Willy pulled the plate closer, blocking it with an arm on the table. "Dog."

Herbie snorted.

"I don't think a dog is the answer." George took the last bite of his frankfurter.

Willy was not about to give up. "There are so many rescues in need of a good home. I volunteer at the shelter. I'll keep an eye out for you."

"You volunteer at the shelter?" Herbie asked. "I hope you're not in charge of feeding the animals."

Willy glared at Herbie. "When I'm not over at hospice or at Arthur Murray, I like to play with the dogs. Walk them."

"Some life," Herbie muttered. "Arthur Murray!"

"Hey," Willy answered. "Don't be such a dick. There are a lot of nice people there. You should come with me."

"I'm sure Arthur Murray doesn't need my help."

"I'm talking about the shelter," Willy clarified. "You'd be great. The puppies can use you as a chew toy."

Herbie waved a hand, dismissing the idea. "I'm not picking up poop."

Willy scowled. "This from a pediatrician. Besides…it's not all about poop. And what's wrong with Arthur Murray? Dancing is great exercise." Willy's voice was emphatic. "George, you'd love it."

George pushed his plate away. He hadn't touched the coleslaw in the tiny paper cup.

Herbie grabbed the coleslaw. "George, come with me to Atlantic Avenue. We'll hit the bars. I need a wingman." He held up the coleslaw. "Are you going to eat this?"

"It's all yours," George said. "And you don't need a wingman. You do perfectly fine on your own."

Herbie attacked the coleslaw with a fork. "True," he said with his full mouth, bits of coleslaw flying free. "But it would be fun. Like when we were young. A drink or two. A lovely lady."

George demurred. "I was never that young. Remember, I married Jeanette when I was twenty-two."

Herbie pointed a chubby finger. "That's your problem. Right there. You should get out into the world. Experience everything. The love of your life could be waiting just around the corner."

Benny exchanged an "uh-oh" look with Willy.

George glared at Herbie. "I just buried the love of my life."

Herbie's face dropped. "George, I'm sorry. I wasn't thinking. It just slipped out. I don't know why I said it. I was just…talking."

"I don't need to be dating," George bristled. "I wouldn't even know how."

"You don't have to date," Willy assured him. "Not until you're ready."

"And what if I'm never ready?" George wondered. "What if I'm through with that part of my life?"

"Then you better find something to do. A man your age shouldn't be alone. You could go nuts," Willy said.

George rubbed his forehead. "I couldn't be like you, Willy. A professional volunteer."

"Don't say it like it's a dirty word," Willy countered. "There are some amazing organizations that need volunteers."

"Damn," Benny yelled as he pounded the table. The plates and glasses jumped. "What's wrong with that goddamn team?"

Herbie nodded in Benny's direction. "Or George, you could wind up like Benny."

"What's wrong with Benny?" George asked.

"Are you kidding? What's right? His whole life is sports. Betting. Pissing away his money on OTB. The guy's a real putz."

Benny squinted as he looked over at Herbie. "I can hear you."

Herbie offered a weak smile. "It's the truth."

"That's how I relax," Benny said, again eyeing the television. "Interception!" he shouted, leaping from the booth, stamping a foot and pumping a fist. A waitress, passing by with a tray, stopped just short of a collision.

"Yes," Herbie quietly observed, "you seem very relaxed."

Willy's eyes lit up. "Hey, I've got an idea, George. Why don't you foster? Help socialize a dog while it waits for a forever home."

Herbie laughed. "*Forever home!* Are you kidding me, Willy? Where'd you come up with that expression?"

George shrugged. "I don't know about a dog."

"You could do a world of good," Willy said as Herbie snatched the pickle from Willy's plate, shoving it in his mouth like a bass might swallow a minnow.

By March, loneliness had finally driven George to follow up on Willy's suggestion and volunteer. The dogs at the Tri-County Animal Rescue in Boca Raton were an energetic group, barking wildly when George came into view. It was his second week of volunteering, and so far, he was having fun. "Settle down, now," he called as he scanned the wire enclosures, leash in hand, searching for Miss Betsy.

"She's a white toy poodle," Ava Hendrickson, the volunteer coordinator, had explained when George reported for his shift. Ava was a small woman, five two with short brown hair in a pixie cut. Her face glowed with a certain freshness. Was it because she didn't wear makeup? Or was her makeup so understated that she looked natural? "Let her come to you. She's really shy. She might be huddled in the rear of the run under a blanket."

George nodded. "How long has she been here?"

"About two weeks. Her mother died and the family was unable to care for her. They turned her over to us for placement."

"Mother?"

Ava smiled. "The woman who raised her from a pup. Now, be careful. She might nip. We haven't had that problem, but a frightened animal is unpredictable. And Miss Betsy is scared."

"Got it," George said. "Is there anything else I should know?"

Ava bit her lip. Her green eyes sparkled as she re-knotted the bottom of the oversized Tri-County T-shirt, accentuating her slim waistline. "Maybe I should go with you."

"I can manage," George assured her. "It's a toy poodle. Not a pit bull."

Ava drew a sharp breath. "That's not fair."

George mindlessly laughed. "I'm just saying…"

Ava's eyes pierced George's friendly demeanor. "Well, stop *just saying*. That breed has been horribly maligned. They're very sweet animals. It all depends on how they're raised."

George couldn't help himself from teasing her. "And what about the kids they've ripped apart?"

Ava offered a steely glare. "For someone who pretends to like dogs, you have a bad attitude."

George glanced down. Maybe he was being a bit harsh. Nonetheless, he couldn't resist. He had to have the last word. "I'm sorry. I didn't realize that violent animals were your favorite breed."

Ava crossed her arms. "Well now you're just being an ass." She stormed off.

George suppressed a laugh. "I'm just saying…" he called to Ava's back. "No sense getting yourself all riled up. You really can't change what people think," he muttered. "Maybe," he said, as if Ava were still near, "you should only rescue pit bulls. Gather them all up and try to stay alive while they lunge at your throat."

The scent of disinfectant caught in George's nostrils as he entered the enclosed area that housed the kennels. George passed rows of pit bull mixes with wide jaws, gleaming teeth, and massive heads. "I'm sorry, fellas, but you all really scare the hell out of me," he whispered as their eyes followed him. He stopped in front of an empty run. He checked the identification card. He'd arrived at Miss Betsy's front door.

No wonder she's hiding. I would too, George thought as he looked around. "Miss Betsy," he called, his voice light and full of sweetness. "Where are you?"

There was a gentle movement under a blue blanket. Sure enough, Miss Betsy had wedged herself in a corner.

George opened the enclosure and stepped inside. He smiled. *This one's got to be adorable,* he thought, eager to get a look at the little poodle. "Miss Betsy," he cooed.

A tiny head emerged from under the blanket. Two big brown eyes looked up at George.

George took a seat on the floor, crossing his legs. "Come here, baby girl." He held out a hand for her to smell. Miss Betsy's nose twitched. *A good sign,* George thought—until Miss Betsy quickly withdrew back under the blanket.

"I know," George said. "The world's a scary place. But I want to be your friend, sugar. Oh—I've got something you might like." He withdrew the bag of liver treats he'd used earlier in the week to reward a terrier mix who'd eagerly followed George's commands during a morning training session. Holding a liver treat in the air, George made a lip-smacking sound.

The blanket moved. Miss Betsy sat up, even though she was still under the blanket.

George laughed. "You're so busted," he said as he held the liver treat low and close to the blanket.

"I've given it a lot of thought," George told Ava two weeks later in the breakroom of the Tri-County Animal Rescue. It was just the two of them. "I'll take her."

Ava sipped her morning coffee as she backed away from George. "She has a name," Ava said, her voiced edged with a certain tension, as if she believed George might have forgotten the little poodle's name.

George couldn't imagine what Ava was thinking. Why was she so cold to him? What had he truly done to so put her off? A little teasing about pit bulls? Could that be it? George sighed. "You know who. Miss Betsy. The terrified little poodle."

Ava stared at George as if she could see into his very soul.

He was suddenly unnerved. Was she not going to allow the adoption? Or was there something else bothering her? Something she saw in him that made him wholly unsuitable?

"It's a big responsibility, George. Are you willing to give her the time she needs? She's been through a lot. She needs to feel safe and loved."

George nodded. "I understand."

She studied him. "But do you?"

George's pulse raced. Was this truly about Miss Betsy? Or was it something else? Did Ava just not like him? Had she decided he wasn't eligible to adopt?

As of late, George had the sense that Ava was avoiding him. When he came to volunteer, she'd typically be hiding in her office. And when they did see each other, she barely acknowledged him. Was she still upset about his killer dog jokes? George thought about apologizing, but he decided against it. *She's not going to intimidate me into an apology*, he thought. *No way.*

George pressed his point. "I don't understand. The goal of the rescue is to get dogs into wonderful homes. I have a wonderful home. What's the issue? I want her. Isn't that enough?"

Ava twitched her nose. George was reminded of the rabbit Peter had had as a child. It had gotten away from him outside and been run over by a car. George hadn't thought of that rabbit in years.

"If you're serious, I'll schedule a visit to your home to check that it's safe for a dog. We'll see if you're ready to provide the care Miss Betsy deserves."

George wondered if the visit was just a pretense to deny his request. "Sure," George agreed, "that makes sense."

"And then I want to see you with her. Is she truly comfortable?"

George gritted his teeth. "Of course she is," he said, suppressing his irritation. "Why wouldn't she be? I hand feed her, walk her. She comes up to me. I'm not exactly a monster."

Ava didn't seem convinced.

"So why has no one adopted her yet?" George asked. A white toy poodle seemed like a natural addition to any family. "She's such a sweet little girl."

Ava's shoulders rose sharply, as if George had encroached on her personal space. "It's the hiding. People don't understand why she's hiding."

"Well, I do," George said. "This place is scary as hell."

Ava nodded. "I'm afraid you're right."

"She must be a smart little girl to try to keep out of sight."

"Yes, but shy dogs don't get picked."

"Well," George said, a thumb pressed to his chest, "I'm picking her."

"Okay," Ava said, her tone conciliatory, yet wary, as she eyed George with suspicion. "When you first volunteered, I thought, oh, there goes Mr. Boca Raton with his George Clooney good looks. He'll be in and out of here in no time. I never pegged you as a guy who wanted to do the hard work, no less adopt a dog. Maybe I was wrong."

George was flattered. "Clooney, huh? Wow. He's one of the good guys."

Ava disavowed George's acknowledgement. "I can't quite put my finger on it. It was just a bad feeling."

"Well," George said, "your feeling is wrong."

"I hope so." Ava smiled, the coldness in her eyes slipping away. "I want you to be successful. I'd love to discover that you're really a sweetheart underneath all that bravado."

George thought about the image he was projecting. He didn't have much patience with his children. That was true. But he was great with animals. Okay, there was that rabbit. But that didn't make him a bad guy. And then there was Puff, the bichon. But Puff's housebreaking issues had been Jeanette's fault. She hadn't been firm with Puff. All of her commands sounded more like questions. Asks, instead of orders.

"The first thing I'm going to do is change her name," George excitedly revealed. "Miss Betsy has got to go."

Ava noticeably stiffened. "She's not a puppy, George. She knows her name."

"But Miss Betsy? I can't have a dog with a name like that."

"Well, you better rethink that, George Elden," Ava said, her face set in a frown. "If there's a name change, no dog."

George lifted Miss Betsy onto the bed. "There you go," he mumbled as the little poodle licked his face. "You like it here, don't you? Well, I like having you."

Miss Betsy rolled over, exposing her soft belly for George to scratch. When the toilet in the master bath suddenly flushed, the little poodle instantly righted herself and faced the bathroom door. She released a growl. Well, it wasn't exactly a growl. It was more of a gurgle. But George recognized it for what it was. A show of protection from his eight-pound buddy.

"What was that?" George cooed as Miss Betsy's throat rumbled. "Are you going to protect me?" George teased as he stroked her back, admiring her beautiful lines. "I hope you do. I need all the protection I can get."

Ava emerged from the bathroom with a towel wrapped about her waist. Fresh out of the shower, she resembled a water nymph. Youthful, energetic, and eternally cheerful. She gave her wet hair a quick shake. "That's a great shower. Really strong water pressure."

It had started with a home visit the Wednesday before.

George had been surprisingly nervous. *This is ridiculous,* he'd thought. *It's just a formality. How can Ava possibly turn me down? I'm the perfect person for Miss Betsy.*

And yet when the doorbell rang, there was a twinge in his gut. It reminded him of the day Peter was born. Judy, his sister-in-law, had squealed with delight, "It's a boy!" as she emerged from the delivery room. Up until that moment, the true gravity of the responsibility of fatherhood had eluded him. He'd been preoccupied with proving himself at work, and somehow, he'd failed to grasp the enormity of the upcoming birth or how he might actually feel the day he became a father. Not until Jeanette went into labor did it truly hit him. And once the baby was in his arms, he was afraid he'd faint. "He's so tiny," he said to Jeanette, even as he was thinking, *Oh, shit. How did I get myself into this?*

"You don't have a fenced-in yard," Ava had observed that Wednesday afternoon as she peeked out onto the balcony, clipboard in hand.

Wasn't that obvious? George thought. *Of course I don't have a backyard. You came up on the elevator.*

"A little dog might slip between the slats in the balcony railing," she pointed out. "I don't like that." She jotted a note.

George nervously rubbed his hands together. "She won't be on the balcony. Why would she be out there?"

"You'll never be on the balcony with her?" Ava didn't sound convinced as she inspected the kitchen.

"No," George said, though he hadn't considered it would be dangerous until Ava mentioned it. "There's a wonderful grassed area on the side of the building. Residents use that for potty time."

Ava glanced his way. "Potty time?" She seemed amused.

George raised a hand in the air. "I just made that up. Isn't that what you were referring to?"

Ava offered a warm smile. It was then that George realized something was different. Ava looked different. She'd become… prettier. Not that she wasn't pretty before, but now she was wearing a dress. A short white dress with spaghetti straps that accentuated her petite shoulders and offered a peek at her cleavage.

"You look different," George awkwardly blurted. "What's going on?"

"Going on?" she innocently asked. "I'm checking your home to see if it's suitable for adoption."

"Right," George said, catching himself. *Keep it professional*, he thought as he waved a hand about the room. "Well, then. Check away."

"What's back here?" Ava headed down the hallway to the master bedroom. "Is this where Miss Betsy will be sleeping?" She walked about the king-size bed. "Are you planning on crate training?"

George leaned against the doorway. "Crate training? She's a big girl. She's already housebroken."

"She's still going to need a crate. At least, until she's completely comfortable in her new home. When you go out, she'll need to be crated. It'll be her safe space." Ava peeked out of the bedroom window.

George couldn't help but notice her shapely calves and ample rear. The clipboard was gone. She must have left it in the living room.

Ava approached George. "Are you still planning to change her name?" Her voice had dropped an octave. It had become sexier. There was fire in her eyes.

Now he understood the tension between them. It had been there all along. He was just too stupid to see the passion burning underneath Ava's manner.

He reached out, and with deliberate slowness, ran a finger down her arm. "Not if you don't want me to."

"I don't," she said, wrapping her arms about his neck, pulling him in as she locked her mouth on his.

By April, George and his three friends, Benny, Herbie, and Willy, were meeting daily to share meals. Though George worried about the expense, he couldn't say no to the guys. How could he explain he was living on the edge? That he was blowing through his available cash, struggling to pay the mortgage and monthly homeowner's association fees? That he still owed on the golf club membership? It all sounded silly. How could he have accumulated so much debt, no less explain it? The mere thought of his financial circumstances made George anxious. He continued to split the tab equally, despite ordering the cheapest items on the menu. He just couldn't let on to the guys about his financial pressures. He was sure his friends would think him a fool for mismanaging his money. For allowing the debt to continue to build unabated. Thank goodness credit cards allowed minimum payments. And since George had four credit cards, he had four ways to keep moving forward.

George slipped into a booth at the very crowded Flakowitz Bagel Inn, a cozy Boca Raton restaurant on Federal Highway. At first glance, the interior resembled a Jewish truck stop, if there ever was such a thing. But the food was excellent. Even if the ambiance was best described as noisy and crowded.

Benny turned over a coffee mug, inspecting the inside. "Have I told you guys I'm thinking of retiring? My financial planner said, 'The end is near.'"

"The end is near. That sounds ominous," Herbie quipped.

"You know what I mean. The end of one stage of life."

Herbie buffed a fork with a paper napkin. "Beware what you wish for. A lot of guys keel over after they retire."

Benny paled.

"Everyone wants to retire," Willy observed as he unfolded a napkin and placed it in his lap, "but no one wants to grow old or die. It's odd when you think about it."

Herbie balked. "I thought you were already retired."

"No." Benny stroked his beard. "Why would you say that?"

Herbie nudged George, the signal that he was about to tease Benny. "Well, it is Tuesday," he said in an impish tone. "We're eating a late breakfast. And the last time I checked, guys who work for a living...work on Tuesdays."

Benny's deep-set eyes darkened. George took a breath. *Here we go.*

"Now don't get mad," Herbie said, waving a hand as if it were a white flag.

"Then what are you doing here?" Benny asked Herbie. "I decided to take the morning off. That's my excuse. You must be retired."

"I'm a part-timer," Herbie gaily answered. "After thirty years of building a pediatric practice, I have the luxury of two young partners. I get to choose my hours. I built the business. I reap the rewards."

"Sounds like slave labor." Benny pointed at Herbie. "They must love seeing patients to feed your kitty." He lowered his finger. "Are you guys getting lunch or breakfast?"

"So you're a part-timer?" Willy asked Herbie as he removed his wire-rimmed glasses, holding them up to examine the lenses. He pulled out a small cloth from his pocket. "You seem to have a lot of time on your hands. My female friends are talking about you. Maybe you should stop dating women who know each other."

"Female friends?" Herbie's cherubic face lit with an inner glow. "Who has female friends?"

Willy blushed. "Women like me. And I like women. There's nothing wrong with that."

Herbie scratched his head. "I haven't understood a word you've said since we sat down."

Willy slipped his glasses back on. "Be careful; that's all I'm saying."

"I'm an innocent," Herbie insisted. "Completely harmless. My God. You buy a woman a drink in Boca and you're practically engaged. They can smell single from across the room. Not to mention money."

"Yours or theirs?" George asked, amused by his timing.

"Mine," Herbie answered indignantly as he looked about. "Where the hell is the waitress?"

George was astonished that Herbie would own up to being wealthy. Herbie had always resisted the obvious truth. "When did you become rich?"

"When did you go gray?" Herbie sniped as a party of three squeezed by, a young family with a child in tow. The little girl, no more than three, stuck her tongue out at Herbie as she waddled by.

George laughed. "Clearly the opposite sex loves you."

Herbie scoffed. "Seriously. Women go nuts for me. What can I do?"

"Yeah, right," Benny said incredulously. "Ladies love Smurfs."

"Maybe," Herbie said, "if you weren't a giant, you'd meet someone nice."

Benny ignored the insult as he looked at George. "I'm thinking of selling my practice. Moving to Mexico. San Miguel de Allende. I could live nicely there."

George saw his opening. He'd been meaning to discuss the condo with the guys. Plant the seed that he wanted out. "I'm still toying with selling my condo. Who needs all that space?"

Willy looked up at Benny. "Leaving the United States is a big decision."

George winced. "Like giving up my condo isn't?"

"I didn't say that." Willy pressed a hand on his chest and took a deep breath. He looked paler than usual.

"Are you okay?" George asked.

Willy shook his head. "I'm fine. Just a bit of stiffness. Are you dead set on selling?" Willy scanned the menu.

"I just said I was," Benny answered.

Willy blinked. "Not you, Benny. I was referring to George and his condo."

"Dead set? What a choice of words," George muttered.

Willy grimaced. "You know what I mean."

"Don't sell. You'll regret it. Trust me," Herbie warned.

"Too many memories," George answered. The pile of medical bills flashed in his mind.

"Maybe that's a good thing," Willy said. "Memories can be comforting."

George thought there was a lot of truth to that sentiment. But in retrospect, he wished he'd let Carole sort through Jeanette's things when he'd had the chance. His refusal to do so had only delayed the inevitable. "Not to me. I've been walking the beach, going to the library, doing anything to get out of there."

"It's good you're getting out." Herbie looked about as if searching for someone he knew.

"It isn't," George answered. "I keep seeing couples everywhere and wishing Jeanette was still here. And then, when I'm in a crowd, I have this urge to run."

Willy rubbed his arm. "Like that guy in the movie? What was his name? The box-of-chocolates guy."

Although George had enjoyed his fling with Ava, he still felt rooted in his marriage. Any dalliance felt like a betrayal. He doubted he could move on with his life as long as he remained in the condo. "All I can think about is Jeanette. It's driving me nuts. I need to move. And I don't want to move near my kids. They have their own lives. They don't need me hanging around."

"What was his name?" Willy muttered. "Tom Hanks played him."

"You can't move." Herbie checked the rim of his water glass. "That isn't what your kids really want."

"They do," George said.

"Kids. They have no idea what's good for them or you," Benny lectured. "My kids are just a pain in the ass. Money, money, money. They always have their hand out. You'd think my son would've been a success by now. I swear, I'm always digging that kid out of one financial jam after another."

George weakly defended his two. "They mean well."

Benny strongly disagreed. "No, they don't!"

"How about they get on with their own lives," Herbie said as he placed the water glass to the side. "You'd think they could wash these things before putting them out again."

George thought of Carole's apartment in Haight-Ashbury. He'd seen pictures. It looked like a hovel. She wanted him to come visit. "Honey, I will," he'd lied, having neither the energy nor desire to get on a plane. "Maybe in another month or so." Meanwhile, Peter was demanding more of George's attention.

While George tried to limit the phone calls to five or ten minutes, Peter rambled on. During one of Peter's downloads, George imagined jumping from the second-floor balcony, keenly aware that such a fall wouldn't kill him. Though it might stop Peter from his incessant complaining.

Willy chimed in. "Herbie's right. Selling your condo won't change a thing. Wherever you go, you'll find yourself there."

George thought Willy sounded like a Hallmark card.

"And as for your kids," Willy continued, "consider yourself lucky. At this age, most kids want nothing to do with their parents."

"I should be so lucky," Benny muttered.

Herbie pointed a finger. "You listen to me, George. Don't be a fool. I've been through this. Remember those four wives of mine? Well, despite the nasty rumors, I did love one or two of them."

Willy shook his head. "Uh, oh. Here we go. Tales of Herbie's love life."

Herbie held his head high. "There's a lot to be learned by sharing the ups and downs of your life, if you had one."

Willy dismissed the insult with a roll of his eyes.

"As I was saying," Herbie went on. "It's not a laughing matter. When you fail, it's a terrible thing. And those marriages were failures."

Willy sighed. "Now there's no stopping him. Here he goes."

Benny laughed. "Does this have anything to do with George?"

"It's time to get real," Herbie said in a somber tone. "The first one, your sister-in-law," he reminded George, "I married for love. I should have held onto her, but I was so damn young. My libido overwhelmed me."

Benny squinted. "I can't imagine you ever being young."

"Libido? Doesn't that sound like a mojito named after Liberace?" Willy mused.

Herbie held up two fingers. "Number two was the affair. Ten years my junior. My office receptionist. Here's one piece of advice." He looked about the table. "Never dip your pen in company ink. And never hire a beautiful blonde receptionist to work for you. We had nothing in common outside of the…supply closet…empty exam room…and eventually, not even there. Number three, well, I'd rather not discuss her. Married twice and I already knew number three was a mistake that first week of the honeymoon. You'd think I'd have learned my lesson."

George checked his watch. "Where the hell is the waitress?"

"Number four, we can discuss later. My point is, I made a huge error. I should have stayed married to number one. She was the one who loved me."

Willy laughed. "I was actually looking forward to hearing again about number four."

Benny covered his mouth and yawned. "Please. How many times do we have to hear the same story?"

George exhaled. There had to be a point to Herbie's outburst. Exactly what, he wasn't sure. "Okay. But what does your sad love life have to do with me selling the condo?"

Herbie shifted. "Is that what we were talking about?"

Benny toyed with an Equal packet. "Herbie, that was one narcissistic segue to nowhere."

"Yeah, Herbie. What was the point?" Willy asked.

"I have no idea," Herbie admitted with a guffaw. "I guess I lost the thread. But I'm sure there was something important in sharing that."

"Sharing what? The stats of your marital follies?" Benny's voice was incredulous.

Willy clapped his hands with excitement. "*Forest Gump*! That's the name of that goddamn movie," he shouted. A moment later, he cried out in pain. With a hand pressed to his chest, he slumped over, his head resting against Benny's arm.

George forced himself to visit Willy at Boca Raton Regional Hospital. It was eerie being back in the hospital where Jeanette had died. Where he'd spent so much of his time that last year of her life. George couldn't help but wander past the intensive care unit. As if being near where Jeanette had taken her last breath might bring her back to him. Emotion defied logic. Logic defied need as he stood outside the unit. He doubted he could stay at the hospital long. He already felt shaky.

"How's he doing?" George asked after he entered Willy's room. The patient was fast asleep. He looked pale and lifeless, like a breathing mannequin.

Benny, seated in a chair by the window, long legs stretched out, rubbed his eyes. "Holding his own. The doctor said he was lucky. They were able to clear the blockage with a stent."

George wanted to flee. Turn and run like a coward. But he held his ground. It took all his courage. "You look beat. How long have you been here?"

"Since last night. I didn't think he should be alone. It was too late to hire a round-the-clock nurse."

Willy's small frame was dwarfed by the hospital bed. George felt a pang of guilt. Maybe he should've relieved Benny earlier. It didn't seem fair that Benny had to sit up all night. "Poor guy. I don't get it. It's not like he's overweight."

Benny stood up, twisting from side to side. Willy didn't wake-up. "The doctor said he had rheumatic fever when he was young."

George arched a brow. "Isn't that private patient information? HIPAA and all."

Benny smiled. "Not if you're a doctor."

"You're a dentist."

"Okay. I lied and said I was his brother-in-law."

It occurred to George that he wouldn't have to lie if it had been Herbie in the hospital bed.

"For now, he's stable," Benny whispered. "But really, what do any of us know about the future? He could have ten more years or kick off tomorrow. By the way, so could you or I. But for now, he's okay. You know heart disease isn't the killer it used to be."

George nodded. "I know. They can do amazing things."

"Now, if they'd only cure cancer."

George felt the familiar pang of regret. Could he have done more to intervene in Jeanette's care? Why hadn't he insisted they go to Sloan Kettering in New York City? Signed her up for an experimental drug trial? It all felt so hopeless.

"Well, since I'm on my feet," Benny said, "and you're here now, why don't I take off and grab a bite?"

George was gripped by fear. He could manage thirty minutes, but no more. He'd have to think fast if he needed to create an exit strategy. "Don't you have patients today?"

Benny rubbed his eyes. "I moved them. So, I'll be back after I eat something."

George calmed down. He wouldn't be required to stay all day. It would only be a short visit. "So your staff called all those people and rescheduled them? Your staff must love you."

Benny yawned, his mouth opened wide to reveal two perfect rows of teeth. "It couldn't be helped. Besides, it was going to be a light day."

George was grateful Benny's schedule ensured his escape. "I bet your office manager didn't think so."

Benny furrowed a brow. "As far as I'm concerned, that battle ax—"

George held up a finger. "Bub, bub, bub. That battle ax keeps your business running like a top."

Benny got ahold of himself. "She does. But sometimes I think I work for her."

"You do," George said with a wry smile, happy to know he'd soon be able to duck out. "Everyone in your office is invested in your success. That's how they keep their jobs."

Benny nodded. "Thank you, Mr. Hospital Administrator. I sometimes forget whom I'm talking to. Anyway, I'm going to get an agency to send a nurse over. They owe me a favor. I worked on the owner last year. The worst case you'd ever seen. His dentures were creating all these sores. He now has a gorgeous, permanent smile. Nearly blinding."

"Great." George took out his iPhone to check his newsfeeds. "Hopefully, someone kind."

"Yes. Someone who can follow him home." Benny headed toward the door.

"That would be great. And not too young. We want someone with a lot of experience who can properly care for him."

While alone with Willy in the hospital room, George's mind drifted to when they'd first met some thirty years earlier. George was attending a three-day healthcare conference at The Fontainebleau in Miami Beach. He'd struggled to focus on the meeting's agenda. All he wanted was to be with his wife.

"I'll be fine," Jeanette had said that first morning as she placed a copy of James Redfield's *The Celestine Prophecy* in a shoulder bag. Sunglasses perched atop her head, she wore no makeup. She stepped into a pair of flip-flops, fussing with a short white tunic she'd slipped over her bathing suit as a cover-up. "Just go do your thing."

George didn't want to do *his thing*. He wanted to do *her thing*.

"Can you see through this?" She spun and pressed the tunic close to her body.

George sat on the edge of the bed, sport coat folded over an arm. "You look beautiful."

"Do I?" she asked with sincere delight.

"Yes, my darling. You do."

Her eyes sparkled as she reached for his pink tie, pulling him up to her. "I like this color on you," she said, the tie acting as a lasso for a kiss on the lips. "Two more days, and I'll have you all to myself. And if you finish early, you can join me on the beach."

George nestled his face into her shoulder, but she pulled away. She rechecked the contents of her shoulder bag. "I think I have everything. Now don't be a grump."

George slipped on the blue sport coat. He examined his reflection in the full-length mirror as he adjusted the pink tie. "It's going to be hard to find you. It's a big beach."

Jeanette came up behind him, wrapping her arms about his waist. She gave him a gentle squeeze. "Maybe we should plan to meet back at the room. Say, three o'clock."

Three o'clock. Their secret rendezvous time. At home on the weekends when the kids were out with friends, they'd connect at three o'clock. It had proven to be the perfect time. Late enough to have accomplished whatever errands they needed to get done. Early enough for a quickie before dinner and the kids returned home.

The day dragged on as George kept peeking at his watch. Lunch seemed the cruelest joke. Sixty minutes passed as a speaker droned on while George struggled with an aching sexual need.

By the close of the last session of the day, excitement coursed through George's body. He imagined Jeanette waiting for him. Riding the elevator to the fourth floor, he thought he'd explode.

She greeted him at the door in a black lace teddy. He stumbled out of his clothes, tripping over his pants. In a flash he was in her arms, his neediness engulfed by her passion.

An hour later, George awoke with a start. Jeanette was standing over him in a robe. She'd just stepped out of the shower. Her hair was wrapped in a towel.

"George, we have a party tonight in Boca. My sister is expecting us at six. Drinks and dinner."

George grunted as he rolled onto his side, turning away.

"Really, George," Jeanette laughed as she poked his back. "I told her we'd be there. She's been upset lately. I want to support her."

George turned about. "Support her? She lives in Boca Raton. She's married to a doctor."

"A pediatrician," Jeanette said as if the clarification was a correction.

"That's a doctor. Herbie went to medical school."

"I know. But a pediatrician doesn't earn the kind of money a surgeon does."

George shifted about. He was wide awake.

Jeanette edged onto the bed. George slid over. She retrieved an emery board from the side table.

"Herbie is the sweetest guy. He has a heart of gold."

Jeanette focused her attention on a nail. "Yes, he is."

George sat up and rested against the headboard, running his fingers through his tousled hair. "So what's the problem?"

"Money, George. They live on everything Herbie earns."

"And that's Herbie's fault?" George asked, irritated. "Your sister better be nice to him." He stretched an arm overhead.

"It's hard to live with a man who likes the finer things in life."

"I don't see your sister living like a pauper. She could get a job."

"George, don't misunderstand. I like Herbie. Truly, I do. But if you're going to marry, you need the financial means to be happy. Right now, they're spending every last dollar."

George looked away. Was it true? Was money the basis for a happy marriage? Maybe Jeanette didn't think he earned enough. Perhaps he should step it up so she could feel more secure. He was only a vice president. He'd hoped to be a chief executive officer. Perhaps he didn't have the temperament to run a hospital.

Maybe he never would.

Judy greeted them that evening at the front gate. She was glowing in a white off-the-shoulder dress. Her skin, a golden tan.

"She certainly doesn't look like she's struggling," George whispered to Jeanette as Judy rushed back to her guests.

Jeanette shot him a dirty look.

"I'm just saying," George muttered as they crossed the threshold and entered a white living room. "And who has white carpeting?" he continued as Jeanette shushed him. "Okay. I'll be good. But take my word for it. Your sister is not starving."

"Not now, George," Jeanette scolded as Judy, standing with a group of women on the other side of the room, called Jeanette's name and motioned for Jeanette to join her. "I'll be back," she said as she crossed the expansive living room.

George stood alone in the hallway. "Great. Just leave me here," he complained, not really upset as he looked among the sea of strangers. He caught sight of his brother-in-law huddled in the corner talking with a guy who looked like he taught mathematics. Or geology. Or maybe chemistry.

George made a beeline to them.

Herbie was his normal cheerful self. "George, it's great to see you. Glad you could make it. This is my friend Willy Krause."

Short and slight with jet-black hair, Willy stood his ground much like a mailbox marks the property: all head and no body.

"Willy was a sprinter in college. Today, he works mostly for nonprofits. He even runs his own charity."

"Foundation," Willy clarified, a hand extended in greeting. "Hey George, nice to meet you. Welcome to Boca."

"George is a hospital administrator," Herbie bragged.

"Really?" Willy said, all teeth. "That sounds interesting."

George couldn't imagine anything less interesting.

"Willy won't tell you, but he's made a fortune investing in start-ups. Lucky son of a bitch. Whatever he touches turns to gold." Herbie shifted his attention to the front door. New people were arriving. He pointed to the bar. "Help yourself to a drink. I'll catch up with you two later."

Willy sipped a martini. "So, you're golfing with us Saturday."

"I'm afraid so," George admitted. "Let me apologize now. Between us, I'm not very good."

"Wow," Willy said, glass held high in the air. "Here's to honesty. Can I tell you a secret?" He waved a finger for George to come closer.

As George leaned in, he caught the distinctive scent of Old Spice.

"Neither am I. Truth be told, neither is Herbie. But Benny, our other friend, he's got the gift. He's a dentist. And you never know when you might need dental work," Willy said with a wink.

"Well, I might be joining your threesome on a regular basis," George admitted. "The hospital I work for has been bought by a Florida-based management company. I'm going to be here quite a lot. This might be the beginning of a great friendship."

Willy smirked as he pointed at George. "Humphrey Bogart. *Casablanca*."

George blinked. "What?"

"You know," Willy continued. "The movie. Claude Rains. Bogart. 'Louie, I think this is the beginning of a beautiful friendship.'"

WILLY'S HEART ATTACK in April jolted George into action. The lingering depression he'd experienced after Jeanette's death was replaced by a new emotion: fear. The fear he could die at any moment, leaving his children to discover the extent of his debts.

George came to a decision.

He had to get his life together. He had to put the condo on the market. And the month of May was the right time to do so. Not too hot. Not too muggy. The perfect weather for northern buyers eager to forgo another harsh winter.

George hoped to work with Big Dave, the Realtor who'd handled the original purchase. But when George called the real estate agency, the receptionist nervously explained that Big Dave had moved on. George wondered if "moved on" meant "died."

That's Boca, George mused. *You don't die. You move on.*

"Sylvia Haddit is our top seller," the receptionist quickly added. "She's wonderful."

George took the recommendation and scheduled an appointment to meet Sylvia at the condo. He had an uneasy feeling about a stranger in his home, critiquing it, especially since he wasn't the best housekeeper. He didn't make the bed or pick up after himself. And even though he had a dishwasher, he wasn't sure how to use the darn thing. Dirty dishes piled up in the sink. Until he washed them. And Miss Betsy's toys seemed to multiply on their own, scattered in every room as if the tiny poodle was marking her territory. George supposed she was.

On the morning of the appointment, George crated Miss Betsy in the master bedroom as he tidied up, kicking dog toys out of the way, shoving some under the sofa and others under the bed. He figured out how to turn the vacuum cleaner on. The correct setting for carpets and hard floors. He discovered the toilet brush hidden inside the porcelain Dalmatian that stood in the corner of the bathroom by the toilet. Using Lysol toilet cleaner, he scrubbed the stains on the side of the bowl, though he doubted the Realtor would inspect the toilet. Just to be sure, he closed the lid. Exhausted, he grabbed a pair of underwear and quickly dusted the tables, releasing tiny particles into the air that caused him to sneeze. He hoped the dust would at least remain airborne until the end of the Realtor's visit.

"Lovely to meet you," Sylvia Haddit said, releasing George's hand and walking past him into the condo. In a red dress that fit like a second skin, Ms. Haddit crossed the room to peek around the corner at the eat-in kitchen. "A little small," she remarked.

It took George a moment to realize she was talking about the space and not her dress.

"It was fine for the two of us," he pointed out.

After inspecting the master bedroom, Sylvia joined George in the living room. Had she looked in the closet? Spotted the vanity in the bedroom with Jeanette's perfume? George hoped she wouldn't mention anything about Jeanette's things.

Sylvia appeared pensive.

Surely, she knew the value of the property. George had been assured she'd sold other units in the complex. It had to count for something that the condo was on the grounds of the Boca Raton Resort & Club. That alone should set the price. And yet, George was nervous. Maybe the décor wasn't quite up to the standards that would show the unit in its best light. Perhaps he'd been too penurious with Jeanette about decorating choices.

Sylvia tugged on an earlobe. "It's one of the smaller units. And the view...well, let's be frank. There is none."

George's stomach churned. Maybe selling the unit wasn't a great idea. "But we're on the grounds of the resort," he said.

"Oh, honey." Sylvia smiled. "Don't get mad. I'm just being honest. I want you to know the limitations before we list. You should be realistic; that's all. You don't need to expound on the value of the location. It's an exclusive address in Boca Raton. But this condo is more of a second home. A place to land. Not live in. At least for my clientele. Of course, if you had a water view, that would be ideal. Small and cozy. Nonetheless, it's a great lock-and-go and the price is going to sell it. I just want you to understand what we're dealing with here. Oh, and before I forget. You'll need to have the carpets cleaned. I spotted that animal in the bedroom."

"She's housebroken," George said, defending Miss Betsy's honor.

Sylvia offered a disingenuous grin. "That's what they all say."

George wondered whom he was dealing with when Sylvia, seated on the sofa next to him, inched a bit too close as she reviewed the specs of similar properties from the MLS listing. *She's a sexy lady*, he thought as Sylvia's arm brushed up against his. Her perfume, a mixture of exotic flowers, permeated his senses. He glanced down, eyes on her cleavage. A diamond-encrusted heart hung from a gold chain and matched the studs in her ears. *They can't be real*, George thought as she pressed harder against him, documents in hand.

"So here are the neighborhood comps," Sylvia said. Her thigh against his.

George swallowed hard, scooting forward to the edge of the sofa. "Which listing is from this building?"

Sylvia scooted up and realigned herself against him. She leaned in, pointing to the bottom of the sheet he was holding. "Over here," she said, her finger on the listing highlighted in yellow.

"I see," George said, feeling increasingly uncomfortable.

"You're shy." She offered a knowing smile. "It's sweet."

"Not really." George let go of the MLS paperwork while Sylvia's finger remained pressed on the page. "It's just that I recently lost my wife."

"Oh honey," Sylvia said, pulling away. "I thought your wife died months ago."

"No. Last week," George lied.

Sylvia scootched further away. "Oh, poor baby. That explains all those things in the bedroom. I'm so sorry. What must you think of me? I had no idea."

George took a breath and looked down, embarrassed by the boldness of his fabrication.

"But you are," Sylvia said, "able."

George arched a brow.

Sylvia giggled as if she'd told a naughty joke.

"Able," George repeated before grasping the meaning. "Of course," he said, blushing at such a personal question.

"Just not ready," Sylvia confirmed, apparently relieved that a failed pass was mostly about poor timing. She tugged on the bottom of her silk blouse. "Now don't you worry, sweetie. When you're ready, you call me. You have my business card."

"I do," George stammered. Did she mean to discuss the listing? Or was she referring to other matters?

"And I'll make you a brisket. Do you like brisket?"

"Doesn't everyone?" George retreated to the corner of the sofa.

"Now let's see. This place will sell quickly, so we'd better do some planning to get you into another property. There are two listings you might potentially be interested in. I can show them, but I need to make a few calls. Give me a sec and I'll take care of that. Meanwhile, why don't you stay seated and make yourself at home."

That's an odd thing to say, George thought as Sylvia stepped out onto the balcony, phone in hand. *This is my home.*

That night, George walked through Mizner Park, the elegant central shopping district of Boca Raton. He didn't notice the other people milling about or the roving violinist playing "La Vie en Rose" for sidewalk diners. Lost in his thoughts, George could have been on an empty stretch of beach with only the ocean for company.

Had he done the right thing? Had he acted impulsively? Were the golf club membership and monthly association fees truly beyond his reach? Or should he have handled it differently? Sold stock to clear the debt despite the tax implications? He'd thought signing with Sylvia was progress, but now, he wasn't so sure. Leaving the condo would be like closing the door on Jeanette. Was he ready to make that move? And larger questions loomed: Where would he go? And what would he do with the rest of his life?

George decided to call Carole as he slipped into a quiet corner between two buildings near the end of the shopping district. Carole had continued to press for the details of his life, but lately, he'd let her calls go to voicemail. How could he talk to his daughter about his fears? In business, he had the vocabulary of a healthcare administrator. Return on investment, strategic planning, quality assurance, facility management. He could discuss healthcare for hours. But his emotions? For that, he had no words. She'd pressed him not to sell the condo. To wait. But now that he'd made the decision, he wanted to tell her. Put it behind him. Get it off his chest.

He'd hoped to leave her a voicemail message, but Carole picked up. Before she'd even said hello, George blurted out, "Carole, I've listed the condo for sale."

He should have texted.

There was a long pause as George waited for the reaction.

"I thought we agreed you'd wait until at least the one-year mark."

George cleared his throat. This was going to be even harder than he'd thought. He wanted to confess that he had no choice. That financial circumstances had forced his hand. But he couldn't admit the truth to his daughter. He just couldn't tell her that he was feeling frightened and lost. Instead, he went on the defensive. "There is no 'we' in the decision."

"I'm surprised. That's all. You caught me off guard." She sounded disappointed.

He wasn't exactly clear on why. Was it his tone? The way he delivered the message? Was it that he couldn't open up and share his true feelings? George rubbed his chin. He'd been grinding his teeth lately. The dentist had said it was from stress. He caught a whiff of Jeanette's perfume. He'd caressed the bottle earlier. Perhaps a droplet had gotten on his finger.

"Carole, please be supportive. What's done is done. I need to move on and I want you to be happy for me."

But George sensed Carole wasn't happy. All he'd wanted was to be reassured that he'd made the right decision listing the condo. Now, he wished he'd never called.

"Daddy, why do you make it so difficult to have a relationship with you? Peter texted me. You aren't returning his calls. Which is interesting, because I'm also having trouble getting hold of you. Why don't you return our calls?"

George's mood soured. He didn't appreciate being cornered. Why were his children so focused on him? Was this a holdover from Jeanette? Had she been too indulgent? Paid too much attention to the details of their adult lives? Why were they draining his energy and trying his patience?

George pressed his eyes shut. "I'm doing the best I can."

"That's what concerns me," Carole snapped. "Your best isn't really very good."

George winced. He couldn't imagine why the call had all gone so wrong. "Carole, this has got to stop. You judging me. Weighing in on my decisions. I don't like it. Tell your brother I'm fine. And the next time Peter complains that he can't reach me, remind him I have a life too."

"We're just concerned. We have no idea what's going on with you." Carole's voice sounded like Jeanette's when she was upset.

A knot formed in the pit of George's stomach. "Going on? What could be going on? There's no great mystery to what's happening here. I'm taking life day by day. I'm living."

"You're not emotionally ready to undertake a move. And it's a lot of work."

"Carole, I'm not enjoying this conversation. You've got to stop worrying about me. I need my space," George said as if he were a rebellious teenager and Carole the parent. "I'll be fine."

"Do you need me to come down and help?"

George was speechless. There was no way out of the endless back and forth. He could hear Carole breathing as he struggled to think of how to answer. "I wish you and your brother lived closer," he awkwardly said, hoping to soften the impending "no."

The overture landed flat. Carole didn't hesitate. "We both know you don't wish that, Daddy."

"Carole, don't be mad."

"I can't help it," she answered, barely audible. "Planes leave every day from Miami to San Francisco. You can easily come visit."

"But honey," he said in a measured tone, "you work. Besides, I have Miss Betsy."

"You can hang out at my place and do as you please. Enjoy the city. Walk the Embarcadero. And bring her with you. She'd love San Francisco."

His gambit at peace had failed.

One more try: a tactic he'd learned in business. If you can't win, change the subject. Sidestep the argument. Better yet, redirect the energy so that the argument shifts elsewhere. "And how long is the flight from San Francisco to Chicago? When was the last time you saw your brother?"

"That's not the same thing. Besides, Peter and I don't get along. You should know that."

"When was the last time you two talked?"

"We don't talk. If we need to, we text. Otherwise, we have separate lives," Carole affirmed. "Let's change the subject."

The ploy had worked.

George was only interested in a short-term, month-to-month rental if and when the condo sold, but Sylvia insisted he see what was available for sale. Though he tried to resist, she was persistent. After a week of pestering, he finally relented to meet her at noon in the lobby of a Boca high rise.

"You'll love this building," Sylvia promised as the elevator doors closed. She was the epitome of Realtor chic in an aqua blouse, strategically opened to offer a glimpse of cleavage, paired with tight black leather pants that emphasized her long, shapely legs. George imagined a whip in her hands. Her perfume, an enticing mix of rose with a hint of vanilla, caught in his throat as the elevator climbed to the fourth floor.

"Willy said your wife was a lovely woman."

George was taken aback. "You know Willy?"

Sylvia fiddled with a tennis bracelet. "We travel in the same social circles. We see each other from time to time. Fundraisers, cocktail parties, gallery openings. I was concerned to hear that he'd been in the hospital. But then, I heard he was released. I called him at home yesterday. He sounded perfectly fine."

Had Willy betrayed his lie? The one he'd told Sylvia about Jeanette when they'd met at the condo? "Jeanette was sick for over a year," George said, uncomfortable discussing Jeanette with an attractive woman.

"That's so sad," she said, her green eyes devoid of any real empathy.

"So, you know Willy. It's a small world."

Sylvia broke into a grin. "Everyone knows Willy."

George nodded as if he understood. But he didn't. Not really.

The elevator doors opened. "Do you drive?" Sylvia asked as they stepped into a long hallway.

George raised an eyebrow. "That's how I got here."

Sylvia laughed. "No, silly. I mean, do you drive at night?" She led the way, her heels creating a tip-tap, tip-tap on the marble floor.

"Yes, I drive at night." George's eyes were glued to the rhythmic swaying of Sylvia's backside as he followed closely behind.

"Well then," she nonchalantly offered. "Handsome, independent, and you drive at night." She swiveled about and caught his eye. "That makes you quite the catch."

"Oh," was all George could manage.

She shifted back into discussion of the property. "It's a great building. One small dog allowed. Everyone is over fifty-five. No small children running around except during the holidays. Actually," Sylvia confided, "you're not allowed to have children stay for more than two weeks. Sometimes grandparents wind up raising their grandchildren. That can't happen here. The bylaws of the homeowner's association forbid it. Well, not directly, but we all know what it means."

Though George was no fan of small children, he thought the rule mean. "Are we getting close?" he asked as they passed the sixth door in what seemed like an endless hallway.

"Not quite," Sylvia said, a girlish tilt to her voice. "Almost there. You'll love it. Trust me."

George doubted it. He should have given Sylvia a budget. Whatever the unit might cost, he could already tell that the place was well beyond his means. Wasn't the whole purpose of selling his condo to pay off debts? Why would he consider buying into such an expensive building? The whole idea was absurd. And he'd certainly never buy a unit with such a long walk from the elevator.

"The walk is worth it," Sylvia assured him as they stopped in front of an elaborately carved mahogany door. With a turn of the key and a jiggle of the lock, the door opened to reveal an expansive space decorated in stark white and charcoal gray. Clean, simple, and very modern.

"Wow. This is quite something," George said as Sylvia raised a remote control from a side table in the entry way. Electric blinds buzzed open to reveal floor-to-ceiling windows in the living room and a gorgeous ocean view.

"Wait till you see the bedroom," she said seductively. "It's heaven."

George worried that heaven was too rich for his wallet. "Sylvia, I'm afraid this property is way beyond—"

Sylvia held up a palm. The light hit her face, revealing the tiniest of lines around her eyes. "Don't say no yet."

Her high heels reverberated along the travertine as he followed. "Check out this gorgeous library," she cooed, a hand expressively introducing the rich mahogany bookcase in much the same way Vanna White displays the letters on *Wheel of Fortune*. With a gentle push, the center bookcase swung open, revealing a hidden doorway. "It's a passageway to the master," she marveled. "You don't have to walk down the hall to get to the bedroom. This is the shortcut. Through the connecting wall."

George had never seen anything like it. He followed Sylvia through the doorway to a spacious bedroom with an attached sitting area. Sylvia turned. Her green eyes flashed a brilliant iridescent. "What do you think?"

George was unsure what to say. Clearly the place was beyond his reach. "Sylvia, I can't afford this."

The slightest hint of a smile crossed her face. "Of course not, silly." She grabbed his hand and pulled him closer. "Besides, it's not for sale." She stood toe to toe with George.

"Then why am I looking at it?" he asked.

"You're not." She ran a finger across his lips. "You're looking at me."

George admired Sylvia's form as she sat on the edge of the bed. The way her strong shoulders transitioned down to her slim waist. He reached over, a finger tracing the small of her back.

"Stop it. I told you, I have to go," she said, pulling away from his touch.

George stretched out, a sheet covering his man parts. He watched her dress. "Where are you going? What's the rush?"

Sylvia searched for a missing shoe. "For one thing, this isn't my condo." She dropped to a knee, running a hand under the bed skirt. "My client might come home any minute."

George leapt out of bed. "Are you kidding?" He scrambled about, gathering his clothes, hopping along as he stepped into his underwear, nearly falling, steadying himself on a dresser. "Why didn't you tell me?" he shouted as he reached for his pants. He sat down to put them on. He had no intention of falling and needing an ambulance to carry him out of a stranger's home clad only in his underwear.

Sylvia covered her mouth, but the raucous laughter was unmistakable. "Oh, look at you. A regular Energizer Bunny. Who knew you could move so fast?"

George reached for his polo shirt at the foot of the bed and slipped it over his head. "I don't see what's so funny!" he shouted as he raced about the room.

Tears gathered in Sylvia's eyes as she grabbed her stomach and bounced with hysterics. "George," she moaned with laughter as she struggled to catch her breath. "They're in New York City. They won't be back until after Thanksgiving. I'm watching the property for them. It's alright."

George offered a hurt look. "Then why'd you lie?" he asked, belt unbuckled, one shoe on.

Sylvia sighed. "You're taking this way too seriously. What do you think is going on here? I'm not looking for a relationship. Or to get married."

George tugged on his waistband. "Married? Who said anything about marriage?"

Sylvia gave a knowing glance. "You've got that desperate look. Those sad, lost puppy eyes."

George blinked as if seeing Sylvia for the first time. "You're wrong. I have absolutely no interest in marrying," he said. "Besides, it's a little early to even consider that. We've only just..." George wasn't sure how to exactly describe what had happened between them. He knew the technical definition, but it seemed impolite to say it out loud.

Sylvia was still laughing as she came close. "Screwed." Her voice transformed. Almost professorial. "Oh yes, George. You very much want to remarry. I can smell it on you. You think a new woman will solve all your problems."

"Well, maybe that's true. Eventually…"

Sylvia tilted her head as if appraising a dress. Did she like the color? Was the cut flattering? Should she bother to try it on?

She gently stroked George's face. "It's the same old story. The first woman who comes along lands the widower. That's fine for some women. I salute them," she affirmed with a nod. "They consider themselves lucky. But not me." Sylvia's eyes traveled across George's broad shoulders as if determining how George might hold up at the dry cleaners.

George clasped his hands together. "So you think I'm desperate?"

"Oh, that's not a nice thing to say," Sylvia said with mock sarcasm. "As if you'd only sleep with me if you were desperate."

George winced. "That isn't what I meant."

"Well, whatever," Sylvia said with a wave of the hand. "It doesn't matter. All I know is that you're not ready for a relationship. That ex-wife of yours—"

"My late wife," George clarified.

Sylvia came close. She tapped George's forehead with a finger. "Yes. Her too. She's in your head. Buried deep inside. She must have been quite a woman. Most widowers are eager to forget the little woman. Some behave as if they were never married at all. Like they have no past."

George didn't understand.

"I know, baby. It seems unfathomable to you. But some men are in so much pain that they refuse to acknowledge they ever loved *that dead wife*. Oh, the games we play to keep ourselves sane."

"That can't be possible."

Sylvia offered a wink. "Trust me. I've seen it all. Men who bury their wives in anger, insisting on remembering every fault. They hold a grudge, as if the little woman died to spite them."

"Well, I'm different," George said. "I'd never disparage Jeanette."

"Yes," Sylvia agreed, offering George a little kiss on the cheek. "That's what makes you so enchanting. Jeanette must have been a pistol."

JUNE CAME AND went in the blink of an eye. Willy was out of the hospital; he was weak, but back on his feet. George continued to meet Benny and Herbie for golf. Willy joined them for meals out, his diet now severely restricted. And just as July broke through the calendar, Willy once again joined them on the golf course. He'd been assured that he was fine. At least, that's what he told his friends that last morning they were together. And then, by the fifth hole, Willy was dead. Lying on the green, Herbie frantically pumping on his chest, calling Willy's name.

The shock of Willy's death made July a particularly unpleasant month. In addition to losing one of his best friends, a third wave of Jeanette's medical bills began to arrive. This time, the invoices were stamped "OVERDUE" in red. Within days, the phone calls started at all times of the day and night. Bill collectors leaving threatening messages.

George was still determined to turn things around. He'd listed the condo with Sylvia back in May. She'd assured him it would be a fast turnaround. But so far, the condo had had few showings. George anticipated that once the condo sold, he'd be able to clean up most of the debt from Jeanette's medical expenses. And if he had to sell stock to make up the balance, he could do so then.

Unfortunately, that plan wasn't working.

Travelers avoided Florida in the humid, hot summer. That meant few buyers. The whole thing felt like a catch-22 as George reviewed his latest credit card bills. Eating out most meals with his friends had spiked the balances close to his credit limit. He could only pay the minimum due.

There had to be something he could do. The lovely bookkeeper at the Golden Funeral Home instantly came to mind. Maybe he could charm her. Get her to give up the information about Willy's family so he could contact them and at least get reimbursed for the funeral expenses. It was a long shot, but worth a try.

George grabbed the phone on the second ring as Miss Betsy danced about demanding to be picked up. The little poodle had hidden her true personality under Tri-County's kennel blanket. Given time and love, she'd blossomed, vocalizing with a low whine whenever George failed to pay her proper attention.

George took a seat on the sofa. Miss Betsy jumped into his lap as a female voice greeted him. "Mr. Elden, this is Jill Winters from The Golden Funeral Home. I'm returning your call."

George's heart raced. How should he handle this? What should he say?

Miss Betsy stood up on his lap, placing her front paws on George's shoulders as she pushed against him, enthusiastically licking George's face, a pink tongue slipping into his open mouth. "Eww," George moaned as the white bundle of love, seemingly satisfied, slid off George's lap and curled up by his side.

"Hello? Hello?" Jill Winters said.

George wiped his mouth with the back of a hand. Any hope of manipulating the situation went right out of his head. "Sorry about that, Ms. Winters. I was wondering. Is there any way that I might persuade you to give up Willy Krause's contact information?"

"Oh," she answered, seemingly disappointed. "Well, tell me. How did everything work out with the donation to FAU?"

George scrambled to remember the lie Benny had told. "Well, we haven't been able to track down the executor of the estate. So, we haven't yet made the donation."

"Oh. I'm sorry to hear that."

There was an awkward silence as George petted Miss Betsy. He hoped Ms. Winters wouldn't be looking for further information on the bogus scholarship. "I was hoping that you might help us out. Is there anything else I can do to make this happen?" George held his breath. It was now or never.

"Well, there is, Mr. Elden. But I'm not sure how to approach it."

George could hear paper crumpling in the background. *Oh no*, he thought. *The funeral home wants more money. They forgot to charge us for something miniscule. Something ridiculous.* George decided that no matter what, he, Herbie, and Benny were through shelling out money. Willy was safely tucked in the ground. The Golden Funeral Home would have to eat any additional costs.

Her voice softened. "I was wondering if you might have dinner with me."

"I beg your pardon?" he said, unsure he'd heard her correctly.

"If you're seeing someone, I understand. I just thought, you being a widower, that maybe…"

"Ms. Winters, how do you know I'm a widower?"

"Please; call me Jill."

"How do you know I'm not married?"

"I recognized your name," she admitted. "We took care of your wife."

George's heart sank. "Of course."

"I know it's unconventional, and I hope I'm not intruding, but it isn't often that an attractive man shows up who *isn't* in mourning. At least, not in the back office."

George was flattered. "I imagine not."

"And I'm not a mortician. I have absolutely no contact with the bodies."

George winced. The conversation had moved from awkward to morbid. "Well, that's a very nice invitation," he said, wondering what Jeanette might think about the phone call.

"So is it a date?"

George remembered the auburn beauty with the great figure. Could he actually do this?

"I understand if you'd rather not."

George thought it had taken a lot of guts for Ms. Winters to ask. Perhaps she'd share the information about Willy's family if they got to know each other. "Sure," George answered, uncertain whether it was a good idea or just downright creepy.

"Then I'll meet you at the bar at Ruth's Chris in Mizner Park at seven p.m. tomorrow."

"Fine," George answered as Miss Betsy licked his hand.

George sat on the edge of Jill's bed, hands cradling his face. "I'm sorry. This has never happened before. I'm usually..."

Something had gone wrong. Was it the two cocktails at the bar? The heavy meal? Why had his mind wandered? He'd tried to focus, stay in the moment, but Jeanette's face had flashed, and then Ava's and Sylvia's. Three women had made an untimely appearance just as George was warming up.

Jill Winters gathered the covers about her.

George pressed his eyes closed. "It's just that, well, I'm still sort of an emotional mess."

Jill sat up, leaning against the headboard. "Don't apologize. These things happen."

George was mortified. "Not to me. It's never happened to me."

"I guess there's always a first," she whispered, hugging her knees in closer. "If this is the first time."

George shifted to face her. "I hope you don't think this has anything to do with you."

"Now, why would I think that?"

Despite her denial, George sensed she was irritated. He'd definitely overstayed his welcome.

"Tell me, George. How many women have you been with since your wife died?"

George hesitated. "Not many. Why?"

"You're a handsome man. Women must be throwing themselves at you."

"A few."

"How many is a few?"

"Two."

"Is that the real count?"

"Yes," George answered.

"Oh. That's different then."

"I'm not following you."

"And how well did you know those ladies? I don't mean sexually. I mean, personally."

George's mouth hung open. "Not very well."

"Why do you think that is?"

George had no clue.

"I have a theory," Jill said. "I call it the Little Boca Boy Syndrome."

George could feel the heat rising in his face.

"Widowers get all this free sex. And for those coming out of long-term marriages, well, they really don't have any dating skills. They look like men, but they're actually adolescent boys, incapable of building a real relationship with a woman. Or too guilty. Or too embarrassed. And why should they stay with one woman? There's a whole garden of lovely flowers to choose from. And this goes on and on, no matter how wonderful the next woman they meet might be."

George thought about Ava from the Tri-County Animal Rescue. Why hadn't he returned her calls?

"Little boys. Just little boys," Jill repeated.

"Wow," George said as he stood up. "You don't think much of men. Making a sweeping judgment like that. I'm not like every man. I'm me."

Jill sighed. "There you're wrong, George. You're just like all the rest. You won't call tomorrow. Even if everything..." She cleared her throat. "Had gone as planned. You still wouldn't have called."

George resisted. "You don't know that."

"I do, George. And just to prove the point, I'm going to give you the name of the family contact for your friend's funeral plot. I shouldn't. But I will."

George didn't know what to say.

Jill stuck her chin out. "Isn't that the only reason you're here?"

George swallowed hard. "I'm here because you invited me to dinner."

"Oh, George, a little honesty would go a long way." Jill slipped out of bed and crossed the room to her dresser, where she retrieved a slip of paper with The Golden Funeral Home insignia.

George took the paper from her. He read out loud the name of the family contact. "Mona Krause?" He was stunned. "Willy had a sister?"

"How much longer to Mona Krause's address?" George asked as he pulled off the freeway.

The sun was beginning to set as Herbie, seated next to him, held up his smart phone. "Another five minutes."

"Then when's the next turn?"

"Just wait. She'll tell us."

A female voice announced, "Make a right on Jog Road."

Benny stretched a leg across the back seat. "How come she only talks sometimes?"

George had no idea what Benny meant. "She always talks."

"No, she doesn't," Benny said as George made a right. "Sometimes she talks, other times she doesn't say anything."

Herbie turned to Benny. "It all depends on which program you use. If you use Siri, she talks. If you use Google Maps, she doesn't."

George looked askance at Herbie. "That isn't true."

"Yes, it is," Herbie said. "Try Google Maps next time. You'll see."

"We *are* using Google Maps," George answered. "I programmed the address into your phone."

Herbie looked down at his phone. "Oh yeah. We are."

George pulled into a strip center parking lot. The female voice spoke again: "Proceed to the route."

"I think we better talk about this first," George said as he shifted the car into park.

Benny winced as he stretched his back. "There's nothing to talk about. We paid for the funeral and now we want the estate to reimburse us."

The female voice spoke again: "Proceed to the route."

"We don't know this woman," George said. "There's no telling how this will go."

Herbie ignored George's concern. "Did Willy even mention a Mona?"

George couldn't remember Willy ever discussing his personal life.

Again, the female voice spoke: "Proceed to the route."

"Oh Jesus." Herbie fiddled with the phone. "How do you turn this off?"

"Something's fishy about this whole thing," George suggested. "It's so odd."

Benny agreed. "It's troubling. And why couldn't she see us earlier in the day?" His tone was so serious that both Herbie and George laughed. "What? What did I say? What the hell is so funny?"

"You are," Herbie answered as the phone once again demanded that they proceed to the route.

"Can you turn her off?" George pleaded.

"It's always two against one," Benny said with irritation. "Ever since Willy died, you two have closed ranks."

George wondered if that was true.

"Oh stop it, Benny," Herbie said.

"No. Really. Now that Willy's gone, you two brothers-in-law—"

"*Ex* brothers-in-law," Herbie corrected.

"—have been riding me, and I don't like it."

"I'm sorry, Benny," George said. "I wasn't aware..."

Herbie waved a hand. "Well, don't expect an apology from me. I've done nothing wrong."

George sighed. "Herbie, don't be an asshole."

"I'm not walking on eggshells with him," Herbie countered. "I'll say whatever I damn well please."

George gripped the steering wheel. "That's just stupid."

"The guy is sixty-five years old. He needs to grow some balls."

George shook his head. “Nice. That’s the way to talk to a friend.”

“Sure,” Herbie said. “I wouldn’t put up with this crap from one of my wives.”

George didn’t miss a beat. “Maybe that’s why you’re alone.”

“Yeah,” Benny said. “So desperately alone.”

“I’m not alone,” Herbie insisted. “Not like you two.”

“You’ve got to admit, your social skills aren’t the best,” George grumbled.

“Hey,” Herbie exploded. “My social skills are fine. And if I ever need advice, you two shouldn’t wait for a phone call.”

“Now Herbie, there’s no reason to get so upset,” George said, hoping to deescalate the situation.

“Yeah.” Benny flashed a grin, throwing Herbie’s words back. “I wouldn’t put up with that from one of my wives.”

“We need to treat each other better,” George said.

“Right,” Benny agreed.

Herbie scoffed at the recommendation. “So what are we going to say when we meet Mona Krause?”

“Proceed to the route,” the phone insisted.

Mona Krause stood in the doorway of her elegant Boca condo perched high in the sky like an eagle’s nest looking down on the denizens below. George thought her the spitting image of matronly with her padded figure and round face. Her dark eyes surveyed the three men before her. It took George but a moment to realize that the surprised expression on her face was her only expression.

“I thought you said you were Willy’s friends.”

George looked at Herbie and Benny in bewilderment. “We are.”

“Well, I’ve never met you. And I know all of Willy’s friends.”

George hardly knew what to say.

"I was the one who arranged for Willy's twenty-four hour nursing coverage when he was in the hospital," Benny said in a huff.

Mona gave him the once over. "Well, I suppose it's alright then. But I don't as a rule allow strangers in my home." She stood aside as they passed through the grand entryway. "Forgive me. The place is a mess. The cleaning crew didn't come yesterday."

The travertine marbled glistened. The tabletops shined. George looked about in awe as they passed through a hallway that opened onto a sunken living room. The ocean view from the penthouse was breathtaking as the sun began to set on the horizon.

No bill collectors here, George thought, feeling sorry for himself.

Mona pointed to a large white sectional in the living room. "You can sit over here."

A little low, George thought as he tumbled into a soft cushion. Benny and Herbie, on either side, knocked into him on the way down. For a moment, he was reminded of a fun house. The only things missing were the mirrors and cotton candy.

Mona positioned herself in a white Barcelona chair. A short woman, her legs bobbed up as she slipped backward. George suppressed a laugh as she struggled to right herself. "And what can I do for you?" she asked, pulling herself to the edge of the leather chair, breathlessly tugging at her skirt.

Benny and Herbie turned to George. George hadn't thought he'd be the spokesperson. Wasn't it Benny who'd gone over what they needed to say to Mona? "Well," George started. "At the funeral, we…I mean the three of us…were asked by the rabbi to kick in—"

Herbie interrupted. "Actually, we paid for the whole enchilada."

Mona did a double take. Her highly arched brows, frozen in place, offered the perfect expression. "You did!"

"Yes," George stammered.

"But why?" Mona asked. "Who are you?"

George looked at Benny for help.

"We're his golf buddies," Benny explained. "The rabbi told us the check to the funeral home hadn't cleared. So for the burial to proceed, we covered the cost."

Mona's hand went to her chest as she released peals of laughter. "Oh no. You didn't," she said, pointing a finger and gasping between chortles. "You three!"

"Well, yes," George answered, uncertain what was so funny.

Mona struggled to regain her composure. "I guess you boys didn't really know Willy."

George was uncertain what Mona meant, but he knew it wasn't good. "Oh, you're wrong. We were close friends."

Mona raised her chin. "You think so, do you?"

George looked at Benny. Benny looked back with a blank stare.

"Is there something you're trying to tell us?" George asked. "Something we should know?"

Mona offered a Cheshire-cat smile. "Clearly, you knew nothing about my ex-husband. If you did, you'd realize how funny this little turn of events is."

"Ex-husband?" George blurted.

Mona arched her back. "Well, who the hell do you think you're talking with? His mother?"

"No," George answered. Mona was obviously too young to be Willy's mother.

"You're sitting in my home and you have no idea who I am," Mona said indignantly. "How did you get my name and phone number?"

"The funeral home," George quickly answered.

Mona's voice hit a new octave. "And Willy never talked about me?"

George looked at Herbie and Benny. They both shook their heads.

Mona's eyes glistened as she took in the information. "And you three say you were his friends?"

Herbie leaned forward. "We wouldn't be here otherwise."

"Well, I'm Willy's second wife."

"So you're family," Benny said, smiling proudly as if putting it all together for the first time.

"No, we're not. You see, Willy walked out on me. One morning he was gone."

George scrunched his brow. "Gone?"

"We had words." Mona looked away for a moment. "We were better as friends. And even though the marriage ended, we remained friends."

George was confused. "Then why did the funeral home have you as a contact?"

"We bought those plots together. It was a kind of wedding present to each other."

Herbie physically recoiled. "I've never heard of such a morbid thing."

Mona blushed. "Willy was concerned that his first wife wouldn't allow him to be buried in the family plot. He was eager to secure another location."

Benny coughed. "Are you kidding?"

Mona puckered her lips. "Now, why would I kid about that?"

George double-clicked the remote as he and Benny walked to the car. The car lights flashed. "It's like Willy had this other life," George said, utterly confused. "How could we not know about two marriages?"

Benny scratched his chin, picking at the hairs. "It makes no sense. And what did Mona mean, we didn't know Willy? It sounded so sinister."

George turned and realized Herbie hadn't followed them out of the building. "Where the heck is Herbie? He came down the elevator with us."

Benny was oblivious. "The way she laughed at us. It gave me the chills."

"To be honest, I'm beginning to think she might be right."

"Hey, listen, George. My back is killing me. How about Herbie and I switch? Let him sit in the back seat. He's smaller."

George peered at the front door to Mona's lobby. Still no Herbie. "He can't. He gets car sick."

"You know, George," Benny said as he squeezed into the back seat of the SUV, "that's what he says, but I don't believe him. He's got more ailments than Carter has pills."

"C'mon, Benny. Be a sport." George settled into the driver's seat.

"I think it's about control," Benny groused. "Herbie just likes to be in control."

George drummed his thumbs on the steering wheel and leaned over to look out the passenger window. He caught sight of the time on the dashboard. It was getting late. Miss Betsy would need to go outside. "Where the heck is he?"

Benny stretched a leg. "George, move your seat up. There's barely any leg room."

"You were fine coming here," George said with irritation.

"Well, that was then. This is now. A fella can change his mind."

George spotted Benny in the rearview mirror. He was sitting at an awkward angle. He didn't look happy. "I can't. If I move closer, I won't be able to brake. Sorry, guy. Really."

The passenger door opened and Herbie slipped into the front seat.

"Where have you been?" George asked.

"With the widow, Mona," Herbie answered, rather nonchalantly. "After you guys stepped off the elevator, I decided to go back."

"Did you need to use the bathroom?" Benny asked.

"No. I just wanted to get her alone."

"Don't tell me she's fallen under your spell," George said. "Gosh, Herbie, some things should be sacred. Like not making a move on your dead friend's ex-wife."

Herbie held a finger in the air. "Think about what you just said, George. There's something so wrong with that sentence. First, dead friend. Like my dead friend still has feelings. Second. Ex-wife. Now, why should that poor women have to suffer alone?"

"Oh, Jesus," Benny moaned. "Here we go."

Herbie turned about. "Benny, not every woman finds me irresistible. I know that's hard for you to imagine. But it's true. I'm just not everyone's cup of tea."

Benny laughed. "Tea, coffee, or cocoa."

"But our Ms. Mona had a lot to share." Herbie shifted to look at George. "She told me what she was unwilling to reveal to the two of you."

George grew increasingly impatient. "We're waiting, Sherlock Holmes."

"First, remember that woman who cried out at The Golden Funeral Home? Something about Willy dying in the prime of life. That was Mona. I recognized her voice as soon as she opened the door and said hello. And second, it turns out that Willy was not who he appeared to be."

"I knew it," Benny said. "He was so quiet. Always secretive. Did you ever notice that?"

George shook his head. "I thought he was just listening."

"Hmm," Herbie hummed. "You'd think so. But it was more than that."

"So get to the point," George said. "What did she say?"

Herbie smiled. "It wasn't what she said; it was whom she told me to talk to."

"Give it up," Benny pressed. "Stop being so damn secretive."

Herbie held up his smart phone. "The name and address of Willy's son."

George and Benny said in unison, "Willy had a son?"

"A son in Miami," Herbie clarified. "The kid's name is Simon."

– 9 –

THERE WAS SILENCE in the car as George and Benny absorbed the news that Willy had a son. "He never talked about a kid," George finally said.

"Apparently, he never talked about a lot of things," Herbie added.

"So what's the next step?" Benny shifted in the back seat.

"We meet the kid," Herbie said. "I'd think that would be obvious."

"The kid," Benny said in confirmation as if they were the Three Musketeers. One for all and all for one.

George checked the clock on the dashboard. "We can't go now. I need to get back to Miss Betsy."

"Are you kidding?" Herbie grumbled. "It's a dog. She can hold it a little longer."

"Not long enough for us to drive to Miami and back. I can't do that to her. Besides, she needs to be near me. We've already been gone a few hours. She must be wondering where I am."

Herbie rolled his eyes. "You've got to get a grip. A dog is a dog."

"Not Miss Betsy. She's special. You don't know her."

"Dear God, George. I'm really beginning to wonder about you."

Benny laughed. "Go easy, Herbie. Haven't you ever fallen in love with an animal?"

Herbie appeared to give the question real consideration. "Absolutely not," he finally asserted.

"Well then, you're missing out on something important in your life," George said. "And I'm not about to screw things up with Miss Betsy."

Herbie turned to face Benny. "I guess we don't have to worry about George and his love life. He's already made a commitment. Miss Betsy's in the running for second wife."

The drive down to Miami on I-95 tested George's nerves. Speeding cars and oversized tanker trucks wove in and out of lanes as George maneuvered through the dark stretch of highway. His fingers ached from gripping the steering wheel. His eyes burned from the glare of the lights of oncoming traffic.

"What are you doing?" Herbie asked as George exited at Northwest Eighty-First Street in Miami.

George pulled into a nearby gas station and glared at Herbie. "You said you had to go to the bathroom. That you can't hold it another minute. There's a restroom inside."

"Oh no," Herbie said. "I'm not going in there. Not in this neighborhood."

"What's wrong with you?" George asked. "It's open. See the sign?" A black paper clock with white hands hung on the inside of a cracked window.

"It's filthy," Herbie answered. "Haven't you ever been in one of those places?"

Benny leaned forward. "It's too dirty for our little Herbie to use the bathroom."

Herbie scowled.

George had no intention of driving around Miami in the dark searching for just the right facility for Herbie's waste product. "Come on, Herbie. Be a man. Do your business and stop being a baby."

"Imagine that," Benny added. "A pediatrician who acts like a baby."

"Shut up," Herbie said as he opened the car door. "When I return, if I return, we're going to find that kid and get the name of Willy's attorney."

George checked the dashboard clock. "Well, you better get a move on. It's already nine."

Benny let out a yawn as Herbie disappeared. "It's nine already? I can't believe I'm still awake." He stretched an arm across the back seat as Miss Betsy stood up. She gave a brisk shake before settling back down at Benny's side.

George wished they were closer to home. He dreaded the drive back to Boca. It would be one long shlep. "What time do you usually go to bed?"

"Nine thirty," Benny sheepishly admitted.

"That's early."

"And you?"

"It depends on whether I've napped."

"Napped?"

George turned to look at Benny. "It's not like I plan to nap. I just fall asleep. It's especially troubling at the movies. Lights go down, I'm out."

"Really?"

"And then later, I can't sleep. Now Miss Betsy likes to go to bed the same time every night. Around eight. Though

I can usually persuade her to stay awake until ten. The trick for me is not to nap. Then I can sleep through the night."

Benny winced. "Sleep through the night. You're lucky. I spend most of my time going back and forth to the toilet."

George laughed. "I know what you mean. You're fine until you lay down. Then suddenly…it's like Splash Mountain."

"As a kid, I was a bed-wetter. I still worry about that."

George would never have guessed. "No."

"Sure," Benny said defensively. "It happens to a lot of boys. It was hell. And embarrassing."

"How old were you when it stopped?"

"Around ten."

"That must have been tough."

"It was. And even after it stopped, I never trusted myself. I still check to make sure the bed is dry when I wake up. Once, our golden Lab, Smitty, had an accident in the middle of the night. There was a thunderstorm and he lost it up on the bed. He was twelve. After that, he slept in his crate. But that night, when I felt the wetness seeping through the top sheet, I panicked. Silly how these traumas stay with you."

"I bet."

"Someday," Benny promised, "I'll tell you how the fear of bed-wetting helped ruin my first marriage."

George could only imagine.

"Here comes trouble," George said, tongue in cheek. "Everything alright?" he asked as Herbie hopped back into the passenger seat.

"Sure," Herbie answered.

"How bad was it?" Benny asked.

Herbie rubbed his hands together. "Your worst nightmare."

George smiled. "Worse than paying for the funeral of a dead friend?"

It was a motor lodge from another era. George guessed it had once been a Howard Johnson's. "Look at the peaked roof. That had to be the front office," he said as he scanned the entirety of the property from the safety of the car. "I'd bet anything that roof was once orange."

Benny shuddered. "It looks like the motel in Memphis where Martin Luther King Junior was assassinated."

George squinted as he looked at the dilapidated structure and then back at the address on the phone. "This is it, gentlemen. No doubt about it."

"Jeez," Herbie sighed. "With all his money, Willy had a kid living like this. I don't get it."

George strained to see the darkened courtyard. It looked deserted. "Do you think it's a drug den?"

"We should have called first," Benny added with a yawn. "It's wrong to come here so late."

Herbie turned to look back at Benny. "I told you. Mona didn't have a phone number. Just an address. It turns out, Willy lost track of the kid. While in the hospital, he asked Mona to hire a private detective to try and find him. A week after the funeral, she received this address. And by the way, it wouldn't be so late if we hadn't stopped at George's to pick up his damn dog."

As if on cue, Miss Betsy sat up and looked about. Benny rubbed the back of her neck. "George, I think I'm taking this one home with me. She's a doll."

"Isn't she?" George cooed.

"Oh, Lord," Herbie moaned. "I can't believe you actually brought that dog."

"I couldn't leave her home," George said indignantly. "She needs attention."

Herbie rolled his eyes. "And you need a good therapist."

"Aww," Benny said. "She's licking my hand."

"Okay, ladies," Herbie sneered. "Can we get back to the matter at hand?"

"Ladies?" George snapped. "Don't use that as an insult. Women are wonderful. If men were more like women, the world would be a better place."

Herbie's eyes bulged. "We'd have zero population growth if men were like women."

"I'm talking about feelings," George clarified.

Herbie covered his ears. "I can't believe I'm listening to this. Can we get on with what we came here to do?"

George wasn't finished. "Herbie, if you ever had a successful marriage or a daughter, you'd know how amazing women are."

Herbie looked at George askance. "I thought your daughter drives you nuts."

"I never said that."

"George, don't lie. I've heard you talk about Carole."

"I've never said anything negative about my daughter. I wasn't complaining. I was…reporting."

"Sounded like complaining to me."

Benny leaned forward. "Next time Carole's in town, I'd like to join you two for lunch. I've been looking for a new piece of art."

George was delighted. "She'd love that."

"Oh my God," Herbie cried. "Listen to you two. Can we please get back to the business at hand?"

George refocused. "I don't know about you guys, but this whole thing feels like a wild goose chase. I don't like it."

Herbie's eyes flashed. "Where's your sense of adventure, George?"

Benny pulled forward, his head between George and Herbie. "The place looks dangerous."

Herbie shook his head. "Our big hero. Maybe you should stay here with Little Miss Thing-of-a-jig."

"Betsy," George corrected. "Her name is Miss Betsy."

Benny lifted Miss Betsy from the back seat and placed her on his knees. Her head rested just under his chin. "I'm just being cautious. It's not like we're young."

Herbie turned sharply about, surprised by the sight of the little dog. He jerked his head back. "Stop making more of this than it is. There's nothing scary about that place. You're scary. One look at you and anyone would think Lurch from the Addams Family had darkened their doorstep."

Benny's voice shot up an octave. "Me? You want me to go in there?"

"Who else?" Herbie said. "You've got the size. No one is going to screw with you."

Silence fell over the car. George glanced in the rearview mirror.

Benny snuggled his head against Miss Betsy's. "Okay, honey." Benny sighed. "I guess the sooner I do this the faster we can get out of this neighborhood."

Miss Betsy closed her eyes as if she was in ecstasy.

"Who loves you?" Benny asked the little poodle. "Georgie porgy? Herbie? Oh, not him. He's a smelly old man. Me? Yes, my little honey. Your big, strong, Uncle Benny."

"Dear God, George," Herbie complained. "You've got to leave that dog at home."

George couldn't help but think about the changes neighborhoods undergo over time. South Beach instantly came to mind. Popular in the 1950s before urban blight set in. And how it had again been transformed into a hot destination. "There was once a time when people vacationed in this rat trap," he said as he eyed the rundown structure.

"Time's funny that way," Benny said. "Nothing stays the same."

"Nothing except the money Willy's estate owes us," Herbie reminded them. "Now come on, Benny. George did Jill from the funeral home. I did Mona, tonight. It's your turn. You're up."

George caught a glimpse in the rearview mirror of Benny's frightened expression. "Okay," George agreed. "I'll go with you."

"Will you, George?" Benny said, his voice hitting a crescendo.

"Sure. I don't blame you." He looked past Herbie out the window at the old motel. "It does look a bit scary."

"Scary!" Herbie chortled. "You girls are killing me."

A full moon lit the night sky as George made his way along the broken pavement on the perimeter of the motel. He was reminded of the night Jeanette had died. The sense of hopelessness. The fear that something terrible was about to happen. Something irreversible and horribly final.

Benny, a few steps behind, cautioned George. "Watch out for the bushes. Someone could be hiding back there, ready to jump out."

George glanced about. The only thing he noticed was Benny dropping farther back. "Hey," he called out. "Where are you going?"

Benny cowered. George had never seen Benny scared. "We shouldn't go any farther. This is definitely a crack house."

George looked through the wrought iron fence past the *Beware of Dog* sign. He refused to give into fear. He pressed forward, entering the motel's small courtyard, certain that the secret to Willy's estate was within reach. To the right was an empty pool with a broken lawn chair on its side at the bottom. In the moonlight, George could see a long row of doors in an L-shape wrapped around the pool.

George steadied himself. "It's just an old motel. There's nothing to be scared of." He hoped he sounded more confident than he felt.

"It's too quiet," Benny warned as an owl screeched in the distance.

"Well, we're here now," George reassured Benny, wishing someone would reassure him. "If what you think is true, there's nothing to fear. Everyone will be drugged out."

Benny's hulking frame morphed into a giant teddy bear. The kind that sits in the corner chair of a newborn nursery, no more fierce than a Great Dane puppy. "My antenna is going way up, George. Way up."

"It's quiet. Everyone's probably asleep. I don't think anyone is going to mess with us."

George was reminded of the latest message on his answering machine: *If you don't call us back, we're sending a bounty hunter to kick down your door.* It was a baseless threat from an overzealous bill collector. *Bounty hunter? Ridiculous,* George had thought. *Bounty hunters don't work on overdue medical bills.* And still, the message had unnerved him.

"We're going to be fine, Benny," George whispered, knowing the reason for whispering undermined his assertion.

Benny didn't seem quite as sure. "It's easy for you to say, George. You're normal height. But ever since I was kid, bullies have taken potshots at me. When you're the biggest kid, you're not always safe. Size doesn't protect you. If anything, you stand out."

George hadn't considered a big kid might be an ideal target. "But we're not kids anymore, Benny. The world has changed. Bullying is totally uncool."

"You think so?" Benny didn't sound convinced.

"Sure." George walked past the darkened office. "I'll knock on one of these doors. Maybe someone will know which room is Simon's."

"It's late, George. We should come back tomorrow. During the day," Benny pleaded.

George thought of the stack of medical bills on his desk. "How do we know anyone will even be here then? Now come on. Buck up. We're here. Let's just do this." George felt a sudden rush of bravery. "Where do you think we should start?"

Benny stepped up to the first door. "I'd say right here."

George jumped as Benny loudly knocked on it. "You should have warned me before you did that," he said, a hand on his heart.

Benny's eyes lit up. He flashed a huge smile. "Look who's scared now. We've got to start somewhere and this door looks as good as any."

"Someone's coming," George whispered.

There was a shuffling of feet. Then, a female voice: "I've got a gun. Get away from the door."

Benny turned to George, who was standing behind him. George wasn't sure what to say. But he had to try something. Willy's funeral expenses needed to be reimbursed. And his Visa balance wasn't going to pay itself. "I'm a friend," he called out.

"I don't have friends," the voice called back.

"We're looking for Simon Krause. Do you know him?"

"I don't know anyone."

"Simon Krause," George repeated. "He's a friend of ours."

"If he's a friend, why are you knocking on my door?"

Benny looked at George with raised eyebrows. It was a good question. "We're attorneys," Benny lied. "His father's died and left him money."

George stepped forward as the chain lock was undone. Benny stepped behind George when the door unbolted.

A woman with round, hollow eyes, her auburn hair in disarray, stared at them. She looked in desperate need of a good meal. Her face was blotchy and covered with sores; when she spoke, George noticed she was missing teeth. He remembered the *before* and *after* photographs of meth addicts he'd seen on a *Dr. Phil* episode. This was definitely the *after*.

"Why should I help you? What's in it for me?" the woman snarled. A ratty bathrobe hung from her bony frame.

George's mouth opened. But what could he say?

Benny reached past George and placed a palm firmly on the door to hold it open. "I'm giving you till the count of three." His sheer size dwarfed the doorway. "After that," he said in a menacing tone George didn't recognize, "I'm coming in to search. And there's no telling what I'll find for the police."

The woman's eyes registered fear as she glanced upward, eyes traveling from Benny's chest to his neck, and then to his face.

Benny offered a scowl.

George thought it an uncanny imitation of Lurch.

All was quiet at the sleepy motel as George and Benny crept along the covered walkway. George was reminded of a *Hawaii Five-O* episode. Not the reboot—the original with Jack Lord and James MacArthur. He fancied himself Lord. Tall, dark, and swarthy. Capable of facing any danger. As long as he didn't really have to.

"Maybe he's out." Benny's voice had a hopeful note as they stood before room 110.

"Maybe. So we have nothing to lose."

"But what's the point of coming here? It's not like the kid is going to reimburse us. Look at this dump. He probably isn't even aware Willy's dead. I bet he hasn't talked to his dad in years."

George couldn't help but agree. "Do you think Willy knew his son lived like this?"

Benny shook his head. "With each passing moment, I'm wondering whether we knew Willy at all."

George was wondering that too.

"Come on." Benny tugged George's arm. "Who knows what we'll find behind that door? Let's get the hell out of here."

George held his ground. "Don't you think we owe it to Willy to check on the kid? At least, see him."

"Oh my God. Really?"

"If it was my son, I'd want my friends to help."

Benny stepped back. "Honestly, George. Willy probably never mentioned the kid because he was ashamed. And some people don't want help. And even if this kid does, we're not qualified to offer it. What do we know about drug treatment programs? I'm a dental implant surgeon. I do teeth. Teeth don't talk back."

"That's because you have your hand in the person's mouth." George stepped forward and rapped loudly on the door. "Open up in there," he shouted. "It's the police."

Benny looked horrified. "George, you're going to get us killed."

George again pounded on the door, this time with the full force of his fist.

There was a scurrying sound before the door swung open. The room was pitch-black. A short, dark-haired man stood on the threshold. The muzzle of a gun pointed directly at George's chest.

"Oh God," George cried, stepping back with his hands in the air, eyes glued to the nose of the gun. Pretending to be the police wasn't such a great idea.

A voice croaked from the shadows of the room. "What do you want?"

Benny threw his voice past the man at the door. "We're looking for Simon. Simon Krause."

"He's not here," the voice called back.

"Hey buddy," George said to the man in the doorway. "Put the gun down. No one wants to hurt anyone."

The man at the door pointed the gun at George's face. "Where's your warrant?"

"We're not cops," Benny answered. The gun shifted direction. Benny raised his hands.

"Then who the hell are you? Federal agents? Narcs?"

"Hell no," George said. "We like to get high. Don't we, Benny?"

"Actually, not that much, George. I hate the feeling of being out of control. And they say it destroys brain cells."

"Benny!" George shouted, nodding toward the guy at the door, reminding his friend that his comments were neither helpful nor pertinent. "Look," George said, his arms growing tired. "We're friends of Simon's dad, Willy."

"My dad?" a voice in the dark asked.

"Yes. Your dad," Benny called out.

"Well, that's different. Hey Carlos," the voice commanded. Light from a small table lamp switched on to offer the barest of illumination. "It's okay."

George squinted as frightened eyes stared back. Some adults were lying on the floor, others on bare mattresses. Some huddled against the walls in a seated position. A mother holding an infant. A father holding a toddler. A small child looked up from one of the two beds in the room, tired eyes searching George's face.

"What's going on here?" George asked as a man in torn jeans, sporting a shaggy beard and a T-shirt with a print of Abraham Lincoln, stepped over a sleeping bag by the door. The sleeping bag moved.

"Let's go outside where we can talk," the man said as George and Benny backed up.

"And you are?" Benny asked.

The man squeezed the tip of his nose with a thumb and forefinger and snorted. "I'm Simon Krause."

– 10 –

SIMON STEPPED OUT of the darkness into the bright moonlight. His compact form reminded George of Willy. Except for the beard, the physical resemblance was striking.

George, shaken from his recent encounter with the barrel of a gun, clasped his hands to stop the trembling. "What's going on in there?" he demanded.

Benny offered a guess. "It's a drug den."

Simon smiled sweetly. It was the calm, patient smirk Willy rendered before offering advice. "Not at all," he said with a snort, giving the tip of his nose another squeeze.

George didn't believe him. Simon's nose action alone told the story. "You're using coke."

"Coke?" Simon said with surprise, seemingly amused. "Allergies. I have terrible allergies and this old motel is infested with mold." He offered George a view of his arm. Instead of needle marks, it was covered in hives. "You know the kind of control it takes not to scratch? It's driving me insane."

"Why the gun?" Benny asked. "I hope you have a permit for that thing."

George had to laugh. "A permit? Benny, look where we are."

Benny nodded, conceding the point.

"So what the hell are you doing here?" George asked Simon. "And why weren't you at your dad's funeral?"

Simon went pale. "He died?"

"Oh my God." George felt the fool. "You didn't know? When was the last time you spoke to your dad?"

Before Simon could answer, there was a rush of footsteps behind them. Herbie's voice rang out, loud and clear. "What the hell are you guys doing? How could you leave me alone for so long in this neighborhood?"

Benny answered. "It wasn't so very long."

"Long enough. Unless you have a death wish." Herbie nervously looked about, Miss Betsy tucked under his arm like a football. "Christ, what a dump. Is this where the kid lives?"

George glared at Herbie. Was there any way to stop him from talking?

"What? What did I say?" Herbie asked. "This place is a rat trap. A place for rummies and hobos."

"*Herbie*," George said, hoping to silence him. Miss Betsy whined as George took the little dog in his arms. The grateful poodle licked his face.

"It's funny," Herbie pondered. "You never hear about hobos anymore. The homeless, yes. But not hobos. Maybe that's because hobos travel by rail and everyone today travels by air."

George cleared his throat, directing his attention to Simon. "This is our friend, Herbie. I'm George. The big guy is Benny. We're your dad's golf buddies."

Herbie stared at the bearded youth. "This is Simon?"

George nodded.

Herbie pointed in Simon's face. "Your damn father stuck us with the cost of his funeral."

"Jesus, Herbie!" George said. "We just told Simon his dad died. He didn't know."

"I had no idea," Simon said.

Herbie seemed contrite. "So that's why you weren't at the funeral."

Benny looked askance at Herbie. "You're a regular Perry Mason."

"Why don't we all sit down?" Benny suggested. There was a picnic table nearby. "How about over there?"

George put Miss Betsy on the ground. "First, we've got to take care of business. Come on, honey." He coaxed the little poodle over to a bush. "Hurry up," he said in a high-pitched voice. "Hurry up. Hurry up."

"Dear God, George," Herbie called out. "The sight of you and that dog is too much."

Miss Betsy squatted, and to George's surprise, as she tinkled, she released a growl in Herbie's direction.

Gathered about the picnic table at the rear of the courtyard, George imagined a family camping trip. Missing: a campfire, marshmallows, and a beer or two. And their friend, Willy. He should have been with them. Instead, they were joined by his son, Simon. A younger version of Willy. A stranger to them. But with the same sure smile. It occurred to George: perhaps Willy too had been a stranger. A congenial, familiar stranger. But a stranger, nonetheless.

George held Miss Betsy on his lap. The glow of moonlight illuminated the foursome, casting a surreal calm. George was no longer focused on Willy's estate. For the moment, he was interested in Simon's story. What had happened to alienate father and son? And how had Simon come to live in the wreck of a motel, crowded into one room with all those people?

Simon met George's gaze. "My dad used to say that in Boca Raton, the moon is so near you could almost touch it."

"We're not in Boca," George said. "This is Miami."

Herbie nodded. "That sounds just like Willy. What a piece of work. No one can touch the moon. Not unless they're nuts. Or an astronaut. Which in my book is the same thing. You'd have to be nuts to ride a rocket to the moon."

"Or brave," George said.

"Or adventurous," Benny added.

"Either way," Herbie clarified, "nuts. So kid, what's the deal? What are you doing here? And when was the last time you spoke to your dad?"

"I'm not a kid. I'm thirty-two." Simon's voice was tense.

Benny squinted. George was reminded of Columbo working a case. All that was missing was the trench coat and cigar. "So, who are all those people in that motel room?" Benny asked.

"They're undocumented."

"And you're holding them for ransom?"

"Of course not," Simon sternly answered. "I'm helping them. This is a safe house. A place for them to land while we search for their relatives and ways to get them where they need to go."

"No offense, kid," Herbie said. "I mean, Simon. There's nothing safe about this place. Nothing."

Benny cocked his head. "So you're working against the government," he said angrily. "Who the hell do you think you are? We have laws in this country. Laws that should be obeyed."

Simon shrugged. "Yes, we have laws. But did you see the faces in that room? Mothers and children. Families. We have an obligation to help."

Benny puckered up as if he had just sucked on a lemon.

Simon was not intimidated. "I don't know where your family is originally from, but my family is from Poland. Do you know how many Jews were wiped out in the Holocaust? Did Willy ever tell you that his parents fled Poland, landing in England before arriving in America? How many had legal documents? Very few. How many died waiting for legal documents that never materialized?"

"That was different," Benny insisted. "They were fleeing the Nazis. They couldn't get legal documents. My God, they'd lost their rights. This isn't the same thing."

"It's exactly the same. Innocent people fleeing drug cartels. Unsafe neighborhoods. Frightened for the future of their children. What do you think is going on in these places? It takes courage to leave everything behind. Everything you know and love to run for your life."

Benny shook his head. "It's just wrong."

Simon dug in. "You know, it's people like you who give America a bad name. Sure, it's okay that you and yours have enough. But why bother to help someone else? It would cut too deeply into your piece of the pie."

"Hey now," George said. "That's enough."

Simon crossed his arms. "It's hardly a beginning."

"It's just not right. If we all behaved like that, it would be bedlam," Benny reiterated.

"I should have figured," Simon groused. "You three are about as selfless as my dad."

"And because of this cause of yours, you live like this?" Benny looked about. "This place is an eyesore. I'm surprised it didn't blow away in the last hurricane."

Simon nodded. "True. But it's part of the sacrifice. If you want to help, you need to be where it's needed most."

George couldn't help but admire Simon's grit. "But where's the money coming from to take care of these people?"

Simon took a breath. "I've already told you too much."

"Did your dad know about this?" George asked.

"My dad!" Simon offered a bitter laugh. "I haven't spoken to my dad in over twenty years. My dad didn't know anything about me." His voice was a mixture of sadness and regret.

George was incredulous. "How can that be?"

"Have you met Mona?"

"Sure."

"What did you think of her?"

George didn't know what to say. "She seemed nice."

"She didn't want dad to have anything to do with me. Dad went right along with her."

"But I don't understand," Benny said. "How long was your dad married to Mona?"

"Officially, two years," Simon answered. "But the marriage ended well before then."

Benny's face registered confusion. "Then why didn't you reconnect with your dad?"

"Reconnect with what? A man who walked away from his son because of his second wife? Now why would I want to have anything to do with him?"

"He wasn't like that," Herbie said.

Simon sighed. "You were his friend. Did he ever mention a son?"

Herbie shook his head.

Simon shrugged. "Of course not. He'd moved on. That's how he was."

"There had to be more to it than that. There must have been more," George insisted.

"What more?" Simon asked. "Do you have children?"

George nodded.

"Now what could anyone say to make you walk away from your son or daughter?"

George didn't answer. He wondered if a new woman would be as accepting of Peter's and Carole's shortcomings. Peter's neediness. Carole's pushiness. *No,* he thought. *I could never walk away from my kids.* The whole idea seemed impossible.

Carole had continued to call George regularly. Too often for George's comfort level. Over time, the conversations followed a regular pattern. A discussion of the artists showcased at the gallery, dates of upcoming events, and Carole's interest in all things cultural in San Francisco. The new exhibit at the Art Institute. The arrival of an exciting Broadway show at the Orpheum Theater. A journey to the Conservatory of Flowers in Golden Gate Park.

George listened politely, stifling a yawn as his eyes wandered to the television where he'd muted the sound. Should Carole inquire into George's life, he deflected to Miss Betsy, doting on the little poodle as if she were the center of the universe. And in a way, George supposed, she was.

He'd rise early each morning to venture along the familiar pathway of fire hydrants, bushes, and trees that riveted Miss Betsy's attention. And if George tried to alter the walk, turning either left or right from the well-traveled route, the little poodle would stop dead in her tracks, twisting her body about to correct George, pulling him in the proper direction much as a guide dog might do to protect a blind companion from a dangerous intersection. With Miss Betsy, mornings had become George's favorite time of day. He and his toy centurion, marching along, enjoying the fresh air. Miss Betsy growling at every wind-carried leaf, every person or dog who dared cross their path.

But after George listed the condo with Sylvia, the nature of the conversations with his daughter changed. Carole pressed to visit. George pressed back.

"Daddy, the gallery is slow and I can leave for a few days. I want to see you. Make sure you're okay."

George nervously shifted on the sofa, waking Miss Betsy snuggled up at his side. "Carole, now's not a good time."

"Not a good time? To see your daughter? Spend time with her?"

George struggled to find the right words. "Carole, I wish I could explain it to you. I just don't have the energy for a visit. I'd be rotten company."

"You don't want to see me," Carole asserted, emotions raw and very real.

George struggled with the truth. How could he tell his daughter that he lacked the patience for her emotional outbursts? That her intensity, even on the phone, overwhelmed him? Carole still craved the attention of Jeanette. He was a poor substitute. He'd only disappoint her. Which is why he'd let so many of Carole's calls go to voicemail. He simply didn't have the stamina. And though he wanted to explain all these feelings, he was afraid she wouldn't understand. Or worse, that she'd refuse to accept his limitations.

"Carole, I'm sorry. I'm just not up to it," he pleaded. "Please understand."

But Carole was not to be put off. "I can help you go through Mom's things. Get all those reminders out of the condo."

They'd been through the conversation before. "Those reminders are what's keeping me sane," George admitted. "I don't know what I'd do if all of a sudden your mother was completely erased."

"But if the condo sells, you're going to need to get rid of Mother's things. You're not going to move them. Or are you? Daddy, this isn't healthy. You should talk with a therapist. Maybe join a grief support group."

"I can't," was the best George could manage.

Miss Betsy hopped into George's lap. She turned about to look into his eyes, pawing at his hand to be petted.

Carole dug in her heels. "I'm coming to visit."

"Oh no, you're not," George said with sudden, unbridled heat.

Miss Betsy jumped off George's lap and scampered out of the room, tail between her legs.

George was incensed. "Maybe you should take time to focus on *yourself*. I'm sure there are plenty of changes you could make if you met with a good therapist or joined a support group. Don't tell me how to behave or live my life. I don't like it, Carole, and I won't tolerate it."

"You don't want to see me. You don't want to get rid of Mother's things. This can't go on. Mom's been gone for months."

George's temper peaked. "Months, years, decades." He grew steadily angrier with each word. "Who the hell are you to tell me how long it should take for me to feel better? To get over your mother's death? My life has been destroyed. I watched the only woman I ever loved, the dearest woman in the world, die a slow, agonizing death. You have no right to make claims about what I need to do. I'll take care of Mom's things when the time comes. I know how to clean out a closet. Make a donation to Goodwill. I'll have you remember your place. You're still the daughter. I get to make my own decisions, young lady. And don't you dare tell me when you're coming to visit. I'll invite you when I'm good and ready. And not one day sooner."

A few moments of silence went by before Carol spoke. "I'm just beginning to realize that I truly don't know you."

Simon walked George, Benny, and Herbie back to the car. "It's not the best neighborhood," he apologized as he shook George's hand. "Thank you for finding me."

"I'm sorry about your dad," George said. "It's too bad."

"Yes." Simon offered a handshake to Benny, and then Herbie.

Back in the car, the three friends were unusually quiet. Miss Betsy, cuddled up next to Benny in the back seat, gently snored as George maneuvered the car through the dark Miami streets in search of the entrance to I-95.

"Herbie, you missed all the fun," Benny reported. "George nearly got us both killed tonight with his 'This is the police, open the door' line. I was certain we were due for trouble."

Due for trouble? George was once again reminded of the golf club dues. A third notice had arrived. There was no way he could pay it. How would he break the news to Herbie and Benny? They'd counted on his club membership. What excuse could he make up?

George struggled to focus. "That's right. I nearly pissed in my pants when I saw that gun. I couldn't stop shaking." He laughed just as he missed the entrance to I-95.

"How could you miss that?" Benny complained. "It was right in front of you."

With barriers and cones everywhere, George searched in the darkness for the next entrance. Was it closed up ahead? Did he need to find another way on? Why was there so much glare on the road? "I'm sorry," George said as he turned down a side street, hoping to find a way to double back. He feared they were hopelessly lost as they passed through the quiet streets of what looked like a warehouse district, then a huge public housing project. "It'll just be a few more minutes till I find the next entrance." But he wasn't so sure.

"I can't wait," Benny complained. "I have to use the restroom. I thought I could hold it, but I can't."

"I know the feeling," Herbie sympathized.

Men and their bladders, George thought as he searched for the next entrance to the highway. "Maybe we should carry one of those plastic urinals they hand out at the hospital."

"Or a pickle jar," Herbie suggested with a snicker.

Benny scooted up, holding onto George's headrest. "Slow down, George. That place over there is open. The lights are on."

George pulled into an empty parking lot off Le Jeune Road and Twenty-Seventh Street, south of Miami International Airport. The property appeared to be a former Waffle House. One streetlight was busted out; the other flashed an eerie yellow glow.

Herbie chuckled. "This place makes my gas station look like the Ritz."

"I have to go," Benny confessed, reaching for the door handle. "Or I'll bust."

"Well, go on then. Hurry up," Herbie called as Benny hopped out of the car and raced to the front door.

Miss Betsy sat up, on full alert.

"Don't say '*hurry up*,'" George whispered as Miss Betsy looked about, yawned, and lay back down. "It's her bathroom cue."

Herbie laughed. "Look at Benny run. He never crossed a football field at such breakneck speed."

"You know, Herbie, you should lay off of him."

"What do you mean?"

George turned about to check on Miss Betsy. She was fast asleep. "Too many jokes. Too much teasing. It gets tiresome."

"For whom? You or me?" Herbie said, suddenly serious.

"For everyone. And Benny doesn't deserve it. He's been a good friend to you. Remember Glades Road?"

Two years earlier, Herbie had been driving on Glades Road late at night, eager to get home after a date. When the light changed, he stepped on the gas, unaware that a teenager speeding toward the intersection was trying to beat the light. When Herbie awoke in the hospital, Benny was with him.

The expression on Herbie's face shifted. The clown was gone.

"Sometimes those jokes are laced with truth."

Herbie balked, waving a hand for George to stop.

"Herbie, you're lucky Benny doesn't deck you."

"He's pretty big," Herbie said under his breath.

"And that's another thing. He doesn't need to be reminded of his size. He knows."

"Hey, giants are good. The Jolly Green Giant."

"Who can really take you seriously when all you do is joke? Here I'm trying to make a point, and you're blowing me off."

Herbie looked away.

"You need to grow up. We're not kids anymore. And the way you're behaving is awful. If you don't stop, you'll find yourself alone."

Herbie exhaled. "Maybe you're right. Maybe I need to dial it down. Has Benny said anything to you?"

"He doesn't have to. I can see the look on his face. Your teasing isn't funny or appreciated."

"I'm sorry about that. You know me, George. When I get excited or I'm having too much fun, it all starts. I guess I'm what you might call obnoxious."

George coughed. "That's a good word for it."

"Ever since I was a kid, I had this gift. To make everyone laugh. If you'd seen how I grew up, you'd understand. There was a lot of tension in the family. My parents didn't get along. My brother and sister were always fighting. I did my best to entertain and distract."

George nodded. "Well, that childhood coping strategy isn't working anymore. You've become annoying. No one wants to be Don Rickles's target."

"Well, you've got to admit, that guy was a hell of a comic."

"That was onstage. You're not onstage. And neither Benny nor I are laughing."

"Got it. Sorry to be such a pain in the ass."

"Don't tell me," George said. "Tell Benny."

There was a loud rap on the driver's side window. George jumped, certain they were about to get carjacked.

"Sorry guys," Benny said with a sheepish grin when George rolled down the window. "I didn't mean to scare you. But they have all these great deserts inside and I thought, if you two were hungry, we could grab some cheesecake."

George eyed the restaurant with the papered-over windows. "Here? Really?"

Benny nodded. "You've got it all wrong. Inside is fine. The outside, well—" Benny glanced about. "It speaks for itself. But inside, it's clean. The bathroom was spotless. And you know what they say about restaurants and bathrooms. Spotless bathroom. Terrific restaurant."

"Now this I've got to see." Herbie turned to George. "Let's do it."

"I can't leave Miss Betsy here."

"Dear God, George. Let the poor animal sleep. She'll be fine."

"Well, maybe I'll cover her with a towel. I have one in the trunk. She likes to hide under towels."

As they walked into the restaurant, George had a thought. "How about we take some food back?"

"Back where?" Benny asked.

"The motel. To Simon."

Benny winced. "George, haven't we had enough of that place for one night? Besides, he doesn't need our help. He looks like he has everything under control."

George disagreed. "I saw the looks on the faces in that room. Those people were hungry."

Benny was quick to respond. "They wouldn't be if they weren't here illegally."

George gave Benny a withering glance. "You're really not going to let that go, are you?"

"The law is the law," Benny insisted.

"Okay, but Simon could use some help. I've got to tell you, right or wrong, I'm impressed he's put himself on the line for other people. Strangers."

"Bleeding liberal," Benny said as they sat down at a corner table.

"Benny," George said with surprise. "You're just full of opinions about this."

"Maybe Benny has a point," Herbie sneered, his voice loaded with sarcasm. "We should be respectful of Benny's feelings."

George caught Herbie's drift. He was throwing George's well-intentioned words back at him. "Herbie, don't twist my words. It just makes you even more obnoxious."

Herbie offered George a jack-o'-lantern smile. Carved in a smirk, hoping to entertain even as it terrified little children.

"George, I can't help how I feel," Benny said. "Whatever you two think, I have my opinion. And I'm sticking to it."

George unfolded a napkin, releasing a fork and knife. "Okay. Feel as you will. That's fine. I might even agree with you. Sure. As a matter of principal, people should be immigrating legally. Absolutely. In an ideal world, we should all be following the rules. But we're not living in an ideal world. And there are children involved. Like it or not, lives are at stake."

Benny looked about. "Is there a waitress?"

"It's different when they're a faceless mob on the news," George continued. "When you can't see anyone's eyes. A lot easier to ignore. You can say, 'Hey, it's not my problem.' But when you see people in need, face-to-face, the only choice is to help."

"I guess if you put it that way," Benny conceded. "But still, it isn't right."

"Fine. It's not right. So what? What are we going to do now?"

"You know, big guy," Herbie said to Benny. "George has been on me tonight. Telling me that I haven't been a good friend to you."

Benny flashed a smug smile. "You've been riding me pretty hard."

Herbie clasped his hands together. "I think I owe you an apology."

"You do?"

"Yes. You're a good guy."

Benny smiled. "Well, thank you. I certainly try."

"And despite your glandular problem," Herbie continued, "I think your heart is in the right place. Though it's located a bit higher than in most other human beings."

Benny laughed. "I knew it," he said to George. "He can't help himself."

"Maybe so," Herbie said in a serious tone. "But that doesn't mean I don't love you. And if anyone else tries to make fun of you, I'd step right in and defend you."

George sighed. "Herbie, can we stick to one topic at a time? What about bringing something back to the motel?"

"My point exactly," Herbie said. "I'm picking on you, Benny, but I love you. So we can bring food back to Simon even though we agree that those folks should be immigrating legally. See how both actions can exist in the same context?"

"Dear God," Benny muttered. "That kind of makes sense."

"I can't believe it!" Simon said after placing the trays of roast beef, turkey, and peanut butter sandwiches atop a small table by the doorway. "You guys are really something. That's very kind of you."

George shrugged. "It's the least we can do."

"The very least," Benny added with a scowl.

A little girl, no older than four, popped her head outside. "Mr. Simon," she sang, her hands reaching up. Simon lifted the little girl in the air, pulling her close. She wrapped her legs about his waist and patted his beard with a little hand.

"This is Marta," Simon said. "Now, what are you doing up so late?"

Marta's brown eyes glowed in the moonlight. "I want to marry you."

Simon turned to George. "Incorrigible."

"How old are you?" Benny asked.

Marta held up all ten fingers.

Simon laughed. "You're not ten!"

"You're very pretty," Benny said. "I had a granddaughter just about your age."

George turned to Benny. "You've never talked about a granddaughter."

Benny held a finger out for Marta to grab. "It really isn't something we talk about."

"Hey, listen," Simon said, "I was thinking. My dad had this friend who was his attorney for years. I can write the name down. I should have thought of it before. Maybe you should check it out. This attorney tried to intercede on my behalf. I'd just finished my studies and was deep in debt. I was hoping my dad might make me a loan till I could land a job and get on my feet."

"What were you studying?" Benny asked in a disparaging tone. "Art history? Philosophy?"

"I'm a Harvard Law School grad," Simon answered.

"Harvard!" George said. "And you're living like this?"

Simon shrugged. "A Harvard law degree still qualifies you for having a heart."

Herbie chimed in. "It seems like wasted potential."

"Not to me," Simon said. "Listen, I know it's hard for your generation to understand, but I wanted to make a difference. Not just make money. I tried that path. Corporate life wasn't for me."

"Hey, we know all about giving back," Benny grumbled. "We were raised with Kennedy's 'Ask not what your country can do for you; ask what you can do for your country.' And we're the generation that protested Vietnam."

"Yes." Simon nodded. "So what have you done lately?"

Benny's eyes bulged. "I vote."

"Well, that's good. But what are your values?"

George held Benny by the arm. "Enough arguing."

But Benny wasn't to be silenced. "So tell me, big shot, did you pay off your school loans?"

Simon winced. "I paid them off."

"I bet," Benny answered. "Working here."

"I don't like to say."

Benny persisted. "If you could do it, other kids can."

Simon smiled. "I don't think so. You see, I have an advantage. I've got a photographic memory. Card counting. All I needed was two weeks in Vegas. They won't let me back at the tables, but I cleared my school debts."

"You're a pretty smart guy," George said.

"Harvard smart," Herbie emphasized. "And this is really what you want to do with your life, kid? I mean, Simon."

"No. This is just what I'm doing now. I've been thinking of moving to Colorado. A change of weather might be good. I've been toying with the idea of getting into the dispensary business."

"Interesting choice," Benny said sarcastically, shaking his head. "Selling drugs. Is that really what we need? More pot."

"Whoa, you guys are behind the curve. I'm not talking about a 'let's get high and have a good time' kind of dispensary," Simon said. "Do you realize the number of people suffering with anxiety and depression? Or chronic pain? Dispensaries offer a lifeline to those who haven't been helped by traditional therapeutics."

George had no doubt of Simon's sincerity, even though he wasn't sure marijuana was the cure-all for man's anxiety. Personally, he'd long ago stopped listening to the news. He found it made him too edgy.

"Before we forget," Herbie said, "how about that lawyer's name?"

Simon passed Marta to Benny to hold before retreating into the motel room.

"You're a doll," Benny said as he softened, gently rocking the child.

She nodded off to sleep, head resting on his shoulder.

When Simon returned, he handed a slip of paper to George. "Here you go."

George folded the paper and tucked it into his pocket. "Thanks. We really appreciate this."

"We'd better head out," Herbie said as he checked his watch. "Or else we'll need to book a room here for the night."

Simon took the sleeping girl from Benny. ""Thanks again. You've done a great thing tonight."

"Right," Benny said. "We've abetted a criminal."

Simon shook his head. "No. You've held a child in your arms who needed you."

Benny sighed, conceding the point.

"You can view this any way you like," Simon said, "as long as you do something. Tonight was a start."

"Preachy bastard," Benny said as he, George, and Herbie walked back to the car.

– 11 –

"So let me get this straight," George said as he checked out the breakfast menu at TooJay's Delicatessen in Boca. Herbie sat next to him; Benny was on the other side of the booth. "Last night, we each chipped in twenty bucks for the food we brought back to the motel. And before we left, we handed Simon another two hundred dollars in cash."

Benny poured cream into his coffee. "That sounds about right."

Herbie dumped a packet of Equal into his own cup. "We're working this all wrong. We're supposed to be recouping our loss. Finding a way to get reimbursed for Willy's funeral. Not continuing to feed the kitty."

George couldn't have agreed more. "I called that lawyer. The one Simon recommended. Jordan Archer. There was a recorded message. The office is closed for a week. Something about a lawyer's conference."

"Oh, no," Herbie moaned. "Not another week before we find the executor."

"If we're lucky," George added.

Benny had a far-off look. "Gee, that little girl last night was adorable."

Herbie chuckled. "It looks like someone lost his heart."

"You know, I've been thinking," Benny said. "I'm going to volunteer when I step away from my practice. I had such a strange feeling last night when we brought that food back to Simon. I don't agree with what he's doing. I know it's wrong. Yet, it felt like the right thing to do. And it isn't as if anyone needed to thank me. It was the very act of doing it that made me feel..." Benny searched for the right word. "Fulfilled."

Herbie shook his head. "Leave it to a rich endodontist to feel good about giving something away for free. Maybe you should cut your practice fees. That might make you feel gloriously ecstatic. I know the toothless in Miami-Dade would be grateful."

Benny blushed.

"Lay off, Herbie," George said as he opened the *Miami Herald*. "That's a great thought, Benny. Good for you."

"Hey, now." Herbie stretched his neck, shifting his gaze across the room. "There's that attractive redhead. She was at Willy's funeral."

Benny twisted about. "She doesn't look familiar."

Herbie nudged George. He pointed a chin in the redhead's direction. "That's the Realtor I told you about. The one from the open house. She couldn't keep her hands off me."

George looked up and winced. He folded the paper back to the "Arts & Entertainment" section. "That's Sylvia Haddit. She's my Realtor."

"The one who's selling your place?"

George wondered if he should have gone with another Realtor. "She promised me the unit would sell quickly. I'm still waiting. And now she's pestering me to look at something to buy." George folded the section over as he checked his horoscope. Aries the ram.

"I thought you wanted to rent." Herbie leaned close, looking over George's shoulder. "You read the horoscopes? Are you kidding?"

"I've told her I only want a rental. But she doesn't take no for an answer. And hey, there's nothing wrong with the horoscopes."

"If you're a total idiot," Herbie said with an impish grin.

George shoulder-bumped Herbie. If he thought the horoscopes stupid, he didn't need to be reading over George's shoulder. "Mine are always dead-on."

"Please, George," Herbie implored. "I have too much respect for you to even answer that."

"I read my horoscope," Benny added.

Herbie nodded in Benny's direction. "Point made."

"Knock it off, Herbie," George warned. "Remember our conversation last night? Do you want me to ask you to apologize to Benny every time you say something mean?"

"Sorry, Benny," Herbie quickly offered as he craned his neck to take in the view across the room. "That Sylvia is a nice-looking woman. Did you..."

George averted his eyes. "A gentleman never says."

Herbie chuckled. "I don't know why you play the virgin, George. You were married. Surely, you learned a thing or two. Didn't you ever cheat?"

George didn't like the question. It inferred that he was less of a man if he had been faithful. "You know I didn't. I loved my wife."

Herbie smiled. "You're confusing love with fear. I saw the way she ruled you. She ran that house."

George grimaced. "I'm not like you, Herbie. I don't run around."

"And that," Herbie stated with authority, "is the reason you're so miserable."

"Miserable?" George closed the newspaper and in a loud, stern voice said, "I may be unhappy, but I'm not *miserable.*"

Two women sitting at an adjacent table turned to give George a disapproving look.

"Keep your voice down," Herbie said. "You want to get us thrown out of here?"

George hunkered down in the seat. Creating a scene was not his thing.

"If you don't behave," Herbie said, pointing at George, "we'll send you back to the Bahamas."

Benny looked up from the menu and laughed.

George wished he hadn't told Herbie and Benny about the trip to the Bahamas. After Jeanette's death, he'd bought an all-inclusive package to Sandals in Emerald Bay. He hadn't realized it was the perfect couples honeymoon destination. Alone and miserable, the week in the Bahamas had proved awful. Despite the sunshine and sandy beach, George was unable to relax. The desire to run away had followed him right to the island. And then, there was no place to go.

"Hey, look," Herbie said. "She's looking this way."

George glanced over. Sylvia waved.

"Very nice." Herbie looked across the room at Sylvia and waved back. "Maybe I should buy some property." He smiled, offering Sylvia a sneak peek at the dental work that had cost him a pretty penny, even with Benny's discount. "I think she's giving me the eye."

"She's not even looking at you," George surmised without looking up from the paper. "It's me. She calls every now and then to see how I'm doing."

Herbie gave George his full attention "And how are you doing?"

George held out his folded newspaper. "I'm busy reading my horoscope. That's how I'm doing."

"You should be bedding that one," Herbie said with a nod in Sylvia's direction. "A Realtor in Boca. She has a job. She's smart. Attractive. She probably does very well financially."

Benny leaned forward and cracked his knuckles. "Have you noticed that all the single women in Boca are Realtors? Do you think Realtor is code for divorcée?"

That night, George thought about letting Peter's call go to voicemail, but at the last moment reconsidered. It had been a month since they'd last connected. George bit the bullet, sat down on the sofa, and took the call. Miss Betsy leapt up to take her place at his side.

"I'm depressed, Dad. I've been spending a lot of time alone."

George summoned his energy. "I thought you had friends in Chicago."

"My friends have families and kids."

"Great. Let them introduce you to a woman. There are plenty of women in Chicago."

"They've set me up," Peter answered. "Nothing has worked out. I don't think I'll ever have what you and Mom had."

George suppressed a sigh. Why did Peter always paint the most negative future? Did he understand the challenges of being in a relationship? A long-term marriage wasn't all fairy dust and ice cream. It was work. More often than not, it was learning how to be together. To listen. To hear and respect the other person's feelings.

"I don't know what women want," Peter grumbled.

George closed his eyes. Same conversation, different day. Always focused on Peter and his troubles. Was there no end to it? "You're too hard on yourself, son. Maybe you should stop pushing. Let things happen naturally. The right woman will find you. She will. You'll see." George wished Peter would grow up. Solve his own problems and be happy. Was that too much to ask?

"It's like I missed an important window in life. Do you know what I mean, Dad?"

George tuned out as Peter rambled on. His eyes settled on the coffee table. There sat a glazed blue-and-yellow bowl decorated with lemons. Jeanette had purchased it on a trip to Italy. With Jeanette gone, the bowl suddenly seemed out of place. Like it belonged back in Santa Margherita Ligure.

George struggled to get to his feet, leaving Miss Betsy asleep on the sofa as Peter droned on, barely taking a breath. The conversation was familiar. All one-way. Peter absorbed in his own story; rehashing every minute detail, this date, that woman, more background information than George cared to know.

George remembered Jeanette's frustration with Peter's calls. *Get to the point,* she'd say. *You're losing me.*

Now George understood why Peter's calls had so soured Jeanette's mood.

George checked his watch. Forty minutes had passed and Peter was still talking about himself. A new world record. What would Jeanette have said? Would she have just gone on listening? How would she have redirected him?

George abruptly interrupted Peter's diatribe about a new dating app. "I also have news. Back in May, I listed the condo. It's only had a few showings, but I'm hoping by mid-August, the unit sells. And I've got my eye on this apartment complex near the beach. It'll be a total change of life."

"I thought you were going to wait a year before making any decisions." Peter sounded disappointed.

George was taken aback. After being supportive of Peter, he'd expected his son to be happy for him. "I don't understand.

I've already battled this out with your sister. Why would selling the condo be a problem? This is good news."

"Gee, Dad, this is the first I'm hearing about it. Why didn't you tell me about it sooner?"

George didn't appreciate being challenged. "Now, you're either with me or against me," George said, a growing tightness in his chest. "I'd like to think you're on my side."

"There are sides?" Peter's voice was softer.

George envisioned a tug-of-war. Carole and Peter holding one end of a rope. George, the other. Jeanette refereeing.

"I just want what's best for you, Dad."

George wasn't so sure. "Now, how would you know what's best for me?" He couldn't wait to hear the answer.

"Maybe I don't," Peter conceded. "You've always been determined to do exactly as you want. We've all tiptoed around you for years. Mom too."

The comment stung. George snapped. "Peter, I don't need anyone's permission to live my life. Maybe there's a lesson in that for you."

"Excuse me? What does that mean?"

"You've got to stop going on and on about your problems." Once George blurted it out, there was no way to get the genie back in the bottle. "You're a grown man. Suck it up. No one is interested in your endless tale of woe. Maybe that's why your friends have abandoned you. And women are staying away."

"I never said my friends abandoned me."

"No one wants to be with someone who constantly complains. That isn't the stuff that maintains friendships."

"That isn't fair."

"And please remember. I'm your father. Not your mother. If you want to talk someone's ear off, schedule an appointment with a therapist."

There was an awkward silence. George stared down at the carpet, shaken.

"Gee," Peter finally said. "How long have you been holding onto that?"

"You need to be aware of other people's feelings. The world is not all about you and your life. Maybe, if you stopped focusing on yourself for a minute, you'd attract a great woman. We all have our troubles," George emphasized. "For instance, I want your mother back." His voice cracked with emotion. "But since I can't have that, well, I'm going to have to jump-start my life. But I'm not going to talk about it endlessly. What would be the point?"

"It's not easy for me. Women are so hard to figure out."

There it was, George thought. *The shift back to Peter.*

"I haven't had that experience." Ava and Sylvia came to mind. Things with them hadn't worked out, but there had been lessons learned. "The ladies in Boca appreciate what I have to offer." As soon as George said it, he wished he hadn't.

"Maybe it's different for men your age." Peter's voice was sullen. "Perhaps the bar is lower."

George marveled. Peter was always the victim.

"You better take care of yourself, Dad, and use protection."

George blushed, unprepared to discuss the details of his sex life with his son.

"There's no need to be embarrassed," Peter guessed. "STDs happen among people of all ages. You should read up on it."

Later that night, George was in bed when his iPhone repeatedly buzzed.

Oh God, he thought when he checked the phone. He'd become the darling of the Boca Raton collection agencies. The vultures were swooping in. Between the angry voicemail messages and repeated texts, George was beside himself. What more could he do? He'd listed the condo. Hopefully, once it sold, he'd be able to clear some of the debt. Stop the bleed. But it wouldn't cover everything. He'd still have to dig into his 401(k). And though George knew he was lucky to have assets, selling stock would reduce his retirement portfolio and generate a huge tax bill.

George tossed and turned, unable to sleep. His mind raced through various scenarios. There was a high-end pawn shop that advertised on television. Jeanette had some good pieces of jewelry. Her diamond engagement ring might generate a few thousand dollars. But the idea of parting with the ring made him wince. Jeanette also had a fur. But nobody wore furs anymore. And could a fur over twenty-five years old have any real value? George doubted it.

He grew increasingly anxious. If the condo didn't sell soon, he'd have to unload a large chunk of stock to cover the debt. Why hadn't he put the condo on the market sooner? Why had he allowed Herbie to talk him out of selling it back in January? And why, for God's sake, had he allowed this financial pressure to go on for so long?

His mind flashed to Willy's funeral. He'd been a fool to split the cost with Herbie and Benny. He wasn't in their financial bracket. And he hadn't anticipated the price of a lead-lined mahogany casket. Who picks a lead-lined casket?

George jerked straight up in bed. *I should never have taken early retirement and bought that cheap health insurance policy. Cancelled Jeanette's life insurance policy. I've jinxed myself. Defied fate. How am I going to dig myself out of this damn hole?*

He leapt out of bed, pacing the bedroom, his mind stuck in a revolving door of worry. Months of inaction had led to this. He shook his fists wildly, hoping to release the surging adrenaline. Every nerve on fire, he rushed into the living room, leaving Miss Betsy curled up alone in bed. Falling to his knees, his breath quickened. *Get ahold of yourself,* he thought as he lay flat on the carpet, body soaked in sweat. *Relax. Breathe.*

But he couldn't reason the moment away.

He stared up at the ceiling, arms flailing as if making snow angels. His brain jumped from one random thought to the next. Willy in the hospital bed, small and helpless. Ava scowling at him: *You Boca Raton men are so entitled.* Sylvia laughing as he struggled to dress. Jill Winters's angry words after his inability to perform sexually. Jeanette in the casket, still and wax-like.

George squeezed his eyes shut.

He couldn't stop the images.

He couldn't escape the horrible feeling of impending doom. And a new terror. The desire to stop the physical discomfort and mind flashes. Even if it meant killing himself.

"Jeanette," he called out, keenly aware that if Jeanette had lived, he wouldn't be struggling. She'd have handled the family finances while he enjoyed a secure retirement. There'd be no medical bills. And though it wasn't her fault, he couldn't help but blame her for his current predicament. She'd insisted they buy on the grounds of the Boca Raton Resort & Club. How was he expected to carry the expenses of such a rich lifestyle? Especially now that she'd abandoned him. Hot tears burned his eyes. "How could you do this to me?"

Carole's voice echoed: *I warned you not to sell the condo. You're not emotionally ready. You should've waited.*

Peter chimed in: *Why don't you ever take our phone calls? Are you really that disinterested in your own children? Have you always been this selfish?*

George covered his ears. He couldn't stop the voices. Voices of disapproval. Voices of lessons unlearned. Voices of impending doom.

Fear racked his body. He realized he was completely and unalterably alone. His unwillingness to ask for help had only amplified his isolation.

His breath quickened; he knew he was destined to die alone. He was overtaken by a sudden urge to move. Jump. Run. As if he'd been infused by superpowers. His heart pumped with the intensity of a NASCAR engine primed at the starting line of the Indy 500. The pressure in his chest became so intense, George was certain he was having a heart attack and about to pass out.

"Dear God, please help me. I don't want to die," he whimpered.

He thought of Jeanette's medical bills stamped *PAST DUE* in red; Carole's snake tattoo as it curled about her neck, forked tongue threatening those who dared to get close; Peter's brown, bushy hair, as unruly as Peter's many problems; Puff, the family Bichon who'd refused to be housebroken, whining after once again soiling the carpet.

And then George remembered Miss Betsy. His beloved poodle fast asleep in the bedroom.

I can't die now, he tried to reason as an intense pain, sharp as a knife, ripped through his chest. *I have to take care of Miss Betsy.*

George rushed back into the bedroom. He spotted the phone on the bedside table. He reached for it and called Herbie. "Do you still have my spare key?" he asked without waiting for the sleepy voice to answer. "You have to get over here, now. I'm having a heart attack. I'm calling for an ambulance. But you'll need to take care of Miss Betsy. She'll be in her crate."

Lying on a gurney in the emergency room at Boca Raton Regional Hospital, George counted himself lucky. He'd cheated death. "It's my heart," he said, a tremor in his voice, when Herbie entered the curtained-off space. George lifted himself up on one elbow. "I'm scared, Herbie. This may be it."

Herbie stood at the foot of the gurney. "You're fine, George. I just talked with the cardiologist. There's nothing wrong with you. You're 100 percent. You can stop worrying. And your little dog is okay, too. I walked her, gave her some kibble, and she's waiting for you in her crate."

George couldn't understand it. He was certain it had been a heart attack. "I couldn't breathe. I was dizzy. I went into a cold sweat."

Herbie leaned forward on the gurney, palms flat. "You had a panic attack. Your basic garden-variety freak-out."

"No," George insisted. "That's not right."

"It happens. You've had an awful past few months. You lost your wife in December. A close friend died in July. And you've put your condo up for sale. You're frightened. It's not so unusual. It happens."

George shook his head. "Am I going crazy?"

"Of course not," Herbie assured him. "You should have seen me when my last wife walked out. Four women! Talk about feeling like a fool. Not to compare, but if they'd died instead of divorced me, I'd have been a happier man."

George moaned. "What a thing to say."

Herbie shrugged. "It certainly would have been cheaper."

George settled back down, head on the pillow. *Oh no*, he thought. He'd just added to his mounting debt with another hospital bill.

"My God, George. Do you know how much I've paid those women over the years?"

George raised his voice. "Can we focus on me at the moment?"

"Sure." Herbie's tone had softened. "Sorry. It's just simple anxiety. You'll need to see a therapist. Stop putting pressure on yourself to be perfect. And start to talk about your feelings."

George sighed. "Are you sure it wasn't a heart attack?"

Herbie crossed his arms, ignoring the question. "Well, old buddy, I don't like to brag, but I've had my share of upsets."

"Upsets?" George didn't believe an upset could simulate chest pain.

Herbie offered George a sympathetic smile. The teasing clown was gone. "I've never told you this, because I didn't want you to think any less of me. But now's the right time. I attend weekly meetings for people with anxiety and depression."

George peered through half-closed eyes. "Are you kidding?"

Herbie took a deep breath, arms outstretched to emphasize the point. "Now why would I kid about that?"

"In Boca?" George asked.

"Boca. Delray. Deerfield Beach. Wherever there's a meeting."

"Every week?"

Herbie shrugged as if it wasn't a big deal. "Yes. And if I'm being honest, sometimes three times a week."

George was astonished. "I can't see you doing that."

Herbie cocked his head. "Doing what? I'm taking care of myself. Honoring my inner child. Soothing the wounds of our modern society."

George shook his head. "I'm not even sure what any of that means. Who are you? And what did you do with Herbie?"

Herbie pointed at George. "Maybe that's your problem, right there. You're not in touch with your feelings. You're going through the motions of life without understanding how it's impacting you. Depression and anxiety are real conditions. Nothing to play around with."

"Well, that's good and fine for you," George began, "but I know what I felt."

Herbie nodded. "You poor bastard," he said in a sympathetic voice. "You think you're better than everyone else. Above life's tragedies and heartaches. Superman. I get it. I know where you're coming from. It's hard to admit you're struggling."

George was stupefied. He wondered if the doctors really knew what they were doing. He was certain he'd had a heart attack. Minor, perhaps. So minor that it wasn't picked up on an EKG. George had read about men who'd experienced health scares and remained undiagnosed until the autopsy. "I don't know, Herbie. Anxiety is really not my thing. Not that there's anything wrong with it. But, I know what I felt. I know who I am."

"You should come with me to a meeting. It'd do you a lot of good."

"I don't think so," George answered. "I'm really fine."

"Well, good then," Herbie said in a resigned tone. "I tried. My job is done. Let's say we get you dressed and out of here. They probably need the gurney. Hey, did you see the cute blonde nurse on your way in?"

George looked at Herbie in disbelief.

"I'm not dead yet. I still get to look. And as much as I like."

"Where people are sick?" George swung his legs over the side of the gurney, slipping off the hospital gown. "Great words of advice for someone in the emergency room."

Herbie reached into the plastic bag at the foot of the gurney. He handed George his shirt. George slipped it over his head.

"As long as they're female and moving, I'm interested." Herbie handed George his pants. "Life's short. Just look around here. Live your life now, George. Don't wait. The end's always a surprise."

"You really think I can go?" George asked. "Maybe they still need me for more tests."

Herbie shrugged. "And you think I'm a hypochondriac!"

George stepped into his pants. "I never said that."

"That's okay; don't sweat it. You're buying me breakfast. Then, we're even."

George zipped his fly. "I'm not sure I should be going to breakfast"

"Why not? You just got over a major heart attack. The fastest recovery in recorded history."

George glared. "Okay, I get it. Ha, ha."

Herbie smiled. "Well, it's not like you don't have it coming. You arrogant prick."

"Nice. Very nice." George ran a hand through his tousled hair. "That's some bedside manner. What a great attitude."

Herbie's eyes flashed and his temperament became serious. "I just told you my deepest, darkest secret. Something I've never shared before, and you dismissed me. I could have told you that I had a head cold and gotten more sympathy. I'm not the one with the bad attitude."

George slipped on his socks. "Come on, Herbie. Don't be angry."

Herbie stood tall. "Why shouldn't I be angry? How often does someone open up to you? Reveal themselves."

George stepped into his loafers. "I don't know what to say."

Herbie glared at George. His body stiffened. "That's obvious. Maybe you have an easier time with life. Maybe you're managing more successfully. Maybe the doctors are wrong. Maybe I'm wrong. Maybe your life is a piece of cake."

George frowned. "Life. Were we talking about life?"

Herbie rubbed the back of his neck as he twisted his mouth into an unfamiliar grimace. "I guess not."

George pretended to understand. "So, you think I should follow up with the cardiologist?"

Herbie's eyes shot daggers. "Holy crap, George. You really don't get it, do you?"

– 12 –

GEORGE REMOVED HIS clothes and placed them on a nearby chair. He slipped under the cool white sheets of the Massage Envy table. Face down, he waited for the masseuse.

Herbie had gifted George the Massage Envy session. "You need this more than I do," he said, much to George's astonishment. Though George appreciated the gift, he was confused about the intent. After all, Herbie was the one who had taken care of Miss Betsy when George had his heart problem. If anything, it was Herbie who deserved a gift.

"Come in," George answered to the gentle knock at the door. The lights dimmed and he closed his eyes.

The masseuse pulled down the sheet covering his back, tucking the corners under his hips.

George took a deep breath and sank into the massage table, face submerged in the cradle, dead weight as he luxuriated in the firm pressure. As he was about to nod off, there was a rumbling below. He'd eaten a late breakfast and the raisin bran was making its presence known. He clenched his buttocks as the masseuse's thumbs pushed down on his lower back. He was now wide awake, struggling to contain what was demanding to be released.

George's toes curled as the masseuse shifted focus to his leg. The rumble in his gut intensified. He couldn't relax. He couldn't drift off. His mind took over as he redoubled his efforts to contain the gas. Perhaps if he thought about Willy's estate, he could distract himself. Stay vigilant.

What was the name of that lawyer? Simon had handed him a slip of paper. He'd only briefly glanced at it before folding it in half and slipping it into his pocket. But then, he did look at it. He'd called the attorney's office. He must remember the name. But somehow, he was blocked. The folded note now waited on his desk, inches away from the pile of overdue medical bills.

Odd, George thought as his discomfort intensified. *If Simon had said the name, I'd remember.*

The masseuse worked on the knots in his forearm. There was a tingling sensation in George's fingertips as he finally remembered: Archer. Jordan Archer.

The gas bubble once again percolated.

George flexed his glutes. His mind flashed back to The Golden Funeral Home. The packed pews. Ladies everywhere. *Who were all those women? How did Willy know them? And more importantly, why is it I know so little about Willy's life?*

George scheduled an appointment to meet Jordan Archer. "We don't all need to go," he said to Herbie and Benny when they met for lunch at Einstein's Bagels on Glades. "According to Simon, he's no longer Willy's attorney. So really, it's just a fact-finding mission. I think I can take it from here."

Herbie wiped cream cheese from the corner of his mouth. "I want to be there." He took another bite of a pumpernickel bagel.

"I don't need to go. I trust you," Benny said between sips of a tall orange juice.

Herbie made a sour face. "This isn't about trust."

George hadn't considered trust a factor. "Then, what is it?"

"I want to understand this whole thing," Herbie admitted. "A friend dies. A guy we think of as shy. All these female mourners show up. He's wealthy, but we wind up paying for the funeral. There's a second wife, Mona. Someone Willy never mentioned. Then, a son. Behold, Simon. Another mystery. Now, I'm not even sure who the hell Willy is. Was. Whatever."

George took in Herbie's assessment as he poked at a piece of half-eaten cinnamon coffee cake with a fork.

"What I'd like to know," Benny added with a sense of irony, "what does this say about us?"

George raised an eyebrow. "You've lost me."

Benny straightened up. "We're friends with Willy for years, but we know nothing about him. Is that because we're lousy friends?"

"Maybe that's just the way it is," George offered. "I'm sure there's plenty about each of you that I don't know."

Herbie stared at George. "You know everything about me. Hell, I'm an open book."

Benny glanced at Herbie. "Some chapters should have been more carefully edited."

Herbie smiled, palms up. "Okay. I overshare. That's my thing. I've always liked people. I'm a *people* kind of guy."

Benny coughed. "Let's not get carried away."

"And you, George," Herbie continued. "I know your story."

"I guess that's not really fair," George answered. "We were related. In-laws and all."

"But Benny's not related to us." Herbie turned to Benny. "Is there anything we should know about you?"

Benny pushed his poppy seed bagel aside. "Like what?"

Herbie scratched his head. "I don't know. If I did, I wouldn't be asking."

Benny stared at them. "Nothing here. You know what I do for a living."

Herbie nodded. "You spend your days with your fingers in people's mouths."

Benny smiled. "It's a noble profession."

Herbie continued. "You're a good golfer. You love baseball."

"All sports."

"You live alone…" Herbie dragged the last word out.

"Correct."

George suddenly remembered: "You have a granddaughter."

Benny looked surprised.

"You mentioned her the other night when we met Simon."

Benny looked away. "Right."

Herbie turned to George. "What else is there to know?"

George shrugged. "Beats me."

Jordan Archer's office was in a Boca strip mall anchored by a nail salon and a wig shop on South Federal Highway. As George pulled into the parking lot, he checked his iPhone. Was he in the right place?

A stunning Black woman dressed in a bright green pantsuit occupied the desk in what appeared to be the waiting room. Her Afro was tight and neat, with a gray streak running down one side. Eyeglasses sat atop her head. She leaned over the desk, squinting. She was engrossed in a magazine. When George closed the door, she looked up as if he'd startled her.

George had no doubt he had.

"Can I help you?" she said, a hand on her heart.

"I'm sorry," George said. "I didn't mean to scare you."

"I thought the door was locked," she confessed. "I usually lock it."

George was confused. "Then how can clients come in?"

The woman offered a deep-throated laugh. "Oh, I open the door for clients."

"And walk-ins?"

"Well," she said with a frown. "I can see through the plate glass window. It's strictly a judgment call. And then I unlock the door."

George took a quick look outside. His car was still parked in front.

Sensing George's discomfort, the woman backtracked. "Don't worry. They don't want your car. They want cash. Drugs and all. Otherwise, they're perfectly harmless."

Exactly who *they* were seemed important to know. "Kids?" George asked.

"Not just kids. Adults too. As you can see, this is not the best neighborhood. We have a lot of homeless folks. Nice people, actually. They're just down on their luck. And some never had any luck."

"Oh," George answered politely, eager to move the conversation forward.

"Now what can we do for you, Mister…"

"George. George Elden."

"Mr. Elden." Her voice was reassuring. Almost melodic.

"I have an appointment with Jordan Archer."

The woman leaned back in her chair and offered George a cryptic look. George was reminded of Angela Davis. Strong and fiery. "Where are you from, honey?"

George was caught off guard. "From here. Boca Raton."

"Now why would a gentleman such as yourself have need for Jordan Archer? Certainly there are plenty of high-priced Boca attorneys eager for your business."

George didn't want to appear rude, but he saw no reason to explain anything to an assistant. "It's a matter of a personal nature."

The woman broke into a big smile. "We don't sell Viagra. You must have confused us with Walgreens." She clapped her hands and laughed, head bobbing from side to side at her own joke.

"Is he in?" George asked, growing impatient. "Can I see him?"

"You sure can," the woman said as she rose to extend a hand in greeting.

George was stunned. "I'm sorry. The name, Jordan. I just thought..."

Ms. Archer smiled. "It was my grandfather's name. A proud man with a proud name."

George swallowed hard as he looked about the cramped space. "I thought this was the reception area and that the office was through there." He pointed to a door off to the side.

"That is my very private twa-lette," Ms. Archer confirmed. "That sounds so much nicer than toilet. Don't you think?"

"Yes." The blood rushed to George's face.

"Well, you might as well sit down," she said, waving him over to a chair. She searched her desk, a palm running over the papers. "Now where are my glasses?"

George cleared his throat. He pointed to the top of her head.

"Of course." She smiled broadly, slipping the glasses down to rest on the bridge of her nose. "There now." She blinked twice. George thought the glasses suited her. She was even more attractive. "And what can I do for you?"

"It's about Willy. Willy Krause."

"William Krause," she said in a dignified manner.

"Yes. Well, we're looking for whomever is responsible for his estate. We have a bill to submit and, well, we're at a loss to know where to submit it."

Ms. Archer crossed her arms. "A bill?"

"For the burial," George explained.

Ms. Archer moved a hand to her throat. "He's dead? You didn't mention that when you made the appointment."

George exhaled. "Sorry. I guess I wasn't clear. He died. Heart attack. And two of my friends and I covered the cost of the funeral."

"For the plot too?"

"No," George clarified. "For the funeral home and burial. You know, the regular stuff. Embalming, casket, hearse, chapel, limo, rabbi, and cemetery fee."

"Now why would you pay for all that? William was a wealthy man."

"We know." George spotted a folder on Ms. Archer's desk with Willy's name on it. He reached for it. "Would you mind if I had a look at that?"

Ms. Archer slammed her palm down on top of the folder. "You bet I do. Client privileged information. I can't share it with you."

"But he's dead," George repeated.

"You did mention funeral expenses," she snapped as if engaged in the cross-examination of a witness.

George tried another tactic. "Why do you still have a file on Willy? Are you still Willy's lawyer? I heard your relationship was terminated."

Ms. Archer wasn't the type to answer questions. She was the type who asked them. "Honey, how did you get my name?"

George attempted to stare Jordan Archer down. From the look in her eyes, he knew he'd met his match. She was one tough cookie. "Simon gave it to me."

Ms. Archer's face brightened. "Oh, Simon. How is he? What's he up to?" She leaned forward. "I haven't heard from him in years."

George didn't know quite how to describe Simon. "He's fine."

"That boy's a prince. I begged William to reconsider," she said with a headshake. "But he wouldn't hear of it."

George nodded, though he wasn't clear on the details of what had transpired between father and son. He'd only heard Simon's version.

Ms. Jordan looked off in the distance. There was a genuine sadness. "Some of these second wives. They can be so tough on a first family."

"What did Simon do to upset Mona?"

Ms. Archer seemed surprised by the question. "Who says he did anything? She was the second wife and Simon had the great misfortune to have ever been born."

George remembered the pained look in Simon's eyes when they'd discussed Willy. Could the reason for the falling out be as simple as all that? It just didn't seem possible.

"It's sad," George pivoted. "But what I really need to know is who is handling the estate. It's not Mona. And it isn't Simon. How am I going to get reimbursed if I can't track down the executor of the estate?"

Ms. Archer appeared to take pity on George. "Willy had a life insurance policy. Now, I can't promise he still had that policy at the time of his death, but if he did, there's an insurance agent out there who can help you find the executor. But, you have to promise me: If there is any money due to Simon, you'll make sure he gets its."

George sighed. Would this search for the executor never end?

"There's an insurance agent," George told Herbie as they waited for Benny at the club for their seven o'clock tee time. "Jordan Archer remembered a life insurance policy, but she didn't remember the name of the agent. She's going to dig around and let me know."

Herbie recoiled. "This is getting ridiculous. How long are we going to have to wait before we get reimbursed? Somewhere there's an estate, and the last time I checked, Willy was loaded. I swear, George, I'm not paying for his damn funeral. And that has nothing to do with friendship," Herbie insisted. "It's a matter of principle."

"I know," George answered, wondering at what price he'd sell his principles to pay off his damn credit cards.

Herbie kneeled to tie a shoelace. "Do you think Willy did this intentionally?"

"You mean, set us up?"

Herbie reached for George's hand. With a yank, Herbie was back on his feet. "It's possible."

"I don't see how. He didn't know he was going to die. And he certainly didn't know we'd be the ones to pay for the funeral."

"We're all going to die," Herbie reminded George. The color drained from his face. "Maybe he did it to teach us a lesson."

George had no idea what could be learned from hiding the executor of an estate.

"If you hate your relatives, you'd hide your assets."

George exhaled. "But you'd have to die to do it. That seems like taking a lesson a bit too far."

Herbie rubbed his chin. "Well, there's still one more opportunity to get to the bottom of this. Remember Mona?"

"Sure. The widow, Mona."

"She's having a gathering at her condo in memory of Willy."

George was thunderstruck. "A shiva?"

"No, no," Herbie said with contempt. "It's too late to sit shiva. You should know that. That happens immediately following the funeral."

George had no idea if that was true. "As far as I'm concerned, you can sit shiva whenever you want."

"Oh, George," Herbie said. "You're really a bad Jew. You know nothing. It's not shiva. Mona's having an afternoon of remembrance. A celebration of life. Nothing religious. Just a gathering of sorts."

"And she invited you?"

"Hey," Herbie smiled. "I can be very charming. And I was one of Willy's closest friends."

George rolled his eyes. "So you've been in touch with her."

"In a way."

"What kind of way?"

"George, do you want to go to this memorial or not? Maybe we might pick up some information. Somebody there might know something."

"So you think a celebration of life thrown by the second wife who was barely married to the guy would include people who truly knew Willy. When were they married? We don't even know the year. I mean, come on. She didn't know us. How could anyone there really have known Willy?"

Herbie sighed. "What other choice do we have?"

George was tapped out. "Maybe we could hire a detective agency." His stomach clenched at even a suggestion of added expense.

Herbie's eyes darkened. "George, we're not searching for the Maltese Falcon, though it might be great to get Bogart on the case."

"Get who?"

"Maltese Falcon. Humphrey Bogart."

"Oh."

"George, don't you watch Turner Classic Movies?"

George was not about to be teased. "Herbie, how old are you? We're living in the twenty-first century."

"I'm the same age as you, George. Give or take a year or two."

"Well, I really don't watch television."

"I bet," Herbie challenged. "Living alone, your television must be on all day. Anyway, *The Maltese Falcon* is a masterpiece. Bait and switch. Just when you think you know what's going on, they upend the story."

"I don't think our circumstance is quite that dramatic."

"I suppose not, but we clearly have no clue about what the heck was going on in Willy's life."

"I think I'm more focused on why the family never showed up at the funeral. And getting our money refunded."

"See," Herbie said, his eyes aglow, "it's a real mystery. A real 'who-done-it.'"

"Minus the corpse, murder weapon, damsel in distress, and a flatfoot or two."

"Flatfoot!" Herbie shouted, an index finger pointed at George. "I thought you don't watch Turner Classic Movies."

"Well," George said, "I might have caught a film here and there."

Benny beamed with pride as the three friends gathered about a high-top table in the clubhouse bar following their round of golf. "That was some game. And the sixth hole. A hole-in-one. You got to admit. Not many golfers can do that," he bragged.

Herbie gave Benny a once-over. "You sure are happy. Now, how do you think that makes us feel when you go on and on about your great shot?"

Benny paused as if giving Herbie's question serious consideration. "If you're my friend, you'd be happy for me."

George laughed. "He's got you there, Herbie."

"I suppose," Herbie agreed as the drinks arrived. "Okay. You were amazing." Herbie raised a gin and tonic. "To Benny."

George was proud of himself. Maybe his talk with Herbie had worked. Perhaps Herbie finally got it. Humor is a judicious gift to be used wisely.

"Now, I have a question," Herbie said. "This Willy thing has really got me thinking. I know this may seem strange, but I'm going to ask anyway. We three have been friends for years. Right?"

Benny and George nodded.

"But in all those years, we haven't always been honest. I think it's time we come clean about our lives."

George nearly choked on his vodka gimlet.

Herbie was serious. "I think we need to trade war stories. There are certain things I know about both of you, but more I don't. And one of the things I've learned through my meetings is the importance of owning your truth. So, in the spirit of brotherhood, I want you each to tell me something I don't know about you."

"Meetings? What's he talking about?" Benny asked George.

George shrugged, unsure what to say.

"Okay. Me first," Herbie said, his glass raised. "I have extreme anxiety. A few years back, one of my patients got very ill. A little girl. Her name...well, that's not important. Anyway, she was hospitalized. I should have gone over to see her, but it was flu season and my office schedule was packed. Besides, there was a hospitalist onsite for her care. That night when I got home, I called the hospital. I wanted to check on her." Herbie sighed. "She'd died that afternoon. Now, being a doctor, I know people die. Even children. But I was devastated. It just knocked the wind right out of me."

George had never heard Herbie talk so passionately. "Herbie. I'm sorry."

"Pediatricians aren't supposed to lose patients. That's the realm of the oncologist. Sometimes the cardiologist. Usually the gerontologist. Not your basic, garden-variety pediatrician. And it isn't as if this was the first patient who'd ever died. It happens in the course of any medical career. So maybe this was the straw that broke the camel's back. I don't know." Herbie sipped his drink. "It wasn't my fault. I wasn't to blame. But I was totally shaken," he admitted. "And then, later on, I was shaking. Now, I don't mean the usual 'Gee, I'm kind of cold.' I mean shaking. Unable to sleep. And that is what essentially wrapped up my fourth marriage. You see, when you marry someone who doesn't really care about you, they exit at the first sign of bad news. My mental health offered her an easy out."

"But you're okay now," Benny said.

"Mostly. I still have moments when I get extremely anxious. That's when my humor ramps up. I'm sorry, Benny. I know you've been the target. But it isn't meant to be mean. It's meant to…I don't know…keep reality at bay. Defuse anxiety."

Herbie looked at George. George was next.

George panicked. What should he say? He couldn't talk about Jeanette. Any difficulties in the marriage were private. Discussing them would seem disloyal. He couldn't discuss his money issues. It was all too shameful. Should he mention the challenge with Carole? Mothering him when he didn't need advice? Or what about Peter? The Peter Pan boy who refused to grow up. Peter's obsessive focus on the opposite sex had made George exceedingly uncomfortable. Peter's railing about the Me Too movement was especially troubling. *These women*, Peter would complain, *are making this all up. Why didn't they report years earlier? Any innocent flirting is now considered harassment. It's open season on men*. After weeks of George stonewalling him, Peter had finally stopped calling. George was relieved to relinquish the role as Peter's emotional support.

"I don't want to play this game," Benny said.

George nearly cheered.

Herbie's head dropped between his shoulders. "It's not a game."

"Then, what would you call it?"

"A moment of clarity. Maybe it will help us get to know each other better."

"My grandmother used to say, 'Beware what you wish for,'" Benny offered.

Herbie pressed back in the seat and folded his arms. "Oh my God. Not your grandmother again."

"Hey," Benny said. "My grandmother was a wise woman."

"No doubt. But there's no reason to be scared," Herbie reasoned. "I know we can do this. It's just sharing. Simple sharing. Go ahead," Herbie encouraged Benny. "Give me your worst. Take a chance. I bet you'll feel better. Why don't you tell us about your granddaughter?"

Benny paled. "I don't think so."

"Go on," Herbie pressed. "You never talk about her."

Benny pushed his Amstel beer aside. He made a fist. "There's nothing to tell."

"How old is she?" George asked. "What's her name?"

Benny sighed. "Rebecca. She was named after my mother."

Herbie turned to George. "That's a pretty name."

"Sure is," George agreed, glad he'd sidestepped Herbie's attention for the moment.

"We called her Becky. She was too small to carry that big name. Just a little thing."

George's curiosity was sparked. "When was the last time you saw her?"

Benny gave it some thought. Biting his lower lip, he frowned. "Can't say."

"What happened?" George asked.

Benny exhaled. "Helen happened."

"Helen?"

"My wife."

"Oh." George was uncertain he wanted to hear the rest of the story. After all, what could possibly be gained by hearing heartbreaking details about Benny and his granddaughter?

He felt compelled to change the subject. George glanced through the menu. "Maybe we should order some appetizers."

Herbie grasped George's wrist. "No, wait. I want to hear this."

Benny looked down. "I think I'd rather not tell it."

Herbie leaned forward. There was a slight burn on his cheeks from the morning sun. "Come on, Benny. You haven't told us anything."

Benny shook his head. "There's nothing to really tell."

"Let's order," George said as a cocktail waitress approached.

"Oh my God," Herbie moaned. "What the heck is wrong with you two?"

The waitress took her cue and withdrew. George closed the menu. "Hey, if he doesn't want to go there, why should he? Life is tough enough without reliving a trauma just to make you happy."

"Make me happy?" Herbie looked at Benny. "Haven't we learned anything from Willy? We should be able to talk to each other. If a hole-in-one is worth our acknowledgement, what about the things we struggle with?"

George wondered how any of this could be helpful. "We golf together. If we have a problem, we should go to a therapist, not burden each other."

Herbie sat back in his chair and ran a hand over his mouth. "I don't get you two. We have a chance to know each other, and instead of sharing, we've agreed to shelter in our own space. Isolated and alone."

"Herbie, that isn't it," George argued. "We'd do anything to help each other. I'm sure Benny or I would always be there for you."

Herbie's eyes bulged. George was reminded of the clown in a jack-in-the-box just at the moment of the big reveal. "How could you be there for me when you don't know who I am? What I need? How can we be friends if we don't know what the hell is going on in each other's lives?"

George flinched. "Now, you're exaggerating."

"Am I?" Herbie leaned forward, palms on the table. "Have either of you asked yourself whether Willy should have been on the golf course?"

Benny shifted uncomfortably in his seat. "He had rheumatic fever as a kid. What more was there to know?"

"We knew about the rheumatic fever from the first heart attack," Herbie said. "What about the second heart attack? Did we ever ask him whether it was a good idea for him to be on the golf course? Of course not. Because we thought it was none of our business. Which means, we essentially knew nothing about Willy."

George wished he was with Miss Betsy. Walking her. Away from all the questions about their friendships.

Herbie pressed on. "And did any of us know about Mona? Or Simon?"

George wasn't sure what to say to make Herbie stop.

"And does Benny know that you had a panic attack and needed to go to the emergency room?"

"Hey." George pointed at Herbie.

"What?" Herbie asked. "Like there's something wrong with Benny knowing you have emotional problems."

Benny turned to George. "Are you okay?"

"I'm fine," George brayed. "Perfectly fine. And I don't have emotional problems."

Herbie leapt from his seat. "You're not fine. You need help. Professional help," he shouted as the waitress, on her second approach, did a quick one-eighty.

George's temper flared. "Herbie, lower your voice. You're making a scene."

"I think a scene is just what needs to be made," Herbie insisted.

The other patrons turned and stared as Herbie slowly slipped back into his seat.

– 13 –

ELEANOR TRIED HER best to get out of attending Willy Krause's celebration of life, but there was simply no arguing with Sylvia. Like a dog with a bone, once Sylvia made up her mind, it was set. God only knows, Eleanor had given it her best shot. But her grit was no match for Sylvia's determination.

"Wait till you see Mona's condo," Sylvia said as they entered the massive lobby of Mona Krause's high rise. "Walls of glass everywhere."

"This feels so wrong," Eleanor confided. "I have no business—"

"Oh sweetie, not this again. You're here with me. Supporting me. We're here together."

Eleanor couldn't help but feel foolish as the elevator climbed, popping her ears.

"This will be a fabulous gathering." Sylvia rushed off the elevator, tripped, and caught herself.

Eleanor offered a steady arm. "Are you okay?"

"Oh, these darn shoes." Sylvia rubbed a calf. "I have weak ankles. Every now and then, one turns out on me."

Eleanor eyed Sylvia's red Valentino pumps. "My word, Sylvia. How much did those shoes cost?"

"If you have to ask, you don't want to know," Sylvia curtly answered.

"Maybe you should get something in a lower heel."

Sylvia was aghast. "Absolutely not. They make my legs look great. Besides, some things are worth suffering for. And high heels take years off."

"Of your life?" Eleanor wisecracked as Sylvia tightly gripped Eleanor's arm, limping along.

"Now remember what we discussed," Sylvia said. "Make sure I meet the men who talk to you. I know these guys. No sense wasting your time on a loser. You only want a man with money."

Eleanor winced. Sylvia was leaning heavily, hurting Eleanor's arm. "Now Sylvia, how many times have I told you that I don't care about a man's wallet?"

Sylvia gasped. "That's what they all say until they're sitting at a neighborhood deli and he's waiting for you to pick up the check. Trust me, doll. Some of these men are boys. Little boys looking for Mommy. You don't want to be Mommy."

Eleanor ignored Sylvia's proselytizing as they reached the open door to Mona's condo.

"Just little boys," Sylvia repeated as she magically righted herself and walked ahead on her own.

Eleanor rubbed her arm, losing sight of Sylvia as her eyes were drawn to the brilliant travertine entryway flanked on either side by five-foot Chinese urns. *Simply gorgeous,* she thought as she passed through a group of elegantly dressed women, cocktails in hand, gathered in the hallway. She caught a glimpse of Sylvia already in the sunken living room, oblivious to Eleanor's absence, busily chatting away as if Eleanor was following closely behind.

"Did you ever see so many people?" Sylvia said as Eleanor caught up to her side.

An expansive space, the condo dwarfed even Eleanor's rather large unit. Eleanor couldn't imagine being comfortable in such cavernous quarters. "Now why would anyone need a condo this size? The entryway alone is obscene," she whispered to Sylvia.

"Yes," Sylvia said. "And there are five bedrooms upstairs."

"Upstairs?" Eleanor turned. There was a sweeping circular staircase in the far corner. "My God. There's a second level?"

Sylvia tossed Eleanor a wicked glance. "Darling, size matters."

Eleanor frowned. She didn't care for sexual humor. She also preferred ladies not curse, and Sylvia frequently disregarded that cue. Eleanor thought to remind Sylvia of the fact just as the crowd parted. "Holy shit," Eleanor gasped as she spotted the enormous wall of glass. From the thirtieth floor, the ocean was a magnificent blue.

Sylvia lifted a piece of lint from Eleanor's blouse. "Lovely, isn't it? I was hoping Mona might sell. But she won't leave. Which goes to show you," Sylvia said as she looked about as if counting the faces of all the people she knew, "it may not have been a happy marriage, but it was financially lucrative."

A large Peter Max painting dominated the living room. At first glance, Eleanor doubted it could be real. What must it have cost? Eleanor leaned in close to Sylvia. "She got all this in a divorce?"

Sylvia puckered her lips. "In a settlement. I bet she has all sorts of stories to tell. But you see, she's not a talker. I've tried to figure it out. But I can't. They were only married a short time. It's a mystery."

"She must have been a very good girl," Eleanor said as she noticed the other oil paintings on the walls.

"Oh, she was," Sylvia answered, oblivious to Eleanor's sarcastic tone. "I wonder where Mona's hiding."

A waiter approached with a tray of champagne. As Eleanor reached for a flute, she couldn't help but feel she was at a cocktail party rather than a memorial.. And though the men were wearing dark suits, none of the women were dressed in somber colors. If anything, Eleanor was reminded of a brightly themed art gala fundraiser she'd attended years earlier on the lawn of a summer estate in the Hamptons.

Sylvia peered through the crowd. "Where can that girl be?"

Eleanor wasn't sure she'd even recognize Mona. Had they ever met? Or was that just another figment of Sylvia's imagination? And did Sylvia really have friends, or were the people she seemed to know just business contacts? Eleanor couldn't quite decide as Sylvia let out an "Oh, hello," or a "Hi, there" as she weaved through the crowd. Eleanor stayed in close pursuit, grateful to be ushered about, feeling important to be with someone so popular.

Despite Eleanor's misgivings, Sylvia's personality remained compelling. She radiated a veneer of outer confidence. Groomed and carried herself to demand attention. Eleanor couldn't help but admire Sylvia's brassy bravado. There was a certain thrill at being friends with such a stylish woman. Eleanor basked in that transformative effect, feeling better about herself for just being in Sylvia's company.

Sylvia pointed the way. "Let's try the kitchen."

Eleanor caught the scent of noodle kugel and freshly brewed coffee. *Well, there's no shortage of desserts,* she thought as they passed through a short hallway that opened into a spacious kitchen that abutted an enormous family room. Cheesecakes, brownies, cookies, and marble cakes lined the long granite countertop.

"There's enough food to feed an army," Eleanor said as she sampled a mini black and white cookie. Rich chocolate with the sweet, sugary taste of a butter cookie. "Delicious! This must be from Rudy's."

Sylvia offered a disapproving look. "Honey, don't. We're not here to eat."

Eleanor swallowed a last bite and rolled her eyes. "Honestly, Sylvia," she said with irritation.

Sylvia searched about. "Oh, I see a spot over there in the corner by the bar. Follow me."

Together they crossed the crowded family room. A man in a blue sport coat, yellow Izod collar turned up, blocked their path. "Ladies," he said, his tone welcoming.

Sylvia pursed her lips. Her cheeks expanded as her mouth magically turned up. Eleanor was surprised Sylvia had the ability to flex her facial muscles in such a descriptive way.

"I'm Herbie Marshall. We've met before. Remember me?"

"Barely," Sylvia said dismissively.

Eleanor recognized Herbie immediately as the cute guy from The Golden Funeral Home.

Herbie raised a brow at Sylvia before turning to Eleanor. "And you are?"

"Eleanor Rifkin."

Herbie took Eleanor's hand. "Lovely. Truly lovely."

"Insufferable," Sylvia sneered.

Herbie nodded formally in Sylvia's direction as if acknowledging royalty, an evil smile breaking across his lips.

"That's it," Eleanor said with delight. "That lecherous smile. Those pearly whites. You look just like Jack Nicholson in *The Shining*."

"Actually, Jack Nicholson got the smile from me."

"Oh, Lord," Sylvia mumbled.

Eleanor laughed. "That's one sexy smile you've got there, *Jack*."

"Herbie," he corrected her as he offered Sylvia a gloating leer that said, *See, I am adorable*.

Sylvia glared back.

"You know," Herbie said to Sylvia, "if you hold that expression too long, your face might freeze. My friend Benny's grandmother used to say that. So it must be true."

Sylvia wasn't buying it. "Friend? A worm doesn't have friends."

Herbie's head shot up in mock indignation. "I certainly do have friends."

Eleanor giggled. "My grandmother used to say, 'If the cat pees, your face will freeze.'"

Herbie's eyes lit up. "I could be wrong, but I think you need to meet my friend George."

Eleanor was disappointed. "Why not Benny? I'd like to meet a man who adored his grandmother."

"Oh, you're too small. You'd need a ladder to connect with Benny. Besides, he's not here. He's at a Marlins game. But," and Herbie took a glance at Eleanor's figure, "you'd be perfect for George. Hey, George," Herbie called to a nearby group of men. A man in a black suit, champagne in hand, turned about. Herbie waved him over.

Eleanor thought the man a dead ringer for a mature Cary Grant.

"George, I want you to meet a new friend of mine. Eleanor," he introduced with a nod of the head before turning to Sylvia and bowing, "and you already know, Red. The Queen of Sheba."

Sylvia offered George a warm smile. "Well, hello stranger," she purred. "I've been meaning to call you. We have a showing scheduled for next week. I'll text you the date and time."

Herbie shrugged. "They should create a Boca dating app, HotRealtor.com."

Sylvia turned, offering Herbie a cold shoulder. "George, this horrible little man couldn't possibly be a friend of yours. He's been annoying us."

Herbie grabbed Sylvia's elbow and pulled her close. "Now don't be that way, Red. Have you tried the brownies?" He led her away despite her obvious objection. "They're just like you. A little bitter. A little sweet."

Sylvia turned, a helpless look on her face as she disappeared with Herbie into the crowd.

"He's quite a smooth operator," Eleanor said. "Do you think we need to rescue poor Sylvia?"

"She'll be fine," George answered. "Herbie's really a sweet guy."

Eleanor couldn't help but stare at George's eyes. He'd such unusually long eyelashes. *Almost pretty*, she thought, suddenly uncomfortable in his presence. "Have you and Herbie been friends for a long time?"

"Long enough," George joked. "And Sylvia. Is she your Realtor?"

"She is. But she's a friend too."

George glanced about as if confirming they weren't in earshot of Sylvia, then whispered, "Sylvia doesn't have friends. Not real friends. She collects people."

Eleanor was instantly put off. Even though she suspected it was true, she felt compelled to defend Sylvia. "I don't think that's a very nice thing to say. In fact, she's been a very good friend to me."

George nodded. "I see."

"And Herbie. Does he collect people? I noticed he wandered off with Sylvia. From the look on her face, it was more of a kidnapping."

George was contrite. "Herbie's an upstanding guy. Unusual, yes. But a good soul."

"I bet," Eleanor quipped. "Faster than a locomotive. Able to reach tall places in a single bound. Look up in the air…"

"Is it a bird? Is it a plane?"

"No," Eleanor said. "It's Herbie."

They both laughed.

Eleanor pressed a palm to her cheek as she gained her composure. "This is terrible. We're at a memorial acting like we're at a singles soirée."

George grinned the kind of grin that made grown women swoon. "Welcome to death in Boca."

"It sounds like a Verdi opera."

"Actually, that would be Thomas Mann."

Eleanor offered a blank expression.

"*Death in Venice* was written by Thomas Mann."

Eleanor tilted her head, giving George another go-over. "You're an opera fan. That's impressive."

"Blame my wife. My ex-wife. I mean…"

Eleanor wondered whether George's hazel eyes might actually be a lighter shade of brown. "So you're divorced."

George reddened. "I'm a widower."

"Oh." Eleanor fixated on George's skin. The man barely had a line. *It's so unfair,* she thought. *Men age so beautifully.*

"And are you single?" George raised a glass of champagne to take a sip.

She noticed his fingernails. Perfectly shaped. Clean and trimmed. *What a marvelous-looking man,* she thought before realizing it was her turn to speak. "Yes. I live alone."

"Well, I suppose it's just the human condition," George went on. "We live, we die. In between, we do the best we can."

Eleanor lost the thread of the conversation in George's sexy half-smile. "I'm sorry. You were saying?" she asked, wondering how his lips might feel on hers.

George looked lost. "I'm not really sure," he admitted. "I'm kind of nervous. I'm not very good at small talk with a beautiful woman."

Eleanor was immensely flattered. "Am I making you nervous?"

George tugged on his tie. "Perhaps it's this whole ritual. Our way of coping with death. What else can we do? We're all afraid we might be next. When you get this close to death, it's better to keep busy. And sometimes, the opposite sex is the only way to make us feel alive."

Eleanor sipped her champagne. She noticed George's black suit with its wide lapels and cuffed pants. Hopelessly out of style and clearly off the rack. She guessed a polyester blend. Her Joel had never shopped off the rack. Everything was custom-tailored. But then Joel was a different breed. Finicky about his appearance. Obsessive about career and home. *Goddamn it, Eleanor*, he'd rail if she dared to rearrange the furniture. *I liked it the way it was.*

George blushed. "I'm just rambling on."

"You're a philosopher. Now, don't be shy," she said, charmed by his boyish demeanor. "It's lovely. Much better than your friend, Speedy Gonzales. At least a philosopher can help you understand the world."

George's gaze shifted. The voices in the room rose. Eleanor heard a woman mention Mona Krause's name as the only woman dressed in black made her way along the perimeter of the room. Her dark hair, pulled back in a ponytail, emphasized a moon-shaped face; her brows were so high on her forehead, Eleanor wondered if it was painful to hold the surprised expression.

Mona held up a champagne flute. With two taps of a teaspoon, the room quieted. "Thank you, everyone, for being here." She looked about. "I know it's been a difficult time. But I so appreciate Willy's friends turning out today."

Eleanor noticed an odd expression on George's face. "Is anything wrong?" she whispered.

"Are these people Willy's friends?"

"I wouldn't know," Eleanor admitted. "I never met the man."

George did a double take. "Then why are you here?"

Eleanor was unsure how to answer. "I was invited by a friend."

George's face registered surprise. "Sylvia."

"Yes," Eleanor innocently answered.

George's eyes shifted back to Mona, who was in the midst of a speech. "Sylvia invited you to attend a stranger's celebration of life?"

Eleanor struggled with how to answer. If she said yes, she'd appear shallow. If she said no, she'd have to explain some connection to Mona or the late Willy. Either way, she feared coming across as foolish and insipid.

George didn't wait for her answer. "Sylvia's not your friend."

Eleanor placed the empty champagne flute on a nearby table. "How do you know?"

Mona's voice hit a crescendo. "Yes, we didn't always get along. And it may not have been a happy marriage. But he was a wonderful man."

"Women like Sylvia don't have friends," George whispered.

Eleanor had no idea why this man, this stranger, felt compelled to insult Sylvia. And though she hadn't known Sylvia long, Sylvia had been kind. Through sheer force of personality, she'd pulled Eleanor out of her lonely existence. "Well," Eleanor said, her tone dripping with sarcasm, "if you know everything about everyone, who should I be friends with?"

George's face went blank. "I didn't mean…"

"What? What exactly didn't you mean?"

George locked eyes with Eleanor. "I'm sorry. I overstepped my bounds."

Eleanor softened. "Maybe we should be paying attention to Mona," she quietly said as Mona wrapped up her speech.

George chuckled. "The last thing anyone should be doing is paying attention to Mona."

Eleanor was shocked. It was bad enough George had gone after Sylvia, but now he seemed to have a negative opinion about the hostess too. "Mister…" Eleanor realized she hadn't caught George's last name. Had he told her?

"Elden. But please, call me George."

"Mr. Elden. You seem to have an angle on everyone."

The noise in the room escalated as Mona retreated and people started talking among themselves. George leaned in.

Eleanor caught a woodsy scent. She briefly closed her eyes. It reminded her of Joel.

"Are you new to Boca?" he asked.

Eleanor nodded. "I bought a condo in March. I live on the grounds of the Boca Raton Resort & Club."

"You do?" George smiled. "Me too. So, you don't really know the ropes yet." A man squeezed past George, forcing him closer to Eleanor. "Maybe we should get together. Share our thoughts on Boca."

Eleanor's heart raced. The physical attraction was powerful. He was certainly easy on the eyes. And even though they'd gotten off to a bumpy start, perhaps there was more to him. He did smell an awful lot like Joel. "Get together?" she said coyly. "I don't have time to get together."

"I meant, would you like to have dinner?"

Eleanor considered the offer. "I think we might be able to arrange something."

"I wondered what happened to you," George said as he spotted Herbie alone on the terrace. A speedboat passed in the distance. The setting sun reflected in the windows of the mansions that lined the Intracoastal

Herbie leaned over the railing and looked down. "Are you afraid of heights, George?"

George sidled up next to Herbie. "Not particularly. At least not with a high railing holding me back."

"Sometimes I wonder what it must be like to fly free. Like the birds. Gliding along the breeze without a care. I wonder if Willy is doing that now. Drifting off somewhere, floating along. Not a care in the world."

George sighed. "I hope so. That would be nice."

Herbie pressed forward on the railing, turning toward George with a dopey smile. "So, was she nice?"

George caught a whiff of Herbie's breath. "How much have you had to drink? You smell like a distillery."

Herbie pressed up against George as they stood shoulder to shoulder. "Me? A few. Lady Sylvia didn't seem to find me appealing. That's happening more and more. Do you think I'm losing my touch? Tell me the truth."

"We need to get you some coffee."

"No," Herbie said. "First tell me about your lady friend. Did she dump you too? No, of course not. Not handsome George."

George didn't want to discuss Eleanor. And certainly not with Herbie in his current condition. "Where'd you go? The last I saw, you were wooing Sylvia with your impressive powers of persuasion."

Herbie bit his lip. "When you take a woman by the arm, and she resists you at every step, you really can't consider that persuasion."

"True," George agreed.

"She was madder than a newborn baby slapped on the ass after a breech birth."

"Nice analogy. Remind me to never repeat it."

Herbie smiled. "She doesn't like me. And to be honest, I'm not so sure she's very likable."

"Sounds like a match made in heaven," George said sarcastically.

"And what about the gal you were with? Ellen?"

George looked over his shoulder. They were still alone on the terrace. "Eleanor. She's nice," he said, downplaying his enthusiasm over meeting a woman he clicked with.

"You're a sad case, George. You need a woman to get your life in gear. Maybe this Ellen is just the right one."

"Eleanor. And what about you, Herbie? What do you need?"

"I'm hopeless," Herbie said wistfully. "A four-time loser. I don't dare try again. Oh sure, I play hit and miss with the ladies. And it's fun. But it doesn't last long. I guess there's not much to me beyond my boyish charm. And I suspect that too is wearing thin. Maybe Jeanette was right. She always thought I was shallow."

"Don't say that, Herbie. That isn't true."

Herbie leaned back, holding onto the railing. "She never liked me, George. Admit it."

"She was hurt for her sister. She blamed you for the failure of the marriage."

"Like a failed marriage can ever be one person's fault. You know, George, it takes two."

George nodded. "Yes. But there has to be someone to blame. Someone who pulled the trigger. And you cheated on Judy."

"Oh sure, that's the easy sign to point to. The cheating. But what about her condescending tone? All the times she rolled her eyes when I spoke. Dismissed my opinion. Made fun of me in front of friends. Those were all betrayals."

"Herbie, you don't need to defend yourself."

"Oh, but I do. You still think I'm to blame. That everything was hunky dory until I stepped out of line. Like I broke that poor girl's heart."

George was startled. "Herbie, take it easy."

Herbie pointed at George. "See what you do."

"What do you mean?"

"You just cut me off."

"No, I didn't," George insisted. "I just don't think you have to explain yourself."

"But if you don't let me explain, you can't possibly know what I'm talking about. What I mean. Who I am." Herbie ran a hand over the railing as if petting a dog. "Tell me, George, how do you do it?"

George swallowed. He wasn't in the mood for an argument. Certainly not at a memorial gathering. "I don't know what you mean." As soon as the words left George's mouth, he regretted them.

"You think you're better than me," Herbie said. "And you have two kids you never speak to. You spend most of your time alone. How do you do it? I'd think you'd be crawling up the walls."

George winced. "I like my own company."

Herbie scrunched up his face. "God, you're a pathetic liar."

"Gee thanks," George said. "Do me a favor. Don't do the eulogy at my funeral."

Herbie chuckled. "I'll make sure Rabbi Sherman does it. He can pretend to be your buddy. Tell everyone what a kindhearted man you were. A wonderful husband and father. A beloved friend. Is that how you'd like to be remembered?"

"To tell you the truth, I don't give a damn how I'm remembered. It's not like I'll be around to hear it."

Herbie's eyes glistened. His mood shifted. Anger replaced by melancholy. "Don't you worry," he said, his voice suddenly solemn. "If I'm there, I'll give you the best eulogy ever." He placed a hand on George's shoulder and gave it a shake. "The best darn eulogy," he repeated as he stepped onto the lower rung of the railing, raising himself up.

George stepped back. "Herbie, maybe you shouldn't be playing around. Get down."

Herbie laughed. "You really love me, don't you, George?"

"I'd love you more if you were standing right next to me. Over here."

"Scared I might jump?"

George didn't like Herbie's tone. "Seriously, Herbie. It's not funny."

Herbie released his grip and raised both hands overhead.

George's heart jumped. He grabbed Herbie by the waist and pulled him down. "Jesus Christ. What the hell is wrong with you?"

Herbie's smile was gone. "I don't know. I was just having fun. So, what about Ellen? What are your plans?"

"Eleanor." George placed a hand back on the railing. "She agreed to dinner. But I'm not sure she likes me. Come to think of it," George said with a nervous laugh, "I'm not sure I like me."

"She likes you, George. Women like you. You're a lucky dog."

"This whole widower thing has me confused. First, you're two people together facing the world, and then, you're alone. It's really cruel when you think about it. No man should live alone. It doesn't seem natural. But to be honest, Eleanor doesn't seem like a long-term bet. There was an odd tension. I couldn't decide if we were getting along or not."

Herbie stepped back onto the lowest rung of the railing and hoisted himself up. "George, you're a catch. You don't have your head in the clouds." A breeze caught in Herbie's curls and they shifted. "Any woman would be happy to land you."

George was touched. "Thank you, Herbie. But please, get off the railing."

"Jeanette trained you well. You haven't had an independent thought in years, which is why you're so screwed up today. You've no clue what to think or how to take care of yourself. You don't know who you are because you were part of Jeanette. I guarantee you, if Jeanette had outlived you, she'd know exactly who she was. But not you. We men are just lost. So, you'll go off with Ellen. And like a good little puppy dog, you'll try to please her. But you can't please her. Because she doesn't really like you. If she did, you'd be good enough as you are."

George hadn't heard Herbie talk with such disdain. So much bitterness. "How do you know she doesn't like me as I am?"

"Experience. I've met more ladies than you have. If they can't change you, they don't want you."

"Wow, that's cynical. How long have you been holding onto that?"

Herbie lifted a foot off the railing, placing his weight to one side. "Don't be offended. It's a fact. You're totally lost without a woman to tell you what to do." There were tears in Herbie's eyes. "I understand only too well."

"Herbie, come down," George insisted. "If you don't, I'm going to pull you down again."

"Don't touch me!" Herbie shouted. "You know what I'm saying is true."

Was Herbie upset about George's life or his own? "Sure, I've had a few bad moments. But I wouldn't say I'm lost."

Herbie harumphed. "Completely lost. Helpless as a baby."

"Okay, Herbie. Whatever you say. Just knock it off. Come on down."

Herbie released his grip on the railing and waved an arm in the air. "Why should I?"

George's pulse raced. Annoyed, he grabbed the back of Herbie's sport coat and tugged hard.

Herbie stepped down.

"What the hell is wrong with you?" George growled. "I swear, you're going to give me a freaking heart attack."

Herbie brushed himself off and straightened his coat. "Calm down. I wasn't going to do anything."

"Well, you could have fooled me."

Herbie took a deep breath. In a sad, self-deprecating tone, he said, "I don't have that kind of courage. If I did, I'd remarry again."

George pulled Herbie in for a tight hug. "Do you know how important you are to me?"

Herbie squirmed away.

George caught Herbie by the wrist. "Are you still going to your meetings? The ones you told me about?"

Herbie shrugged. "I stopped. There's no point to it. No one seems to get better."

George shook his head and sighed. "When's the next meeting?"

"Monday night."

"I'm going with you."

Herbie's face brightened. "You will? You'd do that?"

George nodded, uncertain what he'd just committed to. "Sure. Why not?"

– 14 –

A WEEK AFTER WILLY'S celebration of life, George was eating lunch with Benny and Herbie at TooJay's Deli when a text displayed on his phone. George's face lit up. It wasn't a bill collector. "We've got good news, gentlemen. Jordan Archer, Willy's former attorney, has tracked down the insurance lead. A Valerie Cortland at State Farm sold the policy to Willy." George bit into a hot dog. A mixture of relish, sauerkraut, and mustard covered his mouth as he reached for a napkin. "Now, we just need to contact Valerie and all our problems are solved. We're certain to locate the executor of Willy's estate."

"I don't know," Benny said. "Insurance people are clever. I bet she'll wind up selling you a policy."

"What if Willy dropped the policy?" Herbie asked. "It happens. Especially life insurance. If you're single, what's the point of carrying that kind of coverage?"

George had allowed Jeanette's life insurance policy to lapse once they retired. He'd been concerned about monthly expenses and Jeanette's ability to manage their cash flow, though he'd maintained a life insurance policy on himself to cover Jeanette. He hadn't considered she'd die first, leaving him with a mountain of debt.

Benny nodded. "Willy might have cancelled the policy. Even changed agents."

"Actually," Herbie said as he pointed a fork at a potato knish on his plate, "I don't think she'll tell you anything. I bet the information is confidential."

George sighed. "I say we cross that bridge when we get to it."

Benny pushed his empty plate aside. The corned beef on rye never had a chance. "Fair enough. But maybe you should let me handle this one."

"Oh no," Herbie quickly said. He squeezed a dollop of mustard on top of the knish. "You're a great guy, Benny, but George is faster on the uptake."

George turned in surprise. "Why, thank you, Herbie. That's nice of you to say. Especially considering you two are pretty sharp businessmen."

"Yes," Herbie acknowledged, "but neither of us have the experience you have, George. You worked inside a large healthcare system. You know insurance."

George blushed. What would Herbie and Benny think if he shared the scope of his debt? If he explained there was no life insurance at the time of Jeanette's death? They'd think him foolish. A dolt. A complete idiot. "That isn't exactly true," he said, on the brink of confessing his financial quagmire. "You guys have it all wrong."

But Herbie didn't give George the chance to finish. "It's just this, George. We know the agent, Valerie Cortland, is female. I see the way women look at you. You're like bait on a hook. Me, I'm adorable, but sometimes I come across too strong. Benny, well, he's a giant."

"Women love tall men," Benny interjected as he picked at a piece of coffee cake. "Have you ever seen a Laker without a date?"

"That's different," Herbie explained. "They're stars. They come with all sorts of freebies."

Benny shook his head. "Where do you come up with this stuff?"

Herbie waved a hand, dismissing Benny. "Our best chance for getting the information lies with George. He's well-mannered and handsome. And he projects a kind of innocence."

Benny lifted his coffee mug. "That's because he is."

Herbie laughed. "Amen."

"I'm not innocent," George said.

"Big man," Herbie teased George, his mouth full of knish. "Okay. Let's lay our cards on the table. George, how many women have you been with?"

"I'm not answering that."

Herbie looked at Benny. "How about you? How many would you say?"

Benny looked up at the ceiling. "I'd say a good twenty or so. And that's a conservative guess. Mostly after my divorce, but to be honest, I was no virgin when I married."

Herbie raised his eyebrows at George. "I don't need to fill you in on my experience, but for simplicity's sake, let's just say four. Four ladies. All of whom I married."

George swallowed. "So I don't have a lot of sexual experience with multiple partners. Isn't that a mark against me?"

Herbie leaned forward, elbows on the table. "Silly boy. Not at all. Don't you see, George? You're catnip. Women can smell the vulnerability. You're a clean slate. You'd never cheat because essentially, you're a virgin."

George never ceased to be amazed by what came out of Herbie's mouth. "Hardly a virgin. I have two kids."

"Yes, yes," Herbie waved a hand. "But that's different. You're Mr. Fidelity."

"Mr. Fidelity," Benny repeated with a laugh. "You even sound like an insurance policy."

Valerie Cortland's office was on Military Trail in a small shopping center. George spotted the familiar State Farm logo in the window and wondered about the best approach to gathering the information on Willy's estate. Should he pretend to be a relative making an inquiry? Or just a close friend of the family? If he said he was a friend, at least he wouldn't be lying. George had always been a terrible liar. Easily spotted when he stammered through a half-truth.

A bell chimed when George walked through the door of the State Farm office. A young woman, face covered in freckles, was seated at the front desk, engrossed in a crossword puzzle. George waited for her to look up and make eye contact.

She didn't.

"Excuse me; I'm looking for Valerie Cortland."

"Wait," the receptionist commanded, a hand in the air as she studied the puzzle in front of her. "Where's the home of the Taj Mahal?"

"India."

"Where in India? It's a four-letter word."

"Agra?"

"Why, yes," she said as she scribbled away. "It fits perfectly!" She looked up and smiled, a number two pencil in hand. "You're smart. Thank you."

Odd, George thought, *in a day of smartphones and laptops to actually see a pencil.*

She pointed the pencil at George. "What's up?"

"I was hoping to see Valerie Cortland. Is she here?"

"I should be studying calculus instead of this silly *New York Times* crossword, but I'm addicted. It's ridiculous. I'm pre-med and required to take calculus. Now, will someone please tell me how calculus can possibly be helpful to a physician?"

"I don't know," George said, amused by the young lady's inability to focus. "And Valerie. Is she here?"

"Valerie's out at an appointment."

"Oh," George said. "I should have called first."

"Are you a friend?"

George searched for a reasonable explanation he could quickly offer. Something not too complicated.

She stood up. "Oh my God. You're Valerie's younger brother. I've heard you're in town. Come with me," she said as she pulled George by the arm. They passed through a privacy door. "So lovely to meet you. I'm Melissa. Your sister is so excited you're here in Florida. I've heard all about you."

"Wait a second. You've made a—"

Before he could finish, he was in Valerie's private office, sitting in front of her desk, a very proud Melissa gloating at his side that she'd figured it all out.

"Now make yourself comfortable and I'll get you a cup of coffee. Do you take sugar or cream?"

"Cream," George said, "but really—"

The front doorbell chimed. "Oh, wait, I have to check on that," Melissa said with the enthusiasm of a recent bingo winner. "I'll be right back."

George gathered his wits. For a split second, he entertained the thought of rifling through Valerie's desk. But that seemed too extreme. Too secret-agent. Instead, he sat quietly and dreaded the moment Valerie arrived to find him, not her brother, sitting in her office.

How do I get myself into these situations? And why for God's sake did Willy create this mess?

George heard footsteps behind him. He rose and prepared to explain the misunderstanding.

Valerie Cortland arrived in a flash of energy. Her ash-blonde hair was cut in a stylish bob, her mouth a bright red slash on an angular face. George was reminded of Angela Lansbury from *Murder, She Wrote.*

"Can I help you?" she asked, suspiciously eyeing George as she stood anchored in the doorway, a force of nature like the tall, slender palms that lined the streets of Boca.

George broke into a grin. He hoped his smile might help disarm the situation. "Hello. You must be Ms. Cortland."

"Yes," she said. "And you are?"

George extended a hand. She didn't take it. "George Elden."

"Melissa said you were my brother. Did you tell her that?"

"Oh no. It was a case of mistaken identity. Honestly. I tried to—"

"You led her to think you were my brother." Valerie held her ground, seeming reluctant to step into the space with George. Her brown eyes bored a hole through him.

"I never said…I was related. You know, she's a very enthusiastic young lady." George let out a nervous laugh.

"Do you need insurance? Is that why you're here?"

"Um, no. You see, it's a bit of a long story. I got your name from Jordan Archer."

"The lawyer?"

"Yes, that's right. She thought I should talk to you. I should have called for an appointment. I just hoped you'd be in. You see, I just had lunch with the guys and it just made sense to come over and take care of this."

She squinted. "I don't have a clue what you're talking about."

"Of course not," George mumbled, certain he was making a complete ass of himself. "How could you? Let me start from the beginning. Please." George waved Valerie to take a seat.

"I'm not accustomed to strangers in my office. I'm very uncomfortable."

"Well, I didn't mean…I'm certainly not trying to…well to be honest…it was your receptionist's fault. I never told her I was your brother. She just ushered me in here."

Valerie lifted her chin as if deciding whether to believe him.

"She's very insistent," George said. "I tried to tell her." He held his arms out in supplication. "But I knew that Agra was the location of the Taj Mahal and she was certain I was your brother. And that was that!"

Valerie was having none of it. "Will you leave or should I call the police?"

"This really is just a simple misunderstanding," George pleaded, hands in the air as if Valerie were holding a gun.

"Please leave."

"Certainly," George muttered. "No need for the police. I'm going."

Valerie stepped aside for him to pass.

The next morning, George pulled into the LA Fitness parking lot in Deerfield Beach. Herbie stood waiting at the front door. He wore bright red shorts and a blue T-shirt with a red and yellow Superman insignia.

"Holy crap," George said to him.

Herbie stepped back and smiled with pride. "I know. I'm rocking it."

George was momentarily speechless. "I'd say, more off your rocker. Where did you dig up that outfit?"

Herbie jogged in place. "Ever since I started working out, I have so much energy."

George raised an eyebrow. "No doubt. Aren't those red shorts a little high on the leg? Where did you get them?"

"Online," Herbie answered. "A store in West Hollywood." Herbie flexed his arms in a Hulk Hogan downward pose. "They are very in."

"I'm not so sure," George laughed. "Is that your pickle waving at me?"

Herbie tugged on the shorts. "Don't be silly."

George shook his head. "Herbie, really..."

"No," Herbie said, pointing a finger. "This is your problem. I'm comfortable in my own skin. I am in total control of my image. I know what I look like. And I think I've got it going on."

"You've got it going on, all right," George said as they checked in at the front desk.

An effervescent blonde, perky and petite, was busy spooning her way through a cup of yogurt. She looked up as they approached. "Hi Herbie," she gushed. "How's my cutie pie?"

Herbie waved his pass under the infrared scanner. "Great. And you, Ginger?"

"Oh, isn't he sweet?" The blonde directed the comment to George. "He's the only one who comes in here and says hello, goodbye, and remembers my name. Everyone else just rushes by like I'm invisible. Do you know how many people come through that door? And they say nothing. Nothing at all."

Herbie's chest doubled in size with pride.

"Enjoy your workout," she called as they headed to the locker room.

"Isn't she a doll?" Herbie boasted. "She's got a sweet spot for me."

George chuckled. "She must love antiques."

Herbie grimaced. "You're really no fun, George."

"So where's your headband?" George asked, his voice heavy with sarcasm as he slipped his workout bag into a locker.

"Oh, I nearly forgot." Herbie retrieved a red headband from the pocket of his shorts.

George had been kidding. "What else is hidden in there?"

"Wouldn't you like to know?" Herbie teased.

"No," George said, certain of the answer. "I don't think I would."

Thirty minutes later, George, sweating profusely, pedaled away on a stationary bicycle as Herbie stood next to him, talking.

"I thought you were working out," George squeaked in between breaths. "Why don't you go do something? There are weights over there." George nodded in the direction of the weight area. "Go pick something up."

"I don't think so. You know I have a bad shoulder. It's really played havoc with my golf swing."

George rolled his eyes.

Herbie adjusted the band on his head. "So, what did the insurance agent say? And what's the next step?"

George held up a finger. He had to finish the workout before he could really talk. "Wait for me by the juice bar," he grunted. "I'll fill you in then."

Herbie was all ears. "So, what's the story? What did Valerie say?"

"She wouldn't tell me anything." George wiped his face with a towel. "In fact, she found me in her office and was mad as hell. She asked me to leave."

"What? She kicked you out? Why?"

"It's a long story. But, when I was in her office, I noticed something important."

Herbie leaned in as if George was about to reveal the secret to the murder of JonBenét Ramsey.

George took a swig from his bottle of water. "She's a dancer."

Herbie nodded. "That's nice."

"No," George said. "A serious dancer."

Herbie was confused. "You mean a ballerina?"

George shook his head. "Of course not. She's our age, give or take a few years. But she goes to Arthur Murray Dance Studios."

"How would you know that, George?"

"I saw a plaque on her wall. She's an instructor there. She must do it in the evenings. There were all these trophies on her credenza. She's seriously into it."

Herbie shook his head. "Okay. She can dance. What does this have to do with Willy's insurance policy or the estate?"

"Don't you see? All we need to do is sign up for dance lessons, request her as our instructor, and win her over."

Herbie chuckled. "You're losing it, George. That's just ridiculous. It sounds like something I'd suggest."

George realized Herbie was right. Still, it was the only way he could see moving forward. "What other choice do we have?"

Herbie understood. "It'll have to be you or Benny. I can't dance to save my life."

"It can't be me. She already knows me."

"Then it's got to be Benny. Imagine that big horse dancing."

George laughed. "Well, we don't want to kill her."

"No, of course not," Herbie giggled. "Just slow her down enough to give us the information we need."

Benny was already seated at their booth when George and Herbie arrived for lunch at TooJay's Deli. After explaining his unsuccessful interaction with Valerie the day before, George suggested the next step.

Benny scanned the sports scores in the paper. "No way, José. I'm not doing it."

"Benny, you're our last hope," Herbie whined. "Without you, the trail's gone cold."

Benny refused to be swayed. "I'm firm on this. Years ago, I went for lessons with my ex-wife. It was gut-wrenching. Every other Monday night for two months, she dragged me to learn all these fancy steps. I couldn't master them."

George imagined it had to be hard. "Was it a tango, waltz, or the samba?"

Benny looked at George with surprise. "No. Square dancing."

George poked a finger in his ear as if he'd misheard. "Square dancing! How hard can that be?"

"I broke my wife's baby toe when I stepped on it doing one of those 'Swing your partner do si do' things. I've always thought of myself as a graceful guy, but one misstep, and well, it wasn't pretty."

"Maybe we should drop this whole thing," Herbie said, much to George's shock. "What's the point? The money's gone. We're probably never getting reimbursed. It's been nothing but a wild goose chase from the start. I say we cut our losses and move on."

George's Visa balance flashed before him. "Come on, Herbie," he said. "You're the one who said we shouldn't be paying for the funeral of a wealthy man. That it was wrong. You were adamant. And I agree. We've come this far. Surely we can go a little further."

"But Arthur Murray's?" Herbie asked. "It'll cost money to take dance lessons. Doesn't that defeat the whole purpose?"

"No it won't, Herbie." Benny folded back a page of the newspaper. "Check this out. Arthur Murray is running a special. Two free introductory classes. All men welcome."

"That's terrific," George said, a bit too enthusiastically.

Benny broke into a big smile. "My grandmother used to say, 'Everything happens for a reason. Things present as we need them.'"

Herbie looked at George. "What exactly does any of that mean?"

Benny scowled. “I think it’s perfectly self-evident.”

“Dear God,” Herbie hissed. “Please don’t tell us any more of your grandmother’s sayings. I don’t think I can take much more.”

– 15 –

ELEANOR RAN A brush through her hair. She'd chosen a simple pink skirt and white blouse topped with a string of pearls. The outfit lent itself to any occasion as long as her date didn't show up in a ratty pair of jeans. She suddenly wondered if that was possible. Modern men seemed sewn into worn-out jeans, unwilling to jettison them for casual slacks. Ralph Lauren had epitomized the style. Unfortunately, most men in Boca Raton didn't look like Ralph Lauren.

It was a windy August night. Not ideal for a first date.

Eleanor opted for a white hat with a wide brim that framed her face.

But what if he has a convertible? she fretted. So many Boca men drove sporty foreign models. Cars built for speed. How could she get in and out of a tiny car gracefully? And did a sports car mean the man was going through a midlife crisis? Was that even possible when you were sixty years old?

She hadn't asked where they'd be going for dinner. *I'm such an amateur at this,* she thought. *What if I'm overdressed?*

She changed her pumps to white sandals to simplify the look. *God,* she thought as she switched her keys and wallet from one handbag to another, w*hy am I so nervous? It's just a meal.*

In the few moments before George's expected arrival, she paced. Time stood still as she tried to remember George's face. Much to her surprise, she couldn't. "I'm going to dinner with a total stranger," she whimpered, grasping the genuine awkwardness of the situation. "What if we have nothing in common?" She moved a figurine of a fertility goddess on a side table an inch to the left. She'd purchased it on a trip to South Africa with Joel. How long had it been since she'd been physical with a man? Is that something he might expect on a first date? How long had Joel been dead?

She panicked. *I'm not ready for this.*

She took a deep breath, perched between her past and present, struggling to understand why she was giving the moment such weight. The downstairs buzzer rang. She jumped. In a moment he'd be in the elevator for the short ride to the fourth floor. Steps away from her door.

Her heart raced. *I could pretend I'm ill.*

But it was too late for such ploys. She couldn't turn George away at the last minute. Even if she couldn't remember his face. It wouldn't be fair. She had to go through with the date.

Her phone lit up. A text from Sylvia: *Darling, make sure you wear something sexy.*

Eleanor smiled. She wasn't wearing anything of the sort.

A second text: *Have a wonderful time. I want to hear all about it tomorrow.*

Eleanor wished it was already tomorrow. That the stress and nervousness of dating a stranger were a distant memory.

"Joel," she said. "Give me a sign if you think this guy is worth my time. I'll be waiting. Don't let me down."

The doorbell rang.

Eleanor froze. She'd misplaced her purse. *Where did I put that damn bag?* She rushed about in search of it, room to room. *He's at the door, you fool. Answer the door. Let him in.* But somehow, the lost handbag symbolized an impending disaster. *I don't think I can go through with this,* she thought as the moments ticked by.

She spotted the handbag on top of the glass table in the entryway. Exactly where she'd left it.

The doorbell buzzed again.

"It's do-or-die time," she whispered, bolstering her courage.

George waited anxiously for an answer to the buzzer. He held a bouquet of red roses mixed with white lilies. He'd been unsure what to bring. Jeanette had loved roses. George wondered whether he should have selected the yellow ones that symbolized friendship instead of the red that promised love. Did red roses send the wrong message? Was he moving too fast? *I should have selected the white roses.* But then George remembered Jeanette saying that brides might carry white roses on their wedding day as a symbol of true love. George felt dizzy. Yellow, red, white. Did everything have to have a deeper meaning? Couldn't flowers just be a pretty gift?

Had he made a mistake? A date with a woman he barely knew. It all seemed so contrived. Forced. Ever since Jeanette's death, his encounters with other women had been mostly initiated by the woman. There'd been Ava from Tri-County Animal Rescue. Though he thought her a caring person, it was evident that her true love was dogs. Pit bulls, to be precise. George shuddered to think of what her home must be like. An armed encampment of giant dog heads with sharp teeth. And then the lovely Jill. George couldn't get past The Golden Funeral Home connection. The very thought of someone spending the day in that building was enough to put him off. He'd also pressed the flesh with Sylvia. That had been the most disturbing connection of all. George had been roughly manhandled and discarded. Her aggressive style had gotten him into bed, but in the end, left him feeling like a fool. Hardly the security he'd hoped for in a successful coupling.

There was a stickiness in his armpits. He groaned, flapping his elbows as if performing the chicken dance, hoping the increased air flow might relieve the problem. *Great. Perfect. I'm acting like a nervous teenager waiting for my prom date. At least I don't have acne.*

He realized he'd been waiting quite a while for Eleanor to answer the door. Was he being stood up? He pressed the bell once more as he flapped his arms wildly, hoping to cool off.

He waited.

Still no answer.

George turned to leave, arms still flapping, at the precise moment the door opened.

"George?" Eleanor directed the question to the back of George's head.

He turned about, arms flapping. Bouquet in hand.

Eleanor's eyes zeroed in on George's khakis. She scanned up to the untucked baby-blue Tommy Bahama shirt. No sport coat. *Wonderful*, she bitterly thought, grateful for her last-minute change to sandals.

George stopped flapping. "Hello," he said in a barely audible voice. "I hope I'm not intruding."

Eleanor offered George a quizzical look. "We have a date," she answered, checking her watch. "You're right on time."

"Am I?" George answered. "Well then, I suspect this is where you live."

Eleanor squished her face. *How awkward*, she thought. *This is the strangest conversation.* "Yes, this is my place," she said, waving George in. "Can I offer you a drink?"

George thrust the bouquet at Eleanor, catching her off guard. "For you."

Startled, she took the gift and pretended to admire it. "Lovely," she said, the fragrance of the lilies overwhelming her senses. "Thank you." She'd been intensely allergic to lilies since childhood.

George smiled. "I saw them and thought of you."

Her eyes watered. Her nose started to run. "Let me get these in water. I'll be right back." She carried the poison bundle down the hall to the kitchen, leaving George alone in the entryway. She thought about keeping the roses and tossing the lilies into the trash, but hesitated. Instead she dropped the bouquet on the kitchen counter and vigorously washed her hands with soap and water before letting out a sneeze that rocked her to her toes.

"All set to go?" George asked when she reappeared, tissue in hand, dabbing at her eyes.

"Yes, by all means."

They both rushed the door, Eleanor stepping on George's foot as he crossed in front of her.

"Sorry," George muttered as he took a step back.

"Oh, no," Eleanor squeaked. "Excuse me."

In perfect unison, they again stepped forward and collided.

"Forgive me." George stepped away from the door and nodded to Eleanor to proceed. Eleanor opened the door for George to walk through. Once over the threshold, George reached back, and with a palm at the top of the door, struggled to keep the heavy door open as Eleanor passed under his arm.

He released a toot.

Eleanor pretended she hadn't heard George's short burst of song.

Together they stood waiting for the elevator. "So, George. Where are we going for dinner?"

George checked his watch. "I made a reservation at Ruth's Chris."

"Oh," Eleanor said, pleasantly surprised. "That's great."

As she stepped onto the elevator, she struggled to think of the next thing to say. "It was lovely weather today," she offered. "Nice and clear."

"Yes," George agreed. "We've been having a lot of clear weather."

Eleanor focused on the elevator doors. This was going to be harder than she'd thought. Why hadn't she just stayed home? What was the point of getting dressed up to struggle through dinner with a stranger? It wasn't as if she needed a man to take her to Ruth's Chris. She was perfectly capable of going there on her own and eating at the bar. Or getting a table. Or asking Sylvia to join her. She softly shook her head. *Live and learn*, she thought. *Live and learn.*

George suddenly spoke up. "But it did rain briefly at three o'clock."

Eleanor looked up at him, startled. "Yes. So it did," she answered as the doors opened onto the lobby.

Oh God, George thought as they walked out of the building, his car fob in hand. *This couldn't be more awkward.*

An ear-shattering alarm blared as his car lights flashed. "Crap," he muttered. He'd accidently pushed the hazard alarm on the fob.

"Someone's playing your song," Eleanor tittered as she covered her ears.

George fumbled with the fob. He unlocked the door, hopped in, and started the car.

The alarm stopped.

George leaned forward, hands on the steering wheel. *My God, what else could possibly go wrong?* And then he noticed he was alone in the car. He stepped out and rushed to the passenger side. He opened the car door.

Eleanor looked at him as if he'd just escaped from Bellevue Hospital for the mentally deranged.

"I'm so sorry," he apologized. "I don't know what has gotten into me. I'm so nervous."

Eleanor smiled. She placed a hand on his arm. "Really, there's no reason to be nervous. I won't bite. It's just dinner. We're two mature adults on our way to a meal. So, let's calm down, relax, and enjoy the evening."

George appreciated her kindness.

She slipped into the passenger seat, one leg in, one leg out.

George slammed the car door shut.

She screamed.

"Dear Lord," he said, profusely apologizing as he knelt by her side.

Eleanor held her leg, writhing in pain.

"I've never done that before. I don't know what's gotten into me. Are you okay? Do we need to go to the hospital?"

Eleanor waved a hand at the suggestion, her face contorted in a grimace. "No," she managed to say as she rubbed the red gash just above her ankle. "But I think I better go upstairs and clean this off."

"Of course," George stammered. "Right." And he extended a hand to help her out of the passenger seat.

Eleanor leaned heavily on the open door as she gingerly stepped out of the car, placing her weight on her left leg. The right leg, knee bent, was off the ground.

"I'm afraid this hurts too much to walk."

George didn't hesitate for a moment. "Not to worry," he said. "I'll carry you."

"Oh no, that isn't necessary. I'll lean on you and hop."

"Absolutely not. This is my fault, and I'll take care of it." And with that, George lifted Eleanor in his arms, giving the car door a fast kick, almost losing his balance. "You're a light thing," he said as the muscles in his lower back tightened.

"Really, you don't have to do this," Eleanor said as he struggled.

George was slightly winded as they approached the lobby entrance. "Do you have a key?"

"Oh my God," Eleanor cried, "I must have dropped my bag in the confusion."

"Not to worry," George said. "It's probably in the car. I'll just put you down for a moment and go back."

Eleanor flinched when he put her down.

"Are you sure we shouldn't go to the hospital?"

"No hospital," Eleanor said emphatically.

"Really?" George pressed.

"Go get my bag." Eleanor pointed toward the car.

"Right, your bag," George said, suddenly aware he'd left his keys in the car.

Fortunately, the driver's side door was open.

Eleanor retreated to the bathroom to tend to the cut. *Honestly*, she thought. *Can this be any more ridiculous?*

With repeated dabs of a cotton swab soaked in peroxide, she cleaned the wound. A reddish bruise was coming up around the cut. In the morning, it would be a deep purple. She applied an antibiotic ointment and a Band-Aid.

I'm not sure I want to go back out there, she thought as she examined her reflection in the mirror. What was she doing? *Why did Joel have to die?* She thought of London. It would have been their last trip together. Joel had promised he'd take her someplace special once his client's lawsuit settled. She'd waited patiently. But the lawsuit didn't settle.

She checked her lipstick in the mirror. *I wish I was more like Sylvia. Sylvia goes with the flow. She'd never think twice about going on a date. And if she doesn't like the man, she sends him on his way, probably having a drink at the bar alone.*

"Go ahead without me," Joel had insisted with the case ongoing and the tickets to Europe purchased. It was the only logical solution.

"But it won't be any fun without you. I should wait."

"Nonsense. You go ahead. And if the case wraps up, I'll meet you in London."

"But Joel," she said. "I wouldn't know what to do with myself."

"You'll go shopping and to the museums. London is full of terrific sightseeing. The hotel can set you up on tours. It'll be an adventure."

A week in London alone. How many times in their marriage had Joel's career interfered with their time together? How often had he missed family dinners, homework assignments, and Little League games? Eleanor wished she could do it all over again. Maybe this time, it might be different. She'd know the end of the story. Get Joel to cut back on his work schedule. Go with him to the doctor.

Maybe he'd still be alive.

George wandered into the kitchen for a glass of water. He spotted the abandoned bouquet on the counter. Searching through the cabinets, he found a vase. Without hesitation, he unwrapped the bouquet of red roses and white lilies, placed them in the vase, and added water.

Very nice, he thought as he stood back and admired his work just as Eleanor came into sight.

"I hope you don't mind. I was thirsty and I saw the flowers and…"

Eleanor blanched. "Where did you get the vase?"

"I was looking for a glass."

"Did you find one?"

"No," he said lightheartedly. "I forgot all about it when I noticed the vase in the cabinet."

Eleanor appeared annoyed. "Do you always go through a stranger's cabinets on a first date?"

George darkened. "I beg your pardon."

Eleanor released a sneeze. Then two more came in quick succession. "You slam a car door on my leg, and now, I find you rummaging through my kitchen drawers."

"I was looking for a glass," George said. "Not inspecting your china service."

Eleanor sneezed again. "Well, I think it's outrageous. Someone really needs to put you on a leash."

"Do you have a cold?"

"I'm perfectly fine," she said, sniffling.

"You don't seem fine. Your eyes are bloodshot. And your nose is bright red."

Eleanor visibly cringed. "What a thing to say. What's wrong with you? Don't you have any manners?"

George didn't care for Eleanor's attitude. "I think I'll pass on dinner," he said as he turned to leave. "You seem out of sorts."

"So you think this date is over?" Eleanor shouted as she chased after him. "I'm the one who thinks this date's over. You rude, clumsy man."

George clenched his fists. How had this all gone so wrong? He'd dropped thirty-five dollars on those damn flowers. Now he wished he'd bought carnations.

Together they reached the front door. He grabbed for the knob at the same time Eleanor did.

"I can get the door," he shouted.

"I'm not so sure," she said, giving him a push to step back.

But George prevailed, flinging the door open with such force that it hit Eleanor, knocking her to the floor.

George gasped as Eleanor lay splayed out on the travertine. "Oh no," he said, leaning down by her side. "Are you okay?"

Eleanor lifted herself up on one elbow and stared at George. And then she laughed. She laughed so loud, and so insistently, George had no choice but to join in, settling down on the floor next to her.

"How do you like your eggs?" Eleanor searched the refrigerator, shoes discarded, standing in her bare feet. "I have cheddar and broccoli. I can make us an omelet. And I have a leftover baguette." She retrieved it from the refrigerator and gave it a squeeze. "It'll be nice reheated."

George nodded. "Oh, that's fine. Don't go to any trouble."

Eleanor pulled two wine glasses from the cabinet and handed the wine to George with a bottle opener. "And I have a lovely pinot grigio. You can do the honors."

George fumbled with the opener as Eleanor prepared dinner. The difference in his mood was night and day. Why had he been so nervous? What was that all about?

Eleanor set two red place mats on the counter. She retrieved black linen napkins from a nearby drawer. Slowly, the simple meal was coming together. Light and easy.

"Thank you so much for doing this," he said as he poured the wine.

She plated the eggs. "Well, it was clear, we were going to kill ourselves if we tried to go out to dinner."

George laughed. "It was pretty awful."

She joined him at the counter, two dishes in front of them. "Could you imagine the damage we might have caused if we were in a car together?"

"I don't think the car would have started."

"Probably not."

George liked the way she verbally volleyed with him. "You know...you're okay."

Eleanor raised a glass. "Well, that's nice of you to say, considering what we've gone through tonight."

George sipped his wine. It was delicious. Crisp and bright. It had been a while since he'd last felt comfortable with a woman. It was nice to relax and be himself. Not to be focused on the next thing to do or say. He'd let go of his expectations and worries. They were simply together in the moment. Perhaps Eleanor might not be the great love of his life, but he was happy. Content to just sit at the counter and eat a simple meal.

"How are your eggs?"

"Fine," he said as he raised a glass. "To the master chef."

She blushed. "Really, they're just eggs."

"But they're delicious," he added. "A true work of art. You must be a great cook."

She smiled sweetly. "I pour a mean bowl of cereal."

George laughed.

"To be honest, George, I'm a lousy cook. I don't like cooking."

George glanced about. "You have a beautiful kitchen. Wolf appliances. A Sub-Zero."

"Yes," Eleanor agreed. "But I've never had the patience to really cook. Plus, I hate messes. All those dirty pots and pans. Besides." She held up a hand. "Cleaning would ruin my manicure."

George remembered Jeanette in yellow Playtex gloves when she washed a pan. That was before she decided that cleaning pans was George's job.

"My wife would have loved this kitchen," he said without hesitation. As soon as the words left his mouth, he felt guilty.

Eleanor looked about. "She would have?"

"Yes," George answered, uncomfortable that he'd introduced Jeanette, though not by name, into the room.

"Joel would have made fun of me," Eleanor said. She lowered her voice. "Eleanor, are those red knobs on the Wolf oven supposed to match your earrings?"

George leaned back. "Really? That's clever."

"He was a good man," Eleanor admitted. "But a workaholic. When I realized he loved every minute of his job, I stopped fighting about the hours. Some women lose their husbands to Monday night football. Every night after dinner, Joel disappeared into the den. His private lair. You really can't be a successful lawyer and not take work home. But…" Eleanor held her wine glass close to her chest. "I wish I'd been more involved, more focused on making sure he remained healthy."

"Did you have control over that?" George asked.

Eleanor took a sip of wine as she pondered the question. "I guess not. But we're raised to think that wives are responsible for the family. I felt responsible when Joel died. Like I didn't do enough. I'd lay in bed at night trying to figure out what I could have done differently so he'd still be alive. If only I'd made him go back to the doctor. But he was a big boy. He did what he had to do. And I guess, so did I." Eleanor stared off into space. "What's done is done. There's really no point dredging up the past."

George crossed his arms. There was a sadness about Eleanor that underscored her story. He wondered if there was more to tell. "I'm sure you did the best you could."

Eleanor nodded. "I appreciate you saying that. It's hard for anyone who hasn't lost a spouse to understand. It all sounds insane."

"I totally get it."

Eleanor's cheeks glowed. "Do you, George? I hope so. That would be nice. I can't tell you how uncomfortable it is when people ask me to explain how I feel. Or that what I've just said isn't logical. Who can explain why we feel the way we do? I guess a good therapist can help sort it through. And to be honest, I did go to a therapist."

George was intrigued. "How did that go?"

"In the beginning, it was worthwhile. Truly. But given time, I felt like I was just complaining."

"I'd like to complain to a therapist," George admitted.

She tilted her head. "Would you?"

"Hell yes," George answered. "When my wife, Jeanette, died, all I could think about was that I had retired so that we could be together. Isn't that the whole point of retirement? To spend your days with the one you love?"

Eleanor leaned in toward George. "Yes. Of course."

"And then, there you are, alone."

"Right. And your friends have a life. What are you supposed to do?"

"Make new friends," George said with a shrug.

"Easier said than done. And what about your family, George? Tell me about them." Eleanor leaned back in her chair.

"My daughter is constantly questioning me. Criticizing everything I do. I've told her, 'Carole, you need to get a life.'"

"And your son? What's he like?"

George sighed. "I don't really know him. Oh, I know his problems. God knows, he tells me about them often enough. But it's like we're strangers. I wonder sometimes, who raised you? Where did you get your values? And why is it that when we talk, I'm so darn aggravated?" George took a breath. "A young man in his twenties doesn't need a father. He needs life experience. Let life kick the shit out of him. It isn't my job anymore."

"They say once you're a parent, you're always a parent."

George's mood darkened. He thought the observation insensitive.

"But what do I know?" Eleanor quickly added, as if picking up on George's thoughts.

George scratched his neck. "And your kids. Did you say you have two boys?"

Eleanor smiled. *Minefield.* How to explain the situation with her sons? She'd always thought it reflected poorly on her. After all, how could she have screwed up the relationship so much that her sons wanted nothing to do with her? How could she explain that to a stranger? She wasn't sure she understood it herself. Instead, she dismissed the topic, and asked George if he might like a cup of coffee. "There's Entenmann's cheese Danish in the freezer," she whispered as if it was a state secret not to be shared with the Russians.

Out on the terrace, they settled into the divan, coffee mugs in hand. "It's a lovely night," she remarked as George balanced a small plate of cake in his lap. "The wonderful thing about Entenmann's is you can eat it right out of the freezer. I don't know how they do it. Frozen, it still tastes great."

George nodded. "You just cut out the middleman."

Eleanor laughed. "You mean the toaster oven."

George looked out onto the Intracoastal. "Nice, isn't it?"

"It's lovely. That's why I bought the unit. I've spent a lot of evenings out here, enjoying the view."

"The view is wonderful," George acknowledged. "But I meant, being with another person. Comfortable. At ease."

Eleanor understood. "Yes," she agreed.

Had they gone on their date to the restaurant, it probably would have been a stiff and uncomfortable evening. George knocking over the water glass. Eleanor nervously wishing it was already over.

"I think you're a special lady," George suddenly said.

His pronouncement made her blush. Coyly, she answered, "I have my moments." The clouds shifted to reveal a bright moon. "Oh, look, George. Isn't it lovely?"

George looked up. His expression changed. He no longer looked comfortable.

Eleanor couldn't quite put her finger on it, but there was definitely something different about George. "My Joel used to say that a full moon was God's way of letting you know all was well with the world."

"How so?"

"Well, a full moon is the completion of the cycle. And in the Talmud, Shabbat originally fell only once a month on the full moon."

"I never heard that."

"Well, Joel was into all those details. He was fascinated by religion. Me? Not so much. But Joel used to say when he saw a full moon, 'Ah, my darling. It's God's way of telling us the month is over and we must rest.'" Eleanor smirked. "'Rest' was code."

"Code for what?"

Eleanor felt herself blush a deep crimson. "I don't think I should say."

George smiled. "That's sweet."

"Thank you for saying so," she stammered, embarrassed that she'd just introduced her sex life with Joel into their conversation. "Would you like more coffee?"

George awoke in Eleanor's guest room. He thought about getting up and dressing. Miss Betsy would be waiting for him. But he didn't want to disturb Eleanor. She was sleeping so soundly curled up on her side. He was reminded of Jeanette. She too preferred to sleep on her side. When he tried to spoon with her, she'd push him away. "George, I love you, but you're too warm."

He'd never have guessed the evening would have gone this way. And yet, here he was. In Eleanor's bed. Thinking about Jeanette. How much he still missed her. Especially when he was with another woman. He couldn't help himself. Jeanette had been his true north. He compared every woman to her. Not that she was perfect. But she was perfect for him.

Eleanor stirred.

He remembered her approach. Leaning in close, lips locked on his, hands searching his body in pursuit of southern delights. He'd thrilled to her touch, and in the dimly lit room, found himself intensely excited as she removed each piece of clothing. It was a slow, steady burn. His face grew warm as their lovemaking became fervent and needy. When it was over, he felt a genuine sense of accomplishment. He'd connected powerfully and fully with the woman in his arms; two souls blended in a moment of explosive combustion.

George wondered if they'd see each other again. Or was this another one-night stand? His sexual escapades since Jeanette had been nothing more than brief interludes. He'd enjoyed each lady's favor, but hadn't felt compelled to see them again. But with Eleanor, it felt somehow different. Was it her manner? Was it that they'd both lost a spouse? And though Eleanor had spoken a bit about her husband, he realized, much to his embarrassment, that he'd dominated the conversation with details about his family.

He now regretted sharing his family story.

He'd told an outsider about the problems he had with Carole and Peter. He should have kept that information to himself. Jeanette believed there were some things you never talked about with other people. Offspring topped the list. "You don't want others to be judging the children or our abilities as parents. Talking about private family issues only invites criticism," she'd say.

He'd been disloyal to the family unit.

But his kids were adults. Surely Eleanor was wise enough to know adults make their own choices. Live their own lives. George was no more responsible for Peter's struggles than he was for Carole's. He hadn't failed his children. And still, the guilt persisted. Why had he brought that all up with Eleanor? Was it an attempt to scare her off? Push her away?

Eleanor let out a snort.

George smiled. *She doesn't seem concerned at all,* he thought as he leaned back and drifted off.

Eleanor opened her eyes with a start. There was the sound of gentle snoring. She'd fallen asleep on her side. She had no idea where she was. It took a minute to regain her bearings. She was in the guestroom, her back to George.

In the longest minute of her life, she slowly remembered.

Her heart lurched. A stranger was in her bed. This was not how she'd imagined the evening. At best, she'd expected a nice dinner and to be home by ten o'clock. She'd thought after Joel had died, this part of her life would be over. There'd be no other men. She'd considered herself too old for sex with a stranger. Not that she didn't have desires. Oh, she had plenty of those. But getting naked in front of a man was asking a lot. After all, Eleanor's body carried the war wounds of a woman's life. Two children had thickened her waist. Breastfeeding had reshaped her bust. And now here she was. In bed with a man. A man she didn't really know.

Eleanor tried not to giggle as she thought about the evening.

How silly it had all been. Two opposing forces, awkwardly colliding. What was the point of all the formality? Getting dressed up. The polite questions. The nervousness. She covered her mouth as she remembered George's reaction when he knocked her down at the front door. In hindsight, it was the perfect touch. A great metaphor for sweeping her off her feet.

Slowly, she slipped out of bed and felt around the floor for her discarded clothing. She tiptoed out of the room. It was midnight. Should she wake George and ask him to leave? She wasn't sure of the proper etiquette. She certainly didn't think he should be sleeping over on their first date. She wanted to call Sylvia for advice, but wasn't sure if it was to get pointers or brag.

Back in the master bedroom, she slipped into casual workout wear, sweats and a T-shirt, and headed to the kitchen.

The scent of freshly brewed coffee permeated the air as she worried about what to do next. Coffee in hand, she knocked on the guest room door. "George," she whispered. Another rap on the door and she entered. "George, are you awake?" she asked, louder this time.

Slowly the body began to move. George sat up. "I'm sorry," he apologized. "I was really out." He rubbed his eyes.

"I brought you some coffee," she said, offering him the cup.

"No, thank you," he demurred. "If I drink coffee this late, I can't sleep."

She wasn't sure what to say or do. Whatever intimacy they'd shared had vanished. For Eleanor, George was simply a stranger holed up in her guest room. She was grateful she'd led him to the guest room. It had occurred to her at the very last second to use the guest room instead of the master. It was one thing to dirty the sheets in the guest room, but to have a stranger in her own bed was too much.

"Can I fix you a snack?" she offered, hoping to get him up, into his pants, and on his way to the kitchen, which was closer to the front door than the bed in the guest room.

George didn't pick up on the hint. "No, I don't think so," he said.

Eleanor panicked. What else could she do or say to get him out of the condo? She wished she'd gone over this with Sylvia. Sylvia must have known a hundred and one tricks of getting a man to leave.

What would Sylvia do?

Eleanor racked her brain. *Perhaps he needs some privacy*, she thought as she plotted her exit. "Well, I'm going to have a little something to eat. Come join me in the kitchen when you're ready." And she left him alone, hoping he'd realize it was time to leave.

She checked the time. Twelve thirty. All she wanted to do was curl up in bed with a good book. Alone. Most definitely, alone.

She heard footsteps in the hall.

George popped his head into the kitchen. He was fully dressed. "I think I'll head out. I have a dog to take care of."

She refrained from saying, *Must you go so soon?* Instead, she jumped up to show him to the door, eager to see the back of his head. "Well, thank you for a lovely evening," she said, her manners overtaking her good sense.

– 16 –

GEORGE PULLED INTO the parking lot of the Arthur Murray Dance Studio. "Why am I always driving?" He spotted a woman getting into her car. He pulled up and waited for the spot.

"Is that a real question?" Herbie asked, the newspaper coupon outlining the two free introductory dance lessons in his lap. "You have an SUV. My car's a two-door. And Bigfoot in the back drives a truck. Why a dentist needs a flatbed is beyond me."

"A big, manly, blue truck, thank you very much," Benny added.

George parked and turned off the engine. He shifted to face his passengers. "We need to talk before we go in. What's the plan?"

Herbie grunted. "Do we really need a plan?"

"Do you think we'll have to dance?" Benny asked.

George doubted it. "Not unless you want to," he teased.

"I don't know," Benny admitted. "I've been thinking. Maybe square dancing wasn't my thing. Too much wild stepping about.

I wouldn't mind learning how to do something controlled. Like a tango."

Herbie turned about. "You're really a big girl, aren't you?"

"Herbie!" George groaned.

Benny laughed. "It's okay, George. We know Herbie can't dance."

"I can dance," Herbie said. "A bit."

"I bet you're light on those little feet," Benny joked.

George shook his head. *Men and dancing. Could anything be more complicated?*

Benny pressed on. "Dancing requires coordination. Dancers are professional athletes!"

"Sure," Herbie said. "Figure skaters, tap dancers, burlesque queens. They're all the same."

"Burlesque queens? What era are you living in?" George asked.

"And they're all *not you,* Herbie. They know how to use their bodies."

Herbie sighed. "I know how to use my body."

Benny smirked. "Okay, big shot. Let's see how you do today."

George rolled his eyes. "So again, what's the plan?"

Benny pulled himself forward. "We don't need a plan. This is dancing, George. Just try not to step on anyone's toes."

Herbie raised an index finger. "And remember to keep time with the music."

"We're not really here to dance," George reminded them.

"You're too inhibited, George. You should be more like me." Herbie swung his shoulders back and forth.

Benny laughed. "Like Carmen Miranda?"

George chuckled. "You guys really need to update your cultural references."

George glanced about the large open studio with its wood floor and mirrored walls. "Wow, check this place out," he said as he wandered over to a glass trophy case that held several awards. One silver cup captured his attention. And then he spotted a photo of Willy decked out in a blue silk costume fringed with gold. He was holding the same silver cup. "Look who's in this picture," he called out.

Herbie and Benny drew closer.

"Holy crap," George said, "Willy was an award-winning ballroom dancer. He was a star here."

As the three peered at the photograph, a female voice came from behind. "Gentlemen, may I help you?"

Heads turned to greet a statuesque blonde in black high heels and dark stockings, sporting a red dress with the skirt split high on the thigh. George's eyes were glued on the split.

"Gentlemen, are you here for dance lessons?"

Benny stepped forward. "I'd love to learn how to tango. Do you think a big guy like me can manage that?"

"Blindfolded," the blonde confidently said as she stared at Benny. "I should have guessed. There's something very Latin in your aura. Is your family from Argentina?"

Benny blushed as George looked on in awe. To George, Benny looked as Latin as Lawrence Welk at a taco bar.

The blonde did a fast twirl. "Just give us twelve hours, and you'll dance the tango like a Latin lover."

Benny raised his hand. "I'm ready now."

The blonde turned to George and Herbie. "Are you two also signing up?"

"Not exactly," George clarified. "We noticed free lessons. And we thought…"

"Of course," the blonde answered as she came closer to George. "That's included with our introductory package."

"Like the thirteenth bagel when you order a dozen," Benny added, eliciting a warm smile from the blonde.

Herbie demurred. "Not me. I'm too busy to commit to weekly lessons."

"Oh, but you must," the blonde seductively said. George was reminded of Marilyn Monroe from *The Seven Year Itch*. "We need someone like you around here. Cute, cuddly, and athletic."

George chortled. The image of Herbie dancing, in spite of persistent maladies with his back, knees, and shoulder, overwhelmed George's imagination. "I'd like to see that!"

The blonde called to the rear of the studio. "Georgia."

A tall brunette sashayed her way over, hips swaying rhythmically with every step. George thought her absolutely lovely. One of the most graceful young women he'd ever seen.

As Georgia got closer, Herbie stepped forward and blocked George's view. "Sign me up," Herbie announced as he introduced himself to the lovely Georgia.

"And you?" the blonde asked George. "Will you be taking lessons?"

George had no intention of spending another dime. Didn't he already have enough money troubles? "Maybe just the two free lessons."

"Such a shame," the blonde cooed. "A good-looking man like you should know how to dance."

"I can dance a bit. My late wife thought I was fairly capable. But it's been a while. I'm probably rusty."

"Well then," the blonde said with determination. "It's time to oil those hinges."

"This really looks like fun, George," Benny said.

"Don't be such a cheap screw," Herbie added as he vibrated his body, pretending to dance. To George it looked like he was simulating electroconvulsive therapy.

George was on the spot. How could he get out of it? He couldn't tell Herbie and Benny about his financial woes. They'd think he was a loser. Or worse, a numbskull. "I don't think so."

"George, you need to do this," Herbie pressed. "You got us into this. You need to see it through."

George supposed Herbie was right. After all, his two buddies seemed reduced to hopeless schoolboys at the mere sight of Miss Split Skirt and the lovely Georgia. There was probably no way they'd ever learn anything about Willy's estate if it was up to Herbie or Benny. "Okay, I'm in," George relented without needing the blonde to unveil another lithe temptress.

"Well good. Then we're all in agreement," the blonde said as Georgia, the graceful seductress, mysteriously withdrew. "Now we have some paperwork to fill out and then we can begin your first lesson this afternoon."

Credit cards scanned, paperwork signed, George, Herbie, and Benny were ushered into a small side room off of the ballroom. Together they waited for their first session to begin.

"This should be interesting," George said. "Do either of you actually remember why we're here?" George caught Benny's eye. "What came over you? And you." George turned to Herbie. "Now we're signed up for dance classes. I thought we were trying to recoup our investment. Not spend more money."

Herbie sighed. "George, of course, we want our money back from the estate. But did you see those women? They're gorgeous."

"And young," Benny added. "When are schmucks like us going to have a chance to spend time with such lovely creatures?"

"Do you really think those women are interested in you?"

Herbie sighed. "Good God, George. You're such a killjoy. Where would Charlie Chaplin be without Oona O'Neill? Or that old guy who married Anna Nicole Smith? And let's not forget Alec Baldwin and his yoga instructor wife."

"Okay. Those are the exceptions. But what I said is still true," George confirmed.

Herbie shook his fist. "That's not the point, George. We know. We're not stupid. But at least we get to look forward to twelve wonderful hours with these exquisitely beautiful women. Twelve hours of holding an angel in my arms. Who could resist?"

George threw his hands in the air. "I give up," he said as the door to the room swung open.

A lovely mature woman approached. Decidedly older than George, Herbie, or Benny, she wore her gray hair pulled tight and up into a bun. Fit and trim, she graced the dance floor with a smooth, sultry air. George recognized her photograph from the awards case.

"Gentlemen," she called out as she approached, a hand extended to George. "My name is Lydia, and I'm your dance instructor."

George took Lydia's strong hand in his. Intuitively, he sensed Lydia took no prisoners.

"Are you ready for your first tango lesson?"

"But where are the other instructors?" Benny asked.

Lydia smiled. "Oh, you mean the girls?"

"Yes," Herbie said.

"They're our front-office sales staff. Lovely. But today, I'm your instructor."

George shot Herbie and Benny a look of irritation. "Oh boy," was all he could manage to say as his friends' faces deflated like punctured tires on a road of loose nails.

"But don't you worry," Lydia wagged a finger. "We'll have you doing the tango in no time flat."

Back in the car, George couldn't stop laughing.

The first lesson had proven unforgettable.

After Lydia had instructed each man in the fine art of walking about the room, placing their weight fully on their heels, she divided the group up. Lydia with George and Herbie with Benny. Together, they practiced walking with a partner. "Keep time with the music," Lydia called out. "Don't rush. The tango is a slow, deliberate, continuous walk. No, Herbie. Don't swing your hips. Benny, put your feet closer together. There should be no space between your knees."

When Lydia had first suggested the pairing, Herbie and Benny had balked. "Now stop that," she said when they refused to rest their hands on each other's shoulders, arms intertwined. "That's just silly. You're men. Men dance together in other cultures. The Jews have the hora. And then, there are the Greeks."

And now, George had thought, *Boca Raton has Benny and Herbie doing the tango.*

Herbie slouched in the passenger seat. "What's so funny?"

George cleared his throat. "You…dancing with Benny. What a pairing."

"I thought I did pretty well." Benny shifted in the back seat. "Lydia mentioned I had potential."

Herbie scoffed. "You're a giant elephant. How many times did you step on my foot? It's amazing I'm able to walk without crutches."

George started the engine and backed out of the space. "You did make a cute couple."

Herbie turned to George. "Enough of your homophobia. There's nothing wrong with two men dancing together. I remember my father telling me stories of service men dancing together in World War II. It's what they had to do when there were no women around. And they didn't care. Why should we?"

George was impressed by Herbie's about-face. "Good for you, Herbie. I know how you feel about being touched by another man. This a real turn in the right direction."

Herbie furrowed his brow. "It wasn't another man. It was my dear friend, Benny."

George checked the rearview mirror. Benny's eyes lit up. "Thank you, Herbie."

"Sure. And though an elephant has a great memory," Herbie said with a smirk, "don't ever believe a pachyderm can learn to dance. You won't see it at a zoo. You won't see it at a circus. And you won't see it in Boca Raton. It just can't be done. And it never will."

George knew it. The same routine. Give Herbie an inch, he took the whole ruler.

"Can we be serious for a moment?" George asked. "While dancing with Lydia, she told me about Valerie. It turns out, Valerie and Willy danced together regularly. It seems Willy had been taking lessons for years and Valerie took a liking to him. They danced together in amateur contests representing the studio."

Benny chuckled. "Well, I'll be a son of a bitch. Who knew?"

"Certainly not us," Herbie answered.

"They would send the pair out to retirement communities to entertain with the intent that they might recruit new members. It seems Willy was well-known. As part of the promotion, he'd dance with the single ladies."

Herbie turned to look at Benny in the back seat. "That explains all the women at the funeral."

Benny straightened up. "Of course."

"So, Valerie," George continued, "is an important person. She knew Willy very well. She might hold the answer to the mystery of the estate."

Herbie was impatient. "So how do we get ahold of Valerie?"

George pulled to the side of the road. "Valerie is looking for a new partner. Someone who can step in for Willy."

"And who would that be?" Benny asked.

George smiled broadly. "Someone incredibly light on their toes who already knows the dance moves."

"No," Herbie said with a wave of a hand. "I can't do it. I don't even know the tango yet."

George laughed. "Not you."

Benny lurched forward. “George! She thinks George can do it.”

Herbie seemed disappointed. “George?”

“Yes. Lydia’s going to recommend that Valerie work with me.”

Herbie seemed nonplussed. “That’s absurd. Besides, didn’t you say Valerie threw you out of her office? What makes you think she’ll want to dance with you?”

“My golf may be lousy, but I do a mean rumba. While you two were busy staring into each other’s eyes and walking the floor, I showed Lydia a step or two. I explained about the misunderstanding with Valerie. Lydia said she’d take care of the rest.”

“A rumba is not a tango,” Herbie pointed out.

“No. But if you know how to dance, you can master anything. If Sean Spicer can do a tango on *Dancing with the Stars*, I can learn the tango. Besides, this isn’t about the tango,” George reminded them.

“Right, right,” Benny and Herbie muttered. But neither sounded convinced.

Eleanor grabbed her phone on the first ring. She was sitting at the kitchen counter, a cup of coffee nearby, making out a shopping list, deciding if she wanted frozen peas, broccoli, kale, or spinach. “Hi there, stranger,” she said, trying to be coy.

It had been three days since she’d seen George. Eager for him to leave that first night, she was nonetheless annoyed he hadn’t bothered to call the next day. Or the day after. But mostly, she was irked that when he finally did, she was thrilled to hear his voice.

Sylvia had counseled caution when Eleanor complained about George. She’d asked Sylvia, “Do you think he was abducted by aliens?”

Sylvia didn't laugh. "Take it slow," she warned. "Nothing dies faster than a relationship that starts in the bedroom."

Eleanor thought it odd advice coming from Sylvia, the original bedroom girl.

"I've been thinking about you," George said.

Eleanor attempted an air of indifference. "I wondered what happened to you."

"If I told you the truth," he said, amusement in his voice, "you wouldn't believe me."

She had trouble hearing him. A television set was blaring in the background. A sports telecast. *No,* she decided. George was not contrite. "I thought you might have had a case of amnesia."

George chuckled. "Not quite."

Eleanor doodled on her shopping list. She drew a rat with a long tail. *Well, here it comes: the moment of truth,* she thought.

Another moment of truth had happened two months before she married Joel. His client had called on Thanksgiving Day, and instead of going directly to Joel's parents' home for dinner, they stopped off in a rundown neighborhood in Brownsville, Brooklyn. Eleanor followed Joel into the apartment building, too frightened to stay in the car. She hadn't fully understood the nature of Joel's work.

The stop in Brownsville proved a wake-up call.

They visited the mother of a teenager Joel was defending against a charge of breaking and entering. Inside the dark, cramped apartment, Joel invited the older woman to sit down at her own kitchen table. He sat close to the woman as she wept, placing a hand on hers as he promised to do his best to represent her son. Eleanor was moved by his compassion, but as she looked about, she wondered how the woman could afford Joel's fee.

"I'm doing it pro bono," Joel explained when they'd returned to the car.

"But what if we have a family, Joel? We can't live on kind gestures. We have to be practical."

Within months, Joel had changed direction, taking a position as a New York prosecutor. Two years later, he became a corporate lawyer in the pharmaceutical industry.

Money would no longer be a problem.

George cleared his throat. "Remember my friend Willy?"

"Yes," she said in a monotone, though she'd never met Willy. *This is going to be a dilly of an excuse*, she thought.

"We've been trying to track down the executor of Willy's estate."

Eleanor couldn't imagine what any of that had to do with her. Or why George hadn't called sooner.

"We found out that the person handling the insurance for the estate is a dance instructor. I've been at the studio ever since, practicing the tango."

Tango? Had she missed something in the conversation? "George, what are you talking about?"

"I'm dancing with one of the Arthur Murray instructors at exhibition events around Miami."

Eleanor sighed. "Honestly I'm not following you."

"Don't you see?" George said. Just then, there was a loud roar of a crowd.

"George, I can't hear you," Eleanor snapped, incensed that George thought any excuse forgivable. "The very least you can do is turn down the volume on the television."

There was another loud roar. Eleanor disconnected from the call, her heart pounding. Why was she so angry? Yes, George was rude. Rude enough to warrant her temper. But there was more to the flare-up. An intensity that rocked her. She didn't like the feeling.

Her phone lit up. It was George.

She thought of letting it go to voicemail. *I don't need this in my life*, she steamed as she held the phone, weighing her options. "Yes," she said summarily, hoping he'd be apologetic.

"Sorry about that," he explained. "I'm with my friend, Benny. We're in Jupiter watching the Hammerheads. The Minor League baseball team of the Miami Marlins. I stepped away, and then the team scored. Bad timing. I should have called you after the game."

Eleanor wasn't flattered.

"I apologize for not being in touch. I'd like to make it up to you. How about lunch tomorrow?"

Eleanor bristled. After being put off for two days, why should she be available on a whim? "I don't know," she said, hoping to come up with a reasonable excuse to stall without totally shutting George down.

"She sounded so different," George told Benny when he returned from the concession area after making the call to Eleanor. "There was something odd in her voice. She sounded annoyed."

Benny eyes were glued on the field. "What do you mean?"

"I don't know," George confided. "It's not like I know her. It was just a feeling."

Benny took a swig of beer. "Maybe you caught her at a bad moment. Maybe she was busy. Or rushed. Or tired."

"Maybe. Who knows? Jeanette was so even-keeled. Nothing upset her. She was so easy to be around."

Benny laughed. "Oh, the angelic qualities of the dearly departed wife. Given time, they all achieve true perfection."

George didn't like the turn of the conversation. Jeanette wasn't perfect, but at least their marriage had been a successful one. Sure, they'd had disagreements. Like the time Jeanette insisted George was too stiff around her family. "George, my parents want to get to know you. You need to warm up. Smile. Don't be so deadly serious." Or when Carole had become a demanding teenager, rebelling against house rules.

Staying out late. "Father your daughter," Jeanette had scolded, frustrated by her own inability to control Carole's behavior. Or when Peter got into trouble. George had accused Jeanette of being too lenient. Jeanette had accused George of being too preoccupied with his career. The more George considered the past, the more he realized there were plenty of rough spots in the marriage. Mostly around the children, but still, he and Jeanette hadn't always seen eye to eye.

"Perfect or not, Jeanette was a wonderful woman. I miss her. And yes, she had her faults."

Benny nodded. "We all do. That's the problem with being human. Too many faults. And sometimes those faults obscure the gold. Take Herbie, for instance." Benny bit into a large pretzel covered in salt. "He comes off like a douchebag. But he has a good heart."

George was surprised by the turn in the conversation. He hadn't expected Benny to say something positive about Herbie.

"Do you know that when my granddaughter died..." As soon as Benny uttered the words, he leaned forward, elbows on his knees, chin down. "Herbie was right there with me. He stayed with me that week. Slept on my sofa. He watched me like a hawk." Benny turned to look at George. "He circled the wagons. Understood what I was going through. That ridiculously inappropriate idiot was the best friend I'd ever had. He was there for me. He called me every day for months. Imagine that. Months!"

Herbie had never shared any of the details about Benny's granddaughter with George. George resisted the urge to change the subject. Instead, he sat back and opted to listen.

"I never told you what happened with my granddaughter. Becky was the prettiest little thing. Can you imagine, a big guy like me falling desperately in love with a little baby? Well, it's true. I did." Benny looked up at the heavens. "And when that child was diagnosed with an inoperable brain tumor, I thought I'd go insane."

George's heart jumped in his chest. "I had no idea."

"How could you? You didn't live in Florida back then. And when you came down, we didn't talk. We golfed."

George winced. "There seems to be a lot we didn't talk about."

"That wasn't your fault, George. Helen and I made a pact. We agreed that there was no point in sharing the awful details."

George couldn't remember ever meeting Helen. "How long were you married, Benny?"

"Long enough," Benny said, eyes focused ahead. "It's a funny thing, marriage. It seems to be a lot of work when you're going through it. An awful pain in the ass. And then, when it's over, it's like a dream. Did it really happen? Did she ever love me? Was it worth all the bother? What the heck were we even doing together?"

George understood.

"Sometimes, we were just two bodies bumping into each other, thrashing about." Benny turned to face George. "And I don't mean in a sexual way. There were days when there was just too little space between us, until there was too much. We couldn't find a happy medium."

"Marriage is a tough business."

"And then there were the mindless years. You live together, occupying the same house, but mentally, you're somewhere else. And it works for a while until something awful happens. And then, you realize the person you're living with is a stranger. As if Becky's illness awoke us from our marriage stupor. Tragedies either pull you together or push you apart."

George wondered how he and Jeanette might have fared in the same circumstance.

"Looking back, I can see that my marriage fell apart when Becky was diagnosed," Benny admitted. "My wife decided I was a lousy husband. A bad playmate. And any resentments that were bottled up came rushing out. Broken glass all over the floor as I struggled to cope. I moved out, and in the midst of our estrangement, my granddaughter died."

Benny took a gulp of air as he lowered his head, fingertips pressed to his eyes. "I felt like Jonah from the Bible. My wife didn't want to see me. I stirred up the worst in her emotions, so I stayed away. The day we buried my granddaughter, Herbie went with me to the funeral. Family and friends just stared as if I didn't belong. As if I'd abandoned my family in its hour of need. As if I had killed my own grandchild."

A tear trailed down Benny's cheek. "Herbie got me through that time." Benny lifted his head and offered George a reassuring smile. "Some people aren't exactly how they present. Sometimes, they're better."

George nodded. He couldn't help but wonder if the opposite might also be true. That some people might be worse. Eleanor immediately came to mind.

– 17 –

ELEANOR SLIPPED INTO her favorite white Lilly Pulitzer dress. Sporty casual. Perfect for August in Florida as she bemoaned the state of her hair, which had become frizzy after a morning on the balcony watching the yachts along the Intracoastal. "Humidity is my friend," she softly said, determined to ignore the frizz and refocus on the benefits to her skin. She checked the clock. George would be picking her up in front of her building at noon. She'd have to get a move on if she hoped to be on time for lunch.

The very thought of George brought a smile to her face. His awkward clumsiness, which had once been so annoying, now seemed endearingly sweet. She smiled as she prepared to apply lipstick. Joel had said she suffered from resting bitch face. "Joel, that's an awful thing to say," she'd complain, though she suspected it was true. Still, it had been mean of Joel to point it out. It had only heightened her insecurities.

She grabbed her phone on the first ring. Sylvia's voice boomed. "So, he finally called!"

It was their morning ritual. Each day, around eleven o'clock, Sylvia would check in. Eleanor appreciated the attention. It made her feel less alone. More connected. She imagined the call provided Sylvia with an anchor, too.

"You know, he has no real money. Trust me. I'm his Realtor. I know all."

Eleanor bridled. "Oh, Sylvia. I don't care about such things."

Sylvia's voice radiated disappointment. "Eleanor, really."

They'd been through the discussion time and again. "I just want a man I can enjoy. A man who is educated. And George is kind. You can tell by his eyes."

Sylvia made a clucking sound. "Kind! A man who fails to call a woman after an intimate evening is not kind."

It was true. Eleanor was irritated by George's casual behavior after their evening together. But it wasn't as if there were rules for dating. And if there were such rules, how could George possibly know them if Eleanor wasn't sure of them herself? Still, she couldn't help but agree that George had been disrespectful. But then, maybe her own casual behavior had given him the wrong impression.

It was all so confusing.

Sylvia was adamant. "You should stand him up."

Eleanor thought about it. But hurting a man like George was totally out of the question. "No, I can't do that."

"And why not?"

"It's so petty. If I didn't want to go on the date, I'd have said no."

"You're too nice, Eleanor. Men will walk all over you."

Was she being too nice? And had Joel also taken advantage of her good nature? Certainly, a marriage was different than a date. But was she setting a pattern? Shouldn't a date be held to the same standards of respect?

Eleanor was certain of one thing. "I don't want to turn him off. He radiates a certain warmth."

"Dear, he radiates clumsy with a capital C."

The memory of Sylvia's comment made Eleanor laugh as she waited for the elevator. She recalled George's face when he'd knocked her to the floor. How his eyes had popped. She giggled as she stepped onto the elevator. When the doors closed, the giggle morphed into uncontrollable laughter. She caught her happy expression in the reflection of the elevator's metal doors.

There's got to be a lot of good in a man who can make you laugh, she thought as the elevator started its descent.

George checked his watch. Eleanor had excused herself to go to the restroom after they'd ordered lunch. He'd assumed she wanted to wash her hands. But now, after a fifteen-minute absence, he wondered if her plan was to ditch him at The Cheesecake Factory. He looked in the direction of the restroom, growing increasingly impatient. This was not the way to start off a date.

Herbie's voice shocked George back to reality. "George! Is that you? What are you doing here?" He slid into the seat reserved for Eleanor.

George looked about, hoping Eleanor might suddenly emerge. "I'm on a date."

"Really?" Herbie said. He leaned forward in a conspiratorial fashion and whispered. "What table is she sitting at?"

George straightened up. "She's sitting right where you're sitting."

Herbie leapt to his feet. He addressed the empty chair. "Oh, excuse me, madam."

"Very funny," George said, again checking his watch. "She's in the restroom."

Herbie sat back down. "Okay then. Before she returns, what did Valerie say? Did she tell you the name of the beneficiary of the policy? When can we get our money back?"

"I don't have the answer yet."

"I'm not giving up on this," Herbie said, a finger pressed on the table.

George took a deep breath as if he were drowning and about to go down for the last count. "I'm doing the best I can. But Valerie is a tough cookie."

Herbie was having none of it. "Like hell. She's a woman, George. You're a man. Charm her. I know you were married a long time, but you still remember how to charm a woman."

George wasn't so sure. Not with his date currently missing.

"What exactly did Valerie say?"

George blushed. "I need to control my hips when doing the tango. I seem to have loose hips."

Herbie's eyes widened. "Hips. Tango. Are you kidding me?"

George was dead serious. "I've spent two nights dancing with her. Two three-hour sessions. I couldn't get a word out of her. And let me tell you, that woman is light on her feet." George momentarily closed his eyes. "It's like dancing on a cloud."

"George, dancing wasn't the point of wooing Ms. Valerie."

"I know," George admitted. "But I just got caught up in the dancing. The music. The studio. Valerie's very sexy style."

"George, Valerie must be seventy, if she's a day."

"So what? We're in our sixties. Besides...she's ageless. Believe me. She's got the moves, Herbie."

Herbie's jaw dropped. "I don't believe this. You have the hots for your dancing teacher."

George laughed. "Not the hots."

"Well, I'm going to take care of this."

"What are you going to do?"

"Clearly, George Elden, you're useless."

"What does that mean?"

"When is your next appointment?"

"Tomorrow afternoon. Twelve to three."

"I'm going in your place."

George shook his head. "You don't have the stamina."

"To dance? Trust me. I have plenty of stamina." Herbie's phone beeped. "My date's here. I've got to go. By the way, where's your date?"

George checked his watch. "Still in the restroom. She went in about twenty minutes ago."

Herbie broke into a smile. "Maybe she's sick. Did you breathe on her? Or was it your face that did the trick? George, have you ever considered your company is toxic to the digestive tract?"

Eleanor held the phone away from her ear as Sylvia's voice bounced off the restroom walls. "Tell me exactly what happened."

Eleanor blushed as the door opened and a teenager passed by on the way to a stall. "There's nothing to tell. We'd just ordered. And then, I had an instant reaction. As if I were allergic to shrimp or peanuts. My stomach lurched and I thought I'd pass out."

"Did he say anything to upset you?"

"Absolutely not."

"So, you're hiding in the bathroom because he did nothing."

Eleanor couldn't explain it. Something had triggered an intense desire to flee.

Sylvia recapped. "The waitress asked for your order. And after ordering the Asian Chicken Salad, you excused yourself and ran to the restroom."

"Something like that."

"But why?" Sylvia pressed. "What did George order?"

Eleanor glanced at herself in the mirror. "Quesadillas," she said in a burst of newfound energy. "That's it. Sylvia, you're a genius."

Sylvia's voice assumed a tone of certainty. "Well, of course I am. Now, I've heard of quesadillas sending someone to the restroom *after* you've eaten them, but not before."

"That was Joel's favorite Mexican dish," Eleanor explained. "I freaked out when George ordered the quesadillas. Sylvia, do you think it was a sign? Joel's way of letting me know he's here with me?"

"In the restroom?" Sylvia cleared her throat. "Are you serious, Eleanor? You know I don't believe in such hokum."

Eleanor examined her face in the mirror. Did she look happy? Had her resting bitch face returned? "I guess I'm just being silly. Or is it wishful thinking? The truth is, I wish Joel were here instead of George."

"Eleanor, I don't believe your marriage was as idyllic as you make it out to be. There's no such thing."

"Well, it was," Eleanor insisted.

"Every relationship has its problems. The best of marriages are challenging. I think you've made Joel out to be someone he never was. The perfect man."

Eleanor suppressed the desire to cry.

"You've got to stop living in the past under this false narrative. Face facts, Eleanor. Marriage is marriage. Men are men. Frankly, you can't expect much from either. Maybe that's why you're so afraid to be with a new man. You don't want to get hurt."

"Sylvia, I'm not like you. I can't go from man to man. I'm not emotionally built that way."

"Well dear, I'm not the one hiding in the restroom at The Cheesecake Factory. If I needed to hide, I'd pick someplace elegant. Like a spa."

A toilet flushed as the conversation hit a stalemate. Eleanor caught sight of the teenage girl coming around the corner. Long chestnut hair and a willowy frame. The girl caught Eleanor's eye in the mirror as she washed her hands. Her freckled face offered a sheepish grin. "I've been listening to your conversation," she shyly said. "I think you should go back and face your fears."

Eleanor's jaw dropped.

The young girl dried her hands with a paper towel. "I know. I should mind my business. But you were sharing all of that while I was...*doing my business*...and I couldn't help but overhear. I just thought you might appreciate what my mother always tells me."

Eleanor closed her mouth, quietly acceding.

The girl smiled. "My mother tells me to run toward those things that scare me. Don't let fear hold you back. Otherwise, your life will never be your own."

Eleanor nodded. "Your mother sounds like a very wise woman."

"She is."

Eleanor couldn't resist: "If you don't mind me asking, how old are you?"

The teenager's head bobbed in a perky bounce. "Fifteen."

"Thank you," Eleanor said as the youngster exited the bathroom.

"Now get back out there," Sylvia hissed through the phone.

By the time Eleanor returned to the table, the waiter had delivered George's quesadillas and Eleanor's Asian Chicken Salad. George had diligently worked his way through the breadbasket. He held up the empty basket and offered a weak apology. "I'm sorry. I was starving. I ate all the butter, too."

Eleanor unfolded her napkin and placed it on her lap. "I can't blame you. I'm sorry for taking so long."

"Are you sick?" George asked. "If we need to cut our lunch short, I totally understand. We can take it to go."

Eleanor shook her head. "No. I'm fine," she assured him.

"Good," George said, now intensely curious about what had kept her away from the table for so long. "Is it a family emergency? One of your children?"

Eleanor poked at the salad with a fork. She shook her head.

"I was certain I'd lost you. I thought maybe you accidentally fell in," George teased.

Eleanor offered a horrified expression. "Is that supposed to be funny?"

"A little," George admitted. "I was thinking of organizing a search party."

Eleanor scowled. "I had to make a quick call."

"Oh," George said, more confused than ever. "You should have told me." He pushed his quesadillas aside. "I trust the call was important."

Eleanor furrowed her brow. "I beg your pardon."

Her tone lacked sincerity; an absence of begging with no hope of a pardon.

George swallowed hard. This was not the way he'd thought lunch would go. Clearly, they were off to another rocky start. "I think it's rude to be on the phone when someone's waiting for you. They served the food ten minutes ago. My quesadillas are already cold."

Eleanor put her fork down. "The call was important. It was an emergency," she said, her face turning bright red.

That seemed odd. She'd just contradicted herself. "If the call was an emergency, why didn't you say so when you returned to the table? I already asked you if it was an emergency. Remember?"

Eleanor pushed her salad away. "Is this a cross-examination, Mr. Elden?"

George steadied his gaze. Why did things have to be so difficult? "Look. I like you. But we need to be able to talk. If you have a problem, just tell me. What's the point of a friendship if we can't actually talk to each other?"

Eleanor offered a cold stare. "I have nothing to say." Her tone was firm and decisive.

"Well then, how about an apology for being rude?"

"I said, forgive me," she shot back.

"That's two words. Hardly an apology. How about, 'George, I'm so sorry, I know it was terrible. I kept you waiting at this lovely restaurant for twenty minutes. Shame on me. I had to make a phone call, and I should have told you, so at least you could have gone ahead and eaten your lunch, and not worried that I'd ditched you. Please accept my heartfelt apology."

"Did you want an apology or a soliloquy?" Eleanor asked indignantly. "Is that what you're waiting for?"

George pursed his lips. "It would have shown common courtesy. That's all."

"Common courtesy? You're hardly one to lecture on common courtesy."

George squinted. "What's that supposed to mean?"

"You should have called me the next day after we slept together."

Suddenly George's throat was dry. *So that's what this is all about*. "I don't get it," he said as the waiter approached. "Why agree to have lunch if your plan was to ruin our time together?"

"How's everything?" the waiter innocently asked. "Is there anything else I can get you?"

George studied Eleanor's face. He wondered if she might actually get up and walk out. Part of him wished she would. Instead, Eleanor miraculously transformed. The harshness disappeared. She looked the epitome of kindness. "Can you bring me a martini straight up with a twist?" she said.

George arched a brow.

"I don't usually drink this early in the day," she defended herself. "But you've got me upset."

George ran a tongue over his front teeth. He looked at the waiter. "Make that two."

Eleanor smiled as the waiter headed off to get their drinks. "Well, I don't know about you, but this should be an interesting lunch. Tell me, George, did you often fight with your wife?"

George was in no mood to discuss Jeanette. "Not really."

Eleanor glared at George in a direct challenge. "George Elden, I think you might be a bit of a liar."

George didn't miss a beat. "And you, Eleanor Rifkin, might be a real pain in the ass."

Eleanor leaned against the headboard in her guest bedroom, covers wrapped about her as she watched George sleep. George seemed to encapsulate the best of the male species. *He's a nice man*, she thought as George gently snored. *A good-looking man. Still in great shape. Intelligent.*

Joel had been a restless sleeper. Kicking the covers off. Shifting. Frequently waking Eleanor. "Joel, honey. I'm going to sleep in the other room," she'd say when Joel's restlessness became too much. The occasional night soon became a regular occurrence. It wasn't her idea to have separate bedrooms. It had just worked out that way. Joel could toss and turn to his heart's delight. She could stay up late reading, spreading out with a good book. She came to enjoy the privacy. The silence. She didn't believe she'd given up on the marriage. She was as committed as ever. Surely married couples need not sleep in the same bed to prove their love.

With a grunt, George rolled onto his side and faced her. Eyes open, he smiled. "Was I snoring?"

"A little," Eleanor answered.

"I'm sorry." George slipped a hand under the pillow. "Jeanette hated when I snored. I think it only happens when I'm on my back. She'd nudge me to roll over."

Eleanor nodded. Point taken. Information to be tucked away and used for another time.

"What are you thinking about?" George asked.

"My husband, Joel."

George looked up at her. "It's hard, isn't it? We live our life with someone, invest all that time and care into the relationship, and then they're gone."

"Yes," she said.

"I think it's wonderful that we can talk about our former spouses. It would be strange if we didn't."

"I don't know, George. I think it's all too sad. And to be honest, I really don't feel comfortable discussing Joel."

George furrowed his brow. "Does that mean you're not comfortable with me mentioning Jeanette?"

Eleanor wasn't sure. "I'd like to keep this thing we have, whatever it is, separate from our pasts."

George sat up. "But why? We are the sum of all the things in our past."

Eleanor disagreed. "Maybe you are, George. I'm not. I'm about the future. Creating a new life. If I wanted to live in the past, you wouldn't be here right now."

The next morning, Herbie ordered his eggs sunny side up. "I've got a surprise for you!" he said as the waitress hovered nearby, waiting to take Benny's and George's breakfast order.

Benny was succinct. "Buttermilk pancakes. A side of bacon. And a cup of coffee. Skim, please."

"I need a few minutes," George said as he flipped the menu over. "Do you have any specials?"

The waitress yawned. Herbie yawned. Benny yawned.

"Never mind. I'll have the oatmeal," George decided. "Bring me some skim too."

"Fascinating," Herbie remarked, his eyes glazed over. "I have important news, and you're eating oatmeal."

"Should I have ordered the steak and eggs?"

Herbie ignored him. "Here's the deal. I was dancing with Valerie."

Benny leaned in. "I thought George was dancing with her."

"We switched," George explained. "I was getting nowhere with her."

Herbie broke into a huge smile. "You'll never believe it."

"I will," George promised.

Herbie's eyes lit up. "Valerie does a mean cha-cha-cha. Her technique is flawless."

Benny shrugged. "Okay, champ, but what did she say about Willy?"

Herbie looked off in the distance. His face registered enormous pride. "She said I was a natural. An amazing dancer."

Benny laughed. "You're a man in Boca. As long as your feet are moving, you're fantastic."

"Hey," Herbie said, a finger pointing at Benny. "That's ageist."

"I'm in my sixties. I don't think it's possible for me to be ageist."

"Then, you'd be wrong," Herbie meekly answered. "You know, if we're not willing to stand up for older people, then who will?"

Benny mumbled under his breath. "I'm just glad I can stand up."

George turned to his former brother-in-law. "But what did Valerie say about Willy's estate?"

Herbie winked. "She's going to set up a meeting when the time is right."

George was losing his patience. "When the time is right for what? What does that mean?" Would he ever get reimbursed for his share of Willy's funeral?

Herbie's eyes sparkled. "But, she wants a favor..."

"Oh no," Benny said. "It can't be possible. Valerie wants you to be her sex slave? Please tell me that isn't true."

Herbie stuck his chest out as if such a suggestion won him points in the sexiest-man-alive contest. "What an imagination! Of course not. But she needs a dancing partner for her promotional work with Arthur Murray. And she wants one of us to do it. She won't set up the meeting until we agree."

Benny leaned in. "What kind of a meeting? With who?"

"With whom," George corrected Benny.

"Oh, George. Don't be such a stickler. With who. With whom. Who cares? Whom cares?"

George made a sour face. "That's never right."

"Valerie wouldn't tell me anything more. She just said it'll be a big surprise. It'll answer all our questions."

– 18 –

"VALERIE RESERVED A private room at Morton's for Friday," Herbie explained to George as their golf cart approached the third hole.

George sighed. "Why the mystery? Couldn't she just tell us the name of the executor of Willy's estate? Besides, Morton's is so damn pricey." George's credit card bills flashed before his eyes. Between meals, golf fees, and living expenses, he was fast approaching his credit limit.

Herbie was unfazed. "Lunch is more affordable than dinner."

"But why a private dining room?"

Herbie shrugged. "She's probably Willy's executor."

That made no sense to George. "Then why keep it a secret? She could have been upfront and told us at the start. This damn thing is really getting on my nerves."

Herbie stopped the cart and stepped out. He grabbed a driver, walked over to the tee, and placed his ball. He gave George a confident smile before taking his swing. The ball soared down the fairway. He shielded his eyes from the sun with a hand. "I guess some things just can't be rushed. George, did you see where my ball landed?"

"Somewhere up ahead," George answered dismissively.

Herbie chuckled. "Oh, that's a big help."

George was next to address the ball. A clean swing and the ball disappeared with a whoosh, evaporating in the bright sunlight.

"I don't get it," Herbie said as George joined him in the golf cart. "Why are you so upset about Willy's estate? We're close to getting reimbursed. It's not like we're going to get stiffed. What's the matter with you, George?"

George wanted to tell Herbie about the financial pressures he was under—the bill collectors, the rising credit card debt—but he couldn't bring himself to open up. "I'm just tired of chasing after it, Herbie. Now, we have a lunch set up. What's next? Tea at the hotel? A Mardi Gras in New Orleans? Maybe we should all meet at the Haunted Mansion at Disney World in Orlando? This is getting ridiculous. I don't like it. Not one bit. And now, you seem so calm about it all. Weren't you the one who thought Willy ripped us off?"

Herbie pulled the cart over and stopped. "I was wrong to get so upset. I've given it a lot of thought. That just isn't who I am."

George shook his head in disbelief. "No way. There's no way you changed your mind on this."

Herbie tugged at the front of his shirt as if giving himself room to explain his change of heart. "It didn't happen overnight, George. I had to discuss this with my group."

"Your group?"

"Remember when you were in the emergency room?"

George did.

"I told you I go to meetings to manage anxiety."

Right, George thought. And he also remembered the discussion on the terrace at Willy's celebration of life. George had forgotten to follow up with Herbie. He never did go to that Monday support meeting. He felt a sudden pang of guilt.

"They really helped me get my arms around the whole thing. There's no rushing any of this. We'll get paid when the time is right."

"Herbie, I'm sorry," George apologized. "I was supposed to go with you to that meeting."

Herbie put a hand on George's shoulder and gave it a squeeze. "George, it isn't your responsibility to get me there. I had to do it myself."

"So what did your group tell you to do?"

Herbie offered an astonished look. "They don't tell me to *do* anything. They just give me the space to be myself. I usually come to the answers that work best. It's quite a process. You should try it."

George dismissed Herbie's suggestion as the cart proceeded along the fairway. "Did you tell Benny about the meeting at Morton's? By the way, where is he?"

"I couldn't get hold of him. He hasn't answered his phone or texts."

The golf cart stopped a few yards from George's ball. A breeze kicked up as he stepped onto the fairway. It was a wonderful day to be alive. To be in the great outdoors, enjoying time with Herbie. He was suddenly grateful knowing that Eleanor was waiting for him. He wouldn't be alone for dinner. He imagined Eleanor's counter lined with brie, olive tapenade, crackers, and other tasty treats. A chilled martini glass. Good conversation. And an evening twilight together on the terrace overlooking the ocean.

George took his swing. It landed on the edge of the green.

"Nice shot," Herbie said. "Wow. Someone seems to have gotten their mojo back. Is it because of Angela?"

"Eleanor," George corrected.

Herbie offered an impish smile. "Are you two playing house?"

George shook his head. "Not quite. We're just…"

Herbie interjected. "Keeping company."

George wondered how best to describe the relationship. "I guess. She's nice. I can talk to her. And we have this crazy energy between us."

Herbie strolled over to his ball. "Energy?" he called back.

George waited for Herbie to complete his swing. The ball landed on the green, just short of the hole.

"I'm comfortable with her," George explained.

"Comfortable! Comfortable is good."

Benny's house sat at the end of a quiet cul-de-sac. George rang the doorbell twice. The rain had just started, the usual Florida downpour that arrived every afternoon in the summer. The sky darkened, and then for five or ten minutes, the rain whipped through in a frenzy. No matter how bright the sun in the morning, or how lovely the noontime hour, the afternoon was sure to offer a tropical downpour.

"Jesus Christ," George muttered as he stepped under an inch of overhang to protect himself. "Hey Benny," he yelled as he pounded on the door. "I'm getting soaked out here. Let me in."

Slowly, the door opened. Benny stood in the doorway, eyes bloodshot, pale as a ghost. He looked older. Somehow smaller. As if he'd been out in the rain and experienced shrinkage.

"Holy shit, Benny," George said as he pushed his way in. "It's a monsoon out there. Do you have a towel? I'm soaked."

Benny disappeared down the hall as George removed his shoes and placed them on a nearby mat next to Benny's shoes. George's were three-quarters the size.

Benny returned with a blue beach towel covered in dolphins. George tousle-dried his hair. "Where have you been?"

He ran a hand through his hair, pushing it off his face. "We missed you this morning. Golf isn't the same without you."

"I haven't been feeling well," Benny answered, a dead look in his eyes.

George followed Benny into his den. "Have you seen a doctor?"

"It's not that sort of problem, George."

George was stumped. "Then what is it?"

Benny sat down in his La-Z-Boy chair. "I don't want to talk about it."

George sat in the matching chair next to Benny. Both faced an eighty-five-inch flat-screen television mounted on the wall. "Holy crap, Benny. That's one huge screen."

"Yup," Benny said.

"You heard about Friday?"

Benny nodded. "Morton's?"

George had never seen Benny so down. "Okay. Stop. What the hell is going on with you?"

Benny lifted his eyes to the ceiling. "It's over."

"Over?" George asked.

"All over."

George nodded as if he understood. "Are we talking about Willy?"

Benny shot George a dark look. "Huh?"

George was losing his patience. "What the hell are you talking about?"

"Remember the attractive saleswoman from Arthur Murray? The one who snagged us at the front door?"

George did.

"Well, I've been seeing her."

George sighed. "That young girl?"

"She's a woman, George."

"That very, very, very young woman?"

Benny nodded.

"She broke up with you?"

Benny offered a stern look. "Of course not. Why would she do that?"

George raised a brow. "I don't know. How could I know? You're not telling me anything."

Benny leaned forward. He covered his face with his hands. "I don't think I can talk about this."

George sank deeper into the La-Z-Boy. Why did everything have to be so hard? Why was a conversation with his buddies like pulling teeth? Oh sure, they could laugh, goof on each other, but the moment something serious came up, guys shut down. George wished it was different. That they could just talk without all the pretense.

"Just blurt it out, Benny. It can't be that bad."

"It is." Benny looked at George, hands covering his face, eyes peeking out from slightly open fingers as if telegraphing the message to George via ESP so Benny didn't have to put it into words.

George shrugged. "I got nothing. I have no idea what you're talking about."

"I couldn't do it," Benny whimpered.

"Do it?"

"Yes," Benny loudly said, cringing.

"Meet her mother? Propose?"

"Perform," Benny said in the barest of whispers.

George remembered his time with Jill Winters from The Golden Funeral Home. He'd chalked that up to cold feet. Discomfort at being with someone who worked in a funeral home. Certainly that had been the reason.

Benny scanned George's face for a reaction.

George tried to appear casual. Unaffected. He didn't want to freak Benny out. "You're not the only man who from time to time hasn't been able to perform. It's not the end of the world. It happens to all of us, now and then." George inwardly winced at the memory of Jill's face.

Benny didn't buy it. "Has it happened to you, George?"

George had no intention of revealing his misfire. "No, but that doesn't mean it won't. And if it does, I hope I have a friend who I can talk to about it."

"Talk is cheap," Benny said.

"Well, how about speaking to your family physician?"

"I couldn't do that," Benny admitted. "I'd be too ashamed."

"Now Benny, that's nuts. Nearly every other medical advertisement on television is targeted to this. You watch sports. How many times do they flash erectile dysfunction commercials?"

"I've just never had the problem before," Benny explained. "Look at me. For Christ's sake, I was a star athlete. I'm a successful oral surgeon."

George wasn't sure what dentistry had to do with the problem. "So what? That's who you are. That doesn't mean you're immune to life. Shit happens, Benny. We all have our little problems to work through. And as we age, those problems start to multiply. But it isn't the number of problems we have; it's how we deal with them. And I'd bet that a doctor could give you any number of reasons why you're having a problem."

Benny didn't seem convinced.

George started to count on his fingers. "It could be a clogged artery inhibiting blood flow. Maybe, low testosterone. You might have a cardiac issue that needs to be addressed."

Benny perked up. "Maybe it's reversible."

"Absolutely," George said. "Let's get you to a doctor before you decide your life is over."

Benny nodded. "Hey George, do me a favor…"

George waved a hand. "I know. This is strictly between us."

"I love it," George said as they sat at a picnic table near a food truck parked along the beach. "And this is your treat?" George asked Eleanor, a Cheshire smile on his lips.

"I think I can manage it," Eleanor said. "It's only tacos. But, I thought it might be something different. Fun."

George scanned the chalk menu on the side of the truck. "I like fun."

"So what will it be? The skies the limit."

"I'll have two beef tacos, guacamole, and brown rice. No salsa."

The ocean breeze whipped through George's hair as he watched Eleanor order at the truck's open window. *This is nice*, he thought as he stretched his legs under the picnic table. He spotted a boy with a yellow and blue kite bumping along behind him. "Run," a man yelled from a distance as the boy started to run. The kite finally lifted off. George clapped, though neither noticed him.

"Here you go." Eleanor placed a plate of Mexican delights before him.

"And what about you? Aren't you eating?"

Eleanor opened her shoulder bag and removed a square green Tupperware. "My salad."

"Oh no," George moaned. "I can't eat all this wonderful food and watch you eat a salad."

Eleanor tilted her head. "Well, there is no other choice. I can't eat that," she said, pointing at the plate. "I'll be up all night. Besides, women don't eat like men. If we did, we'd look like men."

George held up a taco as an offering. "That is the most ridiculous thing I've ever heard. You're beautiful. And you have a great figure."

Eleanor held up her Tupperware. "And why do you think that is?"

"You mean to tell me an adult woman can subsist on salad?"

"I didn't say I liked it."

"No. This can't be." George jumped up and headed to the food truck. When he returned, he had a plate with two chicken tacos, black beans, and rice. "No way are you eating salad."

Eleanor licked her lips. "Okay, but whoever finishes last..." She reached for the taco and took a fast first bite, picante sauce gathering at the corners of her mouth. "They buy the Tums."

"Tums?"

"Okay. Ice cream." Eleanor squealed as she took another bite, bits of taco clinging to her lips. She took a third bite. "Ben & Jerry's," she added as she quickly chewed.

George nodded. "I see this won't be easy."

"Easy?" Eleanor repeated, wiping her face with a napkin.

"To keep you from eating us out of house and home once the brakes are off."

Eleanor chortled. "You don't know what you've started, my friend. I assure you, I can easily eat you under the table. There will be no stopping me."

George watched as Eleanor devoured the second taco. He passed over his napkin, which Eleanor eagerly snatched. "You poor thing. It's like you've spent a lifetime on a diet."

Eleanor wiped her face. "Men have no idea what women go through. I mean, just look around. How many men do you think care about their weight? Honestly, have you ever heard one of your friends turning down a French fry because it was fattening? It makes me so mad. And all these guys running around with their guts sticking out. You'd think half the men over fifty were six months pregnant."

George touched his tummy. He'd never had a weight problem. But then, he'd always tried to stay physically active.

"It's just so unfair, George."

George thought there were a lot of things about life that were unfair. Most men tended to go bald while hair eventually showed in the most undesirable places. And then hemorrhoids seemed the curse of anyone who lived long enough. "Yes, life can be unfair," George agreed as he caught sight of the boy in the distance, kite soaring high.

"Men have it so much easier." Eleanor picked at George's brown rice with a white plastic fork.

"Eleanor, how would you like to meet my children?"

Eleanor stopped eating. She dabbed a napkin at the corner of her mouth. "I don't know, George."

"What's there to know?" He reached for her hand.

"It's too soon. Really. We hardly know each other." She withdrew her hand from his.

George furrowed his brow. "I guess so," he said, disappointment heavy in his voice. "Maybe you're right."

"Let's just enjoy each other's company," Eleanor said. "And if this goes somewhere, well, we can decide all of that later."

George leaned on the table, one cheek pressed against a fist. "When do you think you might know?"

Eleanor looked confused. "Know?"

"Whether this is going somewhere."

Eleanor sighed. "George, there's no magic formula."

"I realize that," George said as he wondered about her hesitation and, more importantly, why she never talked about her family.

"So, I have a question." George rolled over and faced Eleanor.

"Oh, no." Eleanor covered her face with her hands. "Whatever it is, can't it wait? The last thing any woman ever wants is to answer questions while in bed."

George sat up. "No. Not about this. This is fine."

"Fine?" Eleanor said as she pulled the covers tightly to her chin and looked up at George. "Fine? That doesn't sound very good."

"No, no," George mumbled. "Better than fine. Excellent."

"Excellent sounds like a grade. Have you been grading me, George Elden?" Eleanor teased.

George blushed. He swung his legs over the side of the bed, toes touching the carpet. "You're making fun of me."

Eleanor laughed. "You're easy to tease, George. Don't you know that? It's what makes you so adorable."

George hung his head.

"Truly." Eleanor leaned over and wrote her name on George's back with the tip of a finger. "You're the sweetest man, George Elden."

George turned and offered a shy smile. "Then why don't you trust me?"

Eleanor squinted. "Is this about meeting your children?"

George shifted, a knee on the bed. He stared into her eyes. "I know nothing about you and your life."

"I've told you about Joel," Eleanor said, her voice an octave higher.

"Yes, I know there was a Joel. But how long were you married? Were you happy? And what about your children?"

Eleanor pulled away, resting her head on the pillow. "I don't like rehashing the past. There really is no point to it. I don't see why we need to discuss what came…before us."

George stood. "Now, that's crazy. Of course it matters. You're shutting me out. Everything that has happened in your life up until this moment is who you are. How can we be together if you're unwilling to share your history?"

Eleanor sat up, leaning against the headboard with the blanket wrapped about her. "Maybe I want something different. Maybe it's too painful for me to go through the past. Maybe I want to start fresh. No looking back. Only looking forward."

"That's exactly what worries me. This refusal to share. I don't see how we can continue if you put up all these walls.

Heck, for all I know, you've murdered your family and are on the run from the FBI."

"I don't think one can hide very effectively in Boca Raton. Credit card charges alone would reveal your location."

George shrugged. "You know what I mean. You could be anyone. How can I trust you if I don't know you?"

Eleanor pulled her knees to her chest. She wrapped her arms about them. "This is the oddest conversation. It's as if we've reversed roles. I'd imagined any man would agree with my very modern point of view. And yet here you are, disproving my theory."

George looked for his underwear. He found it at the foot of the bed. "Don't be sexist. And please don't confuse the issue with talk of gender roles."

"Gender roles? I'm impressed." Eleanor patted the bed. "Come back over here."

"I can't," George complained. "I'm not comfortable."

"Do you want to stop seeing me?" Eleanor asked. "Is this going to be your excuse for ending it?"

George wondered if perhaps it was best if they stopped seeing each other. After all, he could see no future with a woman who was unable to share herself. And though he suspected it might hurt to lose her, it was still early in the relationship. Perhaps the break would be manageable.

"I'm not sure what I want," he admitted, hedging his bet that Eleanor might feel deeply enough about him to change her ways.

"Okay," Eleanor blithely said. "Let's take a time out. You go your way and I'll go mine."

George was stunned. "Just like that?"

Eleanor nodded. "Why not? It's been fun. But we're not kids, George. I don't think I want anything more serious than what we have. And if that isn't good enough for you..."

George slipped into his pants and searched for his shirt. *A rejection*, he thought. *Clear and simple*. "Fine," he announced with forced detachment as he stepped into a pair of deck shoes.

Eleanor pointed toward the vanity table. "Over there. Your shirt's hanging on the chair."

George pulled the polo over his head. "Dammit," he said as the shirt bunched up around his ears. His arms flailed, his head stuck.

Eleanor roared with laughter as George stumbled about, his head finally popping out of the top of the shirt. "Are you okay?" she asked, mirth in her voice.

"I'm perfectly fine," George said. "I hope you find what you're looking for."

Eleanor smiled brightly. "You don't have to leave, George."

"Yes, I do," George said, wishing he was the sort of guy who could manage casual relationships.

George and Herbie sat at a long rectangular table in one of Morton's private dining rooms as they waited for Benny and Valerie to arrive. It was a far cry from TooJay's Delicatessen or the Flakowitz Bagel Inn. The table was dressed with a white linen tablecloth, pristine china, and gleaming glassware. Soft music tickled the ears as a waiter in a black cutaway jacket and matching bowtie asked for drink orders. George and Herbie declined, opting to wait for the rest of the party to arrive.

"Stop checking your watch," Herbie said. "He'll be here soon."

George couldn't help himself. Benny had skipped Thursday's golf game, and now, when they were on the verge of finding out about Willy's estate, he was a no-show.

"Stop worrying, George. Benny loves Morton's. He's not going to miss lunch."

George had offered to go with Benny to the doctor, but Benny had refused.

"I'm not leaving until you schedule an appointment," George had said that day at Benny's house. Fortunately, Benny was able to get an appointment. Too bad it was the morning of the Morton's meeting.

Benny popped his head inside the door of the private dining room. "Hey guys!" He had a big smile on his face.

Herbie flashed a big smile back. "Well, as I live and breathe. The giant returns."

Benny took a seat next to Herbie, giving Herbie's shoulder a squeeze.

Herbie winced. "Be careful. That's my bad shoulder."

Benny pulled his hand back. "I thought it was the other side."

George smiled. Some things never changed.

"I see whatever was bothering you has come and gone," Herbie said.

"Yes, it has," Benny said in a singsong voice. He offered George a wink. "I'm in great shape."

George was happy to hear the news. The appointment must have gone well. George gave Benny a fist bump as Herbie's phone went off.

"I have to take this," Herbie said, excusing himself as he left the room.

Benny exhaled. "George, I have to thank you."

George leaned back in his chair. "So what did the doctor say?"

"You'll never believe it," Benny whispered. "Tagamet in some cases affects the equipment."

"Tagamet for reflux?"

"Right. Who knew? We're going to switch medications and see if the problem goes away. I was stunned. I've been taking it for so long. I had no clue."

George shook his head. "So, it's fixable."

"Absolutely. I didn't realize so many little things could affect Mr. Manly."

George winced. "Oh please, don't tell me you named it."

"My wife did. It was code in front of the kids. Come to think of it, when we divorced, the kids thought she was having an affair with a guy in the neighborhood."

"Mr. Manly?"

"Mr. Dick Manly."

"Nice," George said as Herbie returned to the private dining room.

"Valerie's running late," Herbie announced as he once again checked his watch. "She should be here in fifteen minutes or so. She said we should go ahead and order."

As if on cue, a waiter appeared to take their drink orders. The three gathered around one corner of the long rectangular table. "This is some nice room," Herbie remarked as he looked about. "I wonder what the surprise is."

"God only knows," Benny said.

Herbie turned to George. "So how's everything going with Angela?"

George had to ask, though he knew the answer. "Who the hell is Angela?"

Herbie was taken aback. "You know. Ms. Celebration of Life."

"It's over," George answered, hoping that would be the end of the conversation.

Benny sighed. "Oh, George. I'm sorry. You liked her."

"She didn't dump me," George assured Benny.

"Hey," Benny said, palms in the air. "It's none of my business. Say no more."

Benny's reaction was exactly how George might have handled the same situation if it was reversed. But now George wondered if that was the best reaction. To skim over difficult conversations. To ignore life's challenges. Avoid anything that made them uncomfortable. Could there be an alternative approach somewhere between dismissive and intrusive? Could there be a way to manage a conversation with his friends on issues that bothered him without shutting down the conversation right out of the gate?

George took a leap of faith. "Guys, have you ever noticed that when something serious comes up, we back away? We don't discuss it."

Benny started to defend himself. "George, I didn't mean—"

"No," George said. "We each do it. Herbie, when he doesn't want to discuss something, makes a joke. Benny, you make it into a secret that we need to keep."

"George!" Benny said, his voice cracking. "That was between us."

Herbie looked from Benny to George. "What's going on? Are you two keeping secrets? What are we, in kindergarten?"

George ran a hand through his hair, leaving it disheveled. "Just listen to us! All I'm saying is that we keep cutting each other off. No wonder we don't know the first thing about Willy's life. How could we? We probably never let the poor guy speak."

"That isn't fair, George," Herbie interjected. "Willy spoke plenty."

"But not about the things that mattered. Not about his life. Remember when he suggested I work at Tri-County Animal Rescue? We were all surprised he volunteered at an animal shelter. And how about Arthur Murray?"

"Honestly, George," Benny said. "I'm not sure he wanted to really share all that."

"Why not?" George asked.

Herbie chuckled. "For one thing, did you see that outfit he was wearing in the picture? We'd have thought he was a big sissy."

George slapped a cheek with an open palm. "How could we be friends and know so little about each other? Tell me, how can that be?"

Herbie pointed a finger at George. "She did dump you."

"That's beside the point," George stressed. "Anyway, I'm the one who ended it."

When the waiter returned with drinks and a basket of hot bread, the conversation stopped. George reached for the breadbasket, flipping back the black cloth that kept the bread warm. The smell of sourdough permeated the air.

Herbie looked askance at George. "I don't believe you. You're not the type to dump a woman."

"Well that goes to show how much you know about George Elden." George sipped his iced tea.

"But why?" Benny asked. "You seemed so happy."

"She won't talk about herself."

Herbie and Benny exchanged confused glances.

"She wouldn't tell me anything about her life. Or her children. It's all a big secret."

"Oh my God," Herbie said, a hand covering his mouth. "That sounds like a dream come true."

"A woman who doesn't go on about her past," Benny said. "Solid gold! How lucky could you get?"

"She wants to keep it casual," George said.

Herbie pressed an index finger into his cheek and did his best Shirley Temple imitation. "Gee. She's a meanie!"

"You fool," Benny said, backing up Herbie. "It should only happen to me."

George checked the menu. He never felt more misunderstood. "Forget it. I'm hungry. Let's get that waiter back and order."

Benny seemed unsure. "Don't you think we should wait?"

"Not me." Herbie twisted off a chunk of sourdough bread. "If Valèrie wants to keep us here, fine. But, I'm eating."

"Me too," George said.

Herbie passed the breadbasket as the door to the meeting room opened. Valerie entered, followed by a man.

"Oh my God." George coughed, bread stuck in the back of his throat.

"What the hell?" Benny cried as he stood up and then dropped back down, stunned.

"Holy crap," Herbie muttered, a hand clutching his chest.

– 19 –

"SURPRISE!" VALERIE SHOUTED.

Five foot seven inches of high energy with ash-blonde hair flung her hands in the air as if she were about to go into a performance of the Charleston. A man with a familiar face trailed behind her. A little man who appeared as if he'd wandered into the wrong room at the wrong time on the wrong day.

George focused on the man's face. How could it be? They were at the funeral home. They'd seen the casket. They'd been to the cemetery. George had even thrown dirt on the grave.

Herbie jumped to his feet. "You son of a bitch," he shouted. "Do you know what you've put us through? We've been heartbroken. And you're not even dead!"

Benny said nothing. His mouth hung open.

"Calm down," Valerie said. "This isn't Willy."

George furrowed his brow. "What?"

"Of course not. If this was Willy, I'd be a miracle worker. I'd have brought the dead back to life."

George stared at the man next to Valerie. He looked exactly like Willy. Well, perhaps there were minor differences. Willy dressed like a bum. T-shirt and jeans. Nothing fancy. But this Willy was dressed in a blue suit and red tie. Did Willy even own a suit?

Benny stood to his full height, fists clenched. An angry bear ready to charge a careless hiker. "Then who is he?"

"Now wait a minute," the little guy in the blue suit said as he slowly backed up, taking a position behind Valerie. "Take it easy."

"He's Wally!" Valerie sang out. "Willy's twin brother."

George had no idea Willy had had a twin. But as he looked closer, he realized the guy wasn't Willy. Or was he? His face was rounder. His body thicker about the middle. Willy had always been trim and fit.

Benny approached the pair. "Is this some sort of sick joke? Because I'm in no mood for this kind of crap. Willy, you shouldn't play these kinds of games on friends. It's mean."

Valerie stepped forward and placed a hand on Benny's arm. "Calm down, big guy," she said. "We're all friends here. Like I said. This is Wally. Willy's twin."

Herbie laughed. "There were two of them," he said to George. "Can you believe this? Two Willys."

Benny was unconvinced. "I don't believe it. Not for a minute. Willy never talked about a twin."

"Well, it's true," Valerie announced, waving a hand at Wally as if she'd conjured him out of thin air.

George wondered what Willy might think of the moment. Would he be amused? Why had he never mentioned a twin? Or did he? George couldn't remember as he stepped forward, hand extended. "So, you're Willy's brother. I'm George."

"Yes," was all the man could manage as he retrieved a white handkerchief from an inside coat pocket and dabbed at his forehead.

Benny raised a fist. "I swear to God, Willy. I'm going to punch your lights out."

Wally took another few steps back. "Maybe this isn't such a good idea," he said to Valerie. "You shouldn't have surprised them. There's too much testosterone in the room."

George noticed a hint of a drawl. "Where are you from? Not New York City."

Valerie pushed on Benny's chest. David before Goliath. "What's wrong with you? You're scaring him."

Wally answered George's question, though his eyes remained fixed on Benny. "I'm from Houston. I now live in West Hollywood. In the hills."

"I don't believe you," Benny snarled, spittle escaping his lips.

Valerie pressed her body against Benny's as he appeared ready to lunge.

George joined Valerie, pulling Benny back. "Take it easy, champ! Get ahold of yourself."

But Benny could not be subdued. "If you're for real, why didn't you show at the funeral? What family doesn't show at a funeral? Willy didn't deserve that."

"Something is seriously wrong with you all," the little man said. He turned and dashed out.

Valerie blocked the door so the rest of them wouldn't leave. "Well, now you've done it," she lectured, arms crossed, clearly agitated. She sounded like a disappointed mother. "What's wrong with the three of you? Acting like a bunch of hoodlums. I'm ashamed to say I know you."

George thought it an odd statement since Valerie really didn't know them. But then, George wondered, how well did they know Willy and each other? Based on the growing body of evidence…not very well at all.

"Did I do the right thing?" Eleanor asked, not really expecting an answer.

She and Sylvia had agreed to meet at noon at The Capital Grille. Sylvia had promised the upscale ambiance would cheer Eleanor. So far, it was having the opposite effect.

Sylvia sipped a martini. "Is there really a right thing?" she asked, eyes slightly bloodshot from a second drink. "Who knows? If it felt right, that should be enough."

Eleanor pursed her lips, dissatisfied with Sylvia's answer. "Am I supposed to confide in a man I just met? Does he really need to know the ugly facts of my life? And do I want to know all his messy secrets?"

Sylvia leaned forward, intrigued. "Ugly facts? You haven't told me anything ugly. What exactly are you talking about?"

Eleanor was at once flustered. "I was just being dramatic," she backtracked. She held a glass of merlot in the air. "It's the wine talking."

"Is it?" Sylvia asked, her tone conveying disbelief. "Why not come clean? Let it all out. Tell Momma everything. Then I can advise you about what to do."

Eleanor nearly laughed out loud. *Like hell I will.* She'd no intention of sharing anything with Sylvia. She'd rather confide in George. At least then, she could shape the conversation. Massage it to her favor. Convey the facts, not as they were, but how she wished them to be. But could she rely on George's discretion not to probe into her past? And what if George didn't let it rest? What if he challenged her, asking for details she didn't want to divulge? Could she really tell only part of the story? Half the truth? Discuss Joel's affair and how her sons had sided with their dad?

Sylvia sipped her martini as an awkward silence settled between them.

Eleanor tried to sound light and breezy. "Sylvia, I hate to disappoint you, but there is really nothing to share. No big secrets."

"This isn't about me," Sylvia answered, shoulders raised in perfect posture. "I'm fine whether you tell me or not. My life will go on," she said dismissively. "It's you I'm concerned about. You have two sons you never discuss. A dead husband you rarely mention. It isn't healthy to hold in psychological pain. Eventually, it expresses itself physically."

Eleanor's stomach had been bothering her. A dose or two of Pepto Bismol had become a nightly routine. She just assumed it was the gift of age. Surely, everyone their age had some problems. A backache. Arthritis. Swollen ankles. An upset tummy hardly seemed important.

Eleanor's eye wandered to the middle of the room where a group of men in suits had gathered for a business lunch. *I wonder how often Joel came to The Capital Grille in New York City*, she thought. *Where would he have sat? In the center of the room? No. He'd have wanted his privacy*. She spotted a red leather booth. *There. Off in the corner of the restaurant. That's where he'd have been hiding*.

Sylvia offered a wanton smile. A cat about to play with its favorite toy. "What's going on in that head of yours?" she purred.

"Maybe I'll call George. Give him a second chance."

"Second chance. After he walked out on you?"

"Now, stop," Eleanor said. "You know he didn't walk out. He was just upset."

Sylvia appeared confused. "I thought you said he broke it off."

Eleanor sipped her drink as she studied Sylvia's expression. *She can't stand it. She has to know every detail. Prying and poking. Like I'd ever tell her the truth. I've probably already revealed too much*. "You know men," Eleanor said. "All they want is our attention. I'll tell him I was wrong and he'll come running back."

Sylvia's eyes glowed with admiration. "Now you're talking. Take charge. Let the chips fall where they may. Use him, like he used you."

Eleanor didn't quite understand. George hadn't used her.

Sylvia straightened up. "Teach him a lesson."

Eleanor didn't want to teach anyone a lesson. Perhaps Sylvia was reacting to her own past relationships. Was her bravado based on being hurt by a man? Wasn't Sylvia the one who used men? Eleanor wanted to ask Sylvia again about her past, but she'd already been down that dead-end road. Instead, she let the moment pass. Her attention shifted to a gray-haired gentleman crossing the room. He was holding the hand of a much younger woman. They followed the hostess.

I wonder if his wife knows where he is.

Sylvia glanced over, following Eleanor's gaze. "Do you know them?"

Eleanor clutched her pearls. "In a way."

The May-December twosome slid into the corner booth.

"That man is only interested in one thing," Sylvia said, her tone self-righteous.

"A steak," Eleanor sarcastically replied.

"Sex!" Sylvia announced a bit too loudly.

Eleanor disagreed. "He just wants to feel young again. Attractive to the opposite sex."

"His wife is a woman," Sylvia said in a dismissive tone. "She could make a fuss over him. Dote on his every word. Pretend he's a living god. Bat her eyelashes whenever he does something amazing. Like fart in the kitchen."

Eleanor winced.

"Darling," Sylvia snapped, "a younger woman equals sex."

"A younger woman is a means of escaping the ravages of time. A confirmation that a man's still virile."

Sylvia shrugged. "Same thing."

"Not really," Eleanor clarified. "Sex is a release of tension. It's a lot of work. It creates a sweat. That man over there is engaged in the willful act of suspended belief. Pure illusion.

If he feels thirty-five, then he is thirty-five. Which makes him a sixty-nine-year-old man pretending to be thirty-five."

Sylvia clicked her tongue. "You see, dear, that's where we differ. I'd wager that later this afternoon, in some dark hotel room, our little gray-haired friend over there will be pretending to be thirty-five while in the act of sixty-nine. See the difference?"

Eleanor cringed. She'd tried to paint Joel's affair as a weakness of character. Something he did to boost his self-esteem. The cheating wasn't about her or how she might have failed him in the bedroom. And it certainly wasn't about the pure act of fornication.

"Sylvia, you really don't understand men." The liquor had loosened Eleanor's tongue. "You'd never be able to be with a man like George. A good man looking for a long-term commitment. All he wants is tenderness and understanding. He'd certainly find none of that with you."

Sylvia flinched. "Well dear, you have no idea what I'm capable of or who I've been with. I assure you that if I was interested in George, he'd be with me right now. And I wouldn't be sitting at a bar drinking my feelings."

George was disappointed when Willy—no, Wally—left the private dining room at Morton's so abruptly. It had seemed like they were so close to unraveling the mystery of Willy's funeral and finally being reimbursed.

"What the hell just happened?" Benny turned to George and Herbie. "This is a freaking nightmare."

"I guess lunch at Morton's was out of the question," Herbie mused. "Willy must now be a vegetarian."

Valerie stood with her hands on her hips. "Are you three insane?"

"We were kind of rough," George admitted. He looked in Benny's direction.

Herbie wasn't about to be serious. "Can you believe he left without even saying goodbye? Don't you think that was rude?" He looked about for confirmation.

Valerie was aghast. "You practically attacked the poor man. He agreed to come here and meet his brother's friends and you three clowns scared him off. I wouldn't be surprised if he went straight to the airport to catch the next flight back to California."

Benny seemed contrite. "You shouldn't have surprised us. Why didn't you tell us Willy was alive?"

Valerie shook her head in disbelief. "Because he's not."

"How do we know that?" Benny asked.

"You three are something else," Valerie answered, stupefied. "Does it matter what anyone says? Do you ever listen?"

George held a hand in the air. "Valerie's right. That wasn't Willy. We know Willy."

Benny scratched his head. "He sure looked like Willy to me."

"Certainly," George said. "But he was heavier. And when he spoke, he didn't sound like Willy."

Valerie sighed. "At least one of you has some common sense."

Herbie plunked down into a chair. "Come to think of it, The Golden Funeral Home embalmed someone. I saw the bill. They didn't make that up."

Benny joined Herbie at the table. "You're right. They're a legitimate business. They have to follow all sorts of codes and regulations. Willy had to be in the casket. No doubt about it."

"Yes," Valerie said. "He wasn't Willy."

"So what do we do now?" Herbie asked.

"We get him back here," George answered.

"Oh, no," Valerie said. "I'm not bringing him back to be ambushed."

George took a seat. "Ambushed?"

"Ambushed," Valerie repeated.

"How about if it's just one of us?" George suggested.

Valerie bit her lip. "Maybe he'll agree. But I can't promise anything."

"Thanks, Valerie. You're the best," Herbie said with genuine warmth.

"I didn't say I could do it," she reminded him. "Besides, what's in it for me?"

George cringed. *Not more money.* "You want us to pay you?"

"Of course not," Valerie answered. "But I still need a partner to go with me to do those promotional events."

"I don't know," Herbie said. "That's a lot of work for no pay."

Valerie turned to George. "How about you, handsome? Do you think I'm doing this again for free?"

George's Visa bill flashed before his eyes. He was close to maxing out all his credit cards as he walked the very edge of his credit limit. He *had* to get the money back from Willy's estate to at least pay off the Visa. "Okay," he reluctantly agreed. "I'm in."

"So which one of you is going to meet with Wally? It won't be you," Valerie said, pointing at Benny. "You're too big and scary."

"George will do it," Herbie suggested. "You can count on George to behave himself."

George closed his eyes and nodded. "Sure. I'll do it."

When George's phone buzzed, he was nestled on the sofa with Miss Betsy, certain it was Valerie following up on scheduling the meeting with *Willy Wally*. The little poodle swatted at his hand as he reached for the iPhone. Her eyes pleaded for George to touch her as she released a soft whimper. George pulled her closer as he spotted the caller ID: it was Sylvia.

It was August and George still owned the condo. He was getting nervous. His condo had been on the market since May, but in four months, it had had very few showings. He'd spoken to Sylvia about his concerns. He'd asked if they should do an open house. Sylvia nixed the idea. "I don't do open houses for exclusive properties. The hotel has enough business during the summer to attract potential buyers. If customers are interested, they'll schedule an appointment."

George doubted that was true.

Florida in the summer was a damp swamp. No one in their right mind would want to spend their time at a fancy resort in such sticky weather. Especially the wealthy with access and privilege. Bargain hunters might, for the hotel's reduced rates. But the wealthy could go anywhere.

Maybe she's scheduled a showing, George thought as he answered the phone.

Sylvia's voice was like velvet. "George, I've been thinking about you. Have you missed me?"

George hesitated. Miss Betsy let out a low moan. George ran a hand over the poodle's face as she wildly mouthed his fingers. A new game was born.

"Well that isn't very flattering," Sylvia said flirtatiously.

"Please tell me we have a showing scheduled."

"George, stop worrying. I've told you. Interest is picking up. I've already heard from three Realtors. Trust me. The unit will sell. And we won't need to adjust the price. You just need a little patience."

Patience was a commodity George was running short on.

"Now, as I said, I think we're going to have an offer shortly. So, we've got to make sure you have a place to land. These offers tend to be cash-only with a fast close. You'll need to move out of the condo quickly. So, I want to show you another property. Just in case."

George was adamant. "No more real estate. I've decided to rent."

"Oh, George, that's a terrible idea. I want you to reconsider. Besides, it can't hurt to just look. Hear me out."

"Sylvia, I'm not interested in anything you have."

The double entendre hung between them.

"But you were interested once," Sylvia teased.

George blushed. He'd been easy pickings then. Vulnerable.

"Sylvia, I'm on my way out to an appointment," he lied.

"George, you're so impatient."

"I'm in a hurry," he said as Miss Betsy released a sharp cry. The sound pierced George's ears. He lifted the little body in one hand and placed her on his lap. She popped up, paws pressed against his chest as she stared into his eyes with a look of sheer delight.

"I've found the most adorable property. It would be perfect for you," Sylvia teased.

George lowered Miss Betsy back down. She settled at his side. "I told you. I'm not in the market."

"Don't say 'no' so quickly, George. This is a once-in-a-lifetime deal."

George hesitated. With Eleanor out of his life, he thought about his last tête-à-tête with Sylvia. She'd treated him pretty badly. Toyed with him sexually and tossed him aside. It might be interesting to see what she was offering. Maybe he could turn the tables. Give her a taste of her own medicine. And then walk out.

"Okay. I'm in."

Sylvia sounded delighted. "Thank you, George, for trusting me. You won't be sorry. Meet me tomorrow at two at my office on Glades and I'll take you to see the property."

"How about I just meet you at the property?" George felt leery of being under Sylvia's control.

"Fine. I'll text the information. Two, then?"

"Yes," George agreed, uncertain about what he'd just let himself in for.

"So what are your plans today?" Herbie asked.

George shushed him and pointed at Benny, who stood at the tee. "Let him take his swing."

Herbie scowled. "It's a simple question."

"I'm meeting Sylvia later." George tilted his head toward Benny.

"*Red!*" Herbie blasted just as Benny took his swing. The ball soared high before dropping directly into the middle of a sand trap.

Benny slowly turned and stared at Herbie and George. "What's wrong with you two?"

"I tried to tell him," George meekly explained, signaling Herbie as the culprit.

"You guys know better. Why do I golf with you? You're so...immature. You don't take the game seriously."

"Oh come on, Benny," Herbie protested. "We're here to have fun. Not win the U.S. Open."

Benny raised a brow. "So what were you talking about that couldn't wait?"

Herbie grinned from ear to ear. "Old George. He and Red."

"Red?" Benny repeated.

"Sylvia." George stepped up to take his shot. "Her name is Sylvia."

"You and Red," Herbie repeated as George took his swing. The ball flew high and long down the fairway. "Good one," Herbie said. "Nice lift."

George stepped back, clearing the way for Herbie.

"So what's the skinny?" Benny asked. "You dumped Angela for Sylvia?"

George shook his head. How many times had he corrected Herbie and Benny? "Yes, Angela," George said sarcastically, determined not to correct them anymore.

Herbie's ball sailed down the fairway, landing safely ahead of the sand trap. "Yes!" he whooped, golf club in hand.

Benny shaded his eyes from the sun. "It's amazing how well you do with that bad shoulder. Notice, we're quiet when you take your swing. It would be nice if you afforded me the same courtesy."

"You know what your problem is, Benny? You're too darn competitive," Herbie said.

George had hoped today would be the day when Benny and Herbie wouldn't bicker. But it seemed impossible to be together without one going after the other. "Can't we table this?" George said, more of a plea than a command.

"I'm here to play golf," Benny said indignantly to Herbie. "Not gossip. Or prank each other. I want to actually be here. If you didn't want to play...you should've stayed home."

Herbie crossed his arms, feet planted squarely in the ground like a fireplug. "Maybe we should stop playing together," he suggested. "Clearly you don't like me."

Benny nodded. "You just might be right."

"Okay," George flailed his arms to signal a time-out. "This has got to stop. When are you two going to knock this crap off? We've already lost one friend. Do we need to lose each other? This is really getting serious."

Benny sighed. "Maybe Willy was the glue to our foursome."

"That's ridiculous." George turned to Herbie. "What do you think?"

"I'm beginning to wonder," Herbie answered, eyes on the ground. "He was always the peacemaker. Smoothed everything over. Heck, I don't remember us fighting whenever Willy was around."

George tried to remember. "Well, maybe that was true. But Willy's gone and we still have history together. Our friendship wasn't based on just one of us. We're still friends. Come on, guys," George coaxed. "Pull yourselves together."

Herbie was the first to acquiesce. "Okay, George. I hear you." He turned to Benny, hand extended. "I'm sorry."

"Me too." Benny grabbed Herbie's hand and pulled him in for a bear hug. "I guess I'm just a hothead."

"Great," George said. "Now I told you I'm seeing Sylvia later."

"Jesus, George," Herbie said as Benny released him. "It's always about you, isn't it? Whenever something major happens, the conversation always reverts back to you."

"You and Angela," Benny added.

George exhaled. "You two are a real piece of work."

George pulled up in front of a two-story Boca condo in gated Paradise Glen. He immediately liked the neighborhood. There were no shared walls, and even though the community was new, the landscaping appeared mature. Bushes and small palms separated the parcels, promising privacy on all sides.

Sylvia greeted George at the door. Nothing much had changed since he'd last seen her. She was still tall and lean, her red hair pulled back into a French twist. Her figure was prominently displayed in a tight chartreuse blouse and tan skirt that hugged her hips. "It's lovely to see you again," she said, hand extended in greeting. "I'm so glad you agreed to see the property. I think you're going to love it."

George entered the spacious entryway with its high ceiling. The white walls and white tile opened onto the living room with a tall fireplace covered floor to ceiling in white marble. There was a direct view to the backyard and the pool.

George imagined living in such a grand space. *Jeanette would have loved this*, he thought, sad to be looking at the condo alone. He still felt pangs of her absence whenever he experienced something she might have enjoyed. A great meal. A lovely walk on the beach. A moonlit setting. A place she'd enjoy decorating.

"Wonderful, isn't it?" Sylvia asked, as if defying him to find something wrong with the property.

George walked along the short hallway to the other side of the condo. "What's over here?" He opened the French doors to reveal the master suite. "Spacious," he called out as he strolled into the empty room and spotted the view of the pool from where the bed would be.

Sylvia followed directly behind. "Of course, without furniture it is hard to truly get a sense of the space."

"Oh no," George disagreed. "It's wonderful. But I think it might be too big. And that second floor. I'm not crazy about a staircase. I wouldn't buy a property with a staircase."

"I thought about that," Sylvia admitted. "But it provides two guest bedrooms upstairs, and once you and Eleanor are married, you'll need the additional space. You both have kids. They'll want to visit. And then, grandchildren."

George popped his head back. "Married? What are you talking about?"

Sylvia clasped a palm over her mouth. "Oh God. Did I say married?"

"Yes. I definitely heard married."

Sylvia appeared flustered. "Well, whatever you two decide to do. Even if you just live together. Either way, you'll need space."

George scowled. "Sylvia, Eleanor and I are no longer seeing each other."

Sylvia paled. "I had no idea. She didn't tell me."

"Did she tell you we were getting married?" he probed, highly suspicious of Sylvia's intent.

Sylvia blinked. "I'm sorry, George. I knew you two had a falling out; I just thought that once she called and explained, you two would have patched everything up."

George was growing annoyed. "There's nothing to patch up. We hardly know each other."

"I see," Sylvia said. "Well, I guess this property isn't for you then."

George took one final look around the master. "What is it with Eleanor? You're her friend. Why does she refuse to reveal anything about herself? What secret is she hiding?"

Sylvia held a hand to her throat. "George, now you know it would be wrong of me to share anything about Eleanor. She's my dear friend. I'd never break a confidence."

George nodded. "The ladies always stick together."

Sylvia tilted her head as a finger entwined the gold chain around her neck. "I wish I could be more helpful," she said. "Really, I do!"

George didn't believe her. "You know something, Sylvia. And you're dying to tell me. Aren't you?"

Sylvia looked away. Her jaw set as she considered. "Okay, but this is strictly between us. Eleanor has come out of a very bad marriage. I'm not sure exactly what happened, but she has two sons. And neither of them are speaking to her."

Valerie was insistent when George returned her call. "I'm not telling you a darn thing until you agree to dance with me at Century Village this Thursday at noon."

George put his phone on speaker. He was stopped at one of Florida's endless red lights. He'd hoped to wrap up the arrangements with Valerie to meet *Willy Wally* while he waited for the light to turn green. "Valerie, you should ask Herbie. He'll do it gladly."

"No," Valerie protested. "He dances like a walrus on ice. It takes a lot of energy to push him around the floor. Besides, you know the steps. And if you don't, you can always fake it. So either you agree, or no Wally."

"I won't do it."

"You will do it if you want to talk with Wally."

George groaned. "I don't get it. Why don't you just give me the guy's number? I don't need you to be the middleman."

"You don't," Valerie agreed. "But I need a dancing partner."

"Dear God. How many men have taken dancing lessons from you? Choose one of them. Maybe they can satisfy your needs."

"Excuse me," Valerie snapped back. "George, I'm not interested in you sexually, if that's what you're alluding to. Is that why you're resisting being my dance partner?"

"No, that's not what I meant."

"Oh, horseshit. You know, George, you're not exactly God's gift to women, no matter how many wealthy ladies jump in your path. So don't get high and mighty with me. You need to check that attitude at the door."

George closed his eyes in exasperation just as the light finally turned green. Horns blared as he stepped on the gas. "Alright, I give up. I'll do it," he said as he spotted the Whole Foods sign up ahead. He prepared to make a right into University Commons.

"Good. Then we have a deal," Valerie purred.

"Yes," George agreed as he found a spot in front of J. Alexander's. "I'm all yours."

J. Alexander's was packed with the noontime lunch crowd. George caught sight of Herbie waving from the back. Benny's head, hidden behind a planter, revealed itself as George came around the corner.

"What took you so long?" Herbie asked as George approached.

"Red lights." George sat across from his two friends. Each had a beer in front of them. "When I die, if God asks me what I'd like as my final request before entering heaven, I'd ask for the time back on earth that I spent waiting for Florida's red lights to turn green."

"We do have some long lights," Benny agreed. He took a swig of beer.

"I think it's a good thing," Herbie added. "It slows down the fast drivers."

"Fast drivers?" George asked. "Where the hell do you live? Some of these old people shouldn't even have a license."

"Hey," Herbie said, pointing a finger at George. "Don't be ageist."

George rolled his eyes. "You just love that word, don't you?"

Herbie nodded. "One of my favorites."

Benny agreed with Herbie. "It's easy for you, George, to say these old coots shouldn't be driving. But how the hell can you live in Florida and not drive a car? It's not like New York City. There's no public transportation. At least none anyone with good sense would use."

"Ever hear of Uber or Lyft?" George shot back. "Two safe ways to get where you're going."

"But older people need the app," Benny added.

"You two are living in the stone age." George held up his phone. "Everyone today has a smartphone. Even old people."

"George," Benny said, "we're not old."

"We're not young," George answered. "Average life expectancy for a man is about seventy-eight."

"Then you can be the first in line to give up your driver's license," Benny gloated.

George scowled. He'd never forfeit his freedom by giving up his car. "Point made."

Herbie handed George a menu. "We know what we want. Decide before the waitress comes back. We're starved."

"So, what did she say?" Benny wanted to know as George scanned the menu.

George assumed Benny was referring to Valerie. "She wants me to dance with her," he answered as he tried to decide between the BLT and the turkey club sandwich. "What are you guys having?"

"Dance? I don't understand," Herbie said.

George shrugged. "I suggested you. But she insisted on me. Sorry."

Herbie was indignant. "Sorry? What's there to be sorry about? I have better things to do with my time."

Benny furrowed his brow as the waitress approached. "I'm not following this conversation," he said before ordering a medium-rare burger with fries. "If Angela likes to dance, why should she dance with Herbie? She's going out with you, George."

"Not Angela," Herbie corrected Benny. "I'll have the same," he told the waitress. "But make my burger medium."

"Make that three," George said with three fingers held up. "I'll take mine well-done."

Benny twirled a fork. "Aren't we talking about Angela?"

"Who the hell is Angela?" George asked, knowing full well Benny was referring to Eleanor.

"We're discussing Red," Herbie explained to Benny. "Red has the hots for George."

"Oh my God," George said with exasperation. "Let's start again. I just got off the phone with Valerie. She wants me to join her at Century Village. If I do that, she'll connect me with Willy. I mean Wally. You know. *Willy Wally*."

"And what about Red?" Herbie wanted to know.

"You mean Sylvia?"

Herbie nodded. "Yeah. Red."

"She wanted to show me some property. She had this idea in her head that I might be getting married."

Benny straightened up. "Married? Because you two danced together?"

"Oh my God," George cried. "That's Valerie. Not Sylvia. Sometimes, it's really hard to talk to you two."

Herbie pointed at Benny. "He means you."

"Not me. I listen," Benny said adamantly. "You're the one who's always busy talking."

"Stop," George blurted out as both Herbie and Benny gave him their full attention. He leaned forward, elbow on the table, a hand cradling his face. "It's both of you."

"Well go ahead, George," Herbie pressed. "Explain yourself."

"Red," George said, "as in Sylvia, shared a lot with me about Angela. I mean Eleanor. At first, she wasn't going to say anything. But then she spilled her guts."

Herbie shifted. "What did she say?"

"Eleanor's marriage wasn't a happy one."

Herbie cleared his throat. "Whose was?"

"And she has kids she never sees."

"To some men," Benny added, "that's a bonus."

"No," George said. "That's sad."

"Or maybe," Herbie said, "she isn't a very nice lady. Sometimes you get what you divorce. I mean, deserve."

George supposed Herbie was right. "It doesn't really matter. We're not seeing each other anymore."

"And you're still taking her dancing?" Benny asked.

George exhaled. It was hopeless.

George hurried through a snack of peanut butter on Ritz crackers, mindful that he needed energy to keep up with Valerie. He'd no intention of looking like a fool in front of the Century Village audience.

"Don't you own anything besides a black suit?" Valerie asked when George entered the community center. "You look so…funereal. No one wants to be reminded of death at Century Village. It's like I'm dancing with the grim reaper. Don't you own a red jacket? Or one in yellow? Or something with sparkles?"

George bristled. "Sparkles? What is this, my bar mitzvah?"

"Oy vey," Valerie said as she eyed him with certainty. "You wore a jacket with sparkles at your bar mitzvah."

George had, though he vehemently denied it. "This is the best I can do." He held out his arms wide. "Take me as I am," he joked in an effort to cut the tension.

"Alright," Valerie said, her face twisted in disgust as she stepped up and grabbed him by the arm. "You'll need to stand up straight. Remember what I said about your posture. Do I need to send you to a posture class?"

George wondered if there were such things.

"Back straight, chin up," she counseled. "And when I start to pull away and travel, make sure you stand still so I can make my way completely around."

"You'll be traveling. North or south?" he joked.

"You don't move until I pass the Rock of Gibraltar."

George had no idea what she was talking about until Valerie reached around and slapped him hard on the rear end. "It's right behind you, George. Now make sure you stand in place, rhythmically shifting your hips when I circle. And for Christ's sake. Stand up straight."

Two hours later, George wiped the sweat from his forehead with the back of his hand. Though the room was air-conditioned, dancing in front of all those women was daunting. He'd tried his best to keep up with Valerie, but she had the endurance of ten stallions. She was a true master, executing showy kicks, literally dancing circles around George as he clenched his Rock of Gibraltar, awkwardly shifting from foot to foot, trying to stay in rhythm with the music. What should have lasted forty-five minutes went on and on as Valerie extolled the different steps the audience would learn and the history of the international dances in her repertoire. George waited patiently for her to finish the pitch.

And then, as if by magic, she finally wrapped up.

"You too can boogie your way onto the floor," she told the audience as she held George's hand up in the air. "Would anyone like to take a spin with George? Ladies?" she called out. "He's free, Jewish, and over twenty-one."

George gasped, unsure whether he was more shocked at her *Jewish* reference or her offer that anyone could dance with him. "No," he whimpered under his breath. "That's not part of our deal."

"Come on, ladies," she beckoned, ignoring George.

Women started to rush to the front of the auditorium. "No, no," George muttered at the kindly faces thrilled with excitement, lined up by Valerie.

"Wonderful," Valerie exclaimed. "But before we do that, I need each of you to sign this sheet. Name and phone number so we can stay in touch."

George started to pull away, but Valerie grabbed the bottom of his coat jacket and pulled him back. "You want to meet Wally, don't you?" she said under her breath. "Then there's just a little more work to be done."

George stood deflated as the first woman, an attractive brunette, grabbed his hand and pulled him in close. "Mrs. Rita Finkelstein," she said. "I'd like to samba." She twitched a shoulder in an intense Latin motion.

And I'd like to end world hunger, George thought as he moved his hips, demonstrating the samba while trying not to step on Mrs. Finkelstein's toes.

By the end of the day, George's feet ached from the afternoon dance session. "Who'd have thought dancing could be such an athletic event?" he complained to Valerie, who looked fresh as a daisy. She shot him a nasty look as if he'd just insulted her. Perhaps he inadvertently had. "And what about Wally?" he asked. "Have you made the arrangements so I can meet him one-on-one?"

Valerie pursed her lips. "George, I know perfectly well what I promised. Are you doubting my word?"

"No," George answered, worried he might be required to perform an Irish jig in order for Valerie to fulfill that promise.

Sylvia twisted a diamond-studded band about her finger as she took in the view from the twenty-fifth-floor balcony of the Doral Plaza, Miami's latest addition to the condominium skyline.

She didn't normally venture this far south, but the client, a friend of a friend, was interested in a Miami condo, and since cash is king, Sylvia had the upper hand in negotiating the deal. *Easy as pie*, she'd thought when she'd agreed to represent the buyer, forgetting about the bumper-to-bumper I-95 traffic, the huge semis, endless roadwork, and multiple accidents that made the journey to Miami from Boca a sheer hell.

The clouds shifted, briefly hiding the sun, creating an effect of light and dark as Sylvia grew impatient. *I wish he'd hurry up.*

The client had insisted on seeing the property a third time. Sylvia, never one to linger on a decision, couldn't fathom anyone being so indecisive. "You either like it or you don't," she'd say with grand bravado. But what she really meant was, *If you don't like it, don't waste my time.* Because time was money, and money was what it was all about. Usually. But this afternoon, as she looked out on the marvelous ocean view, she wasn't focused on the commission. Instead, she imagined the future. Faceless clients and similar terraces. Other showings. Other deals. When had her life become so tiresome? Why was she so bored?

She watched the ocean break on the shore below as she heard her mother's voice. *We each get exactly what we deserve. No more. No less.*

Sylvia's mother, Rose, had been dead for decades, and still, her disapproval echoed in Sylvia's ear. "You should have a husband. A family."

She'd tried to explain to her mother. "I'm not sure I want to marry."

Rose glared at her daughter. "Sylvia, don't be crass. You're not one of those funny girls." Rose's code for *lesbian.* "You need someone to take care of you. Everyone does."

Sylvia wrestled with the memory. Had she finally come around to her mother's point of view? Was it a passing mood or a real fear that time was growing short and she didn't want to end up alone?

Sylvia rubbed her right hand. Arthritis had crept into the thumb. She had to remember not to flex the digit. Otherwise, there'd be a dull ache. And just recently, her podiatrist had recommended flats to relieve the discomfort in her lower back, exacerbated by a sore knee.

Sylvia confronted the truth. Her career had become stale. Chasing after leads. Walking through empty properties. Trying to please others. Was it time she made a change? Please herself? If so, how?

Her mother had not been a happy woman. Always wishing life offered something more. And though Sylvia's life had been different, untethered by a husband and children, she understood her mother's disappointment. Perhaps it wasn't one specific choice that created life's sadness, but the compilation of choices that precluded a happy outcome. Wasn't that how she'd built her own trap?

It was a moment of unpleasant clarity. A taking of account that Sylvia had spent years avoiding through a busy career.

"Excuse me." A male voice came from behind.

Startled, Sylvia turned to face her client, a short, stubby man with salt-and-pepper hair. He had the face of a bulldog.

"Can I take ownership in thirty days?" Mr. Bulldog had been stalling for weeks. Now, suddenly, he wanted to close quickly.

Sylvia should have been excited. Instead, she was irritated. Another demand. Another deliverable. She imagined tossing Mr. Bulldog off the terrace. "Sure. No problem," she said, all smiles. "I'll make a call right now and take care of it."

As she held the phone to her ear, she thought of George Elden. His handsome face. The way his salt-and-pepper hair broke across his forehead. His performance in bed.

She imagined him next to her, enjoying the view. Putting his arm about her waist.

Was it too late? Had she missed her chance?

– 20 –

CAROLE REFUSED TO let it go. "I just don't understand why you'd need a two-level home in a gated community. You're not getting any younger. You could trip on the steps. Hurt yourself. Who would be there to help?"

George squeezed his phone so tightly he feared he might crush it. "Carole, I said I looked at the property. I didn't buy it. And by the way, my health is excellent. I don't take any medications. My balance is great. And I certainly don't need my adult daughter telling me what I can and cannot do. At least, not yet."

George could practically hear the pouting from 3,000 miles away as he glanced at the clock. Three minutes into the call and he was already annoyed. "And what have you been up to?" he asked, hoping to get the conversation back on track.

Carole grunted.

"Have you heard from Peter?"

"No." Her voice was distant and aloof. "Have you?"

George didn't have the energy to deal with his son. "Not this week," he answered, although it had been weeks since he'd connected with Peter.

"Dad, what is it about you and Peter? Why is it so hard for you two to get along?"

How could he explain it to Carole? Could he be honest and say it was possible to love a son but not like him? He'd wrestled with the dilemma ever since Peter had gone through puberty. He wasn't particularly proud of the feeling. He hadn't said anything to Jeanette, but suspected she knew the truth. But then, Jeanette had never asked the question directly. She'd been too busy managing Peter. The social stumbles. His difficulty getting along with others. His struggles with women. Jeanette had been the main go-to while George had buried himself in a busy career.

"Carole, I wish I knew," he answered, though he did know. It was a matter of respect. George didn't respect Peter. It had been easier to pull away. As long as Jeanette had been alive, he could pretend all was well. But in her absence, he couldn't continue the charade.

"Daddy, when do you think I might see you again?"

"Not till after San Francisco's rainy season," George suggested, putting off a visit for another six months. "Maybe you could come to Florida?" He hoped his daughter wouldn't take him up on the invite.

"We'll see," Carole answered in a noncommittal tone.

"Well, you think about it," he said, grateful for the physical distance.

While he was stretched out on the living room sofa, phone in hand, George received a text from Valerie confirming the appointment with Wally: *Next Monday. Wally will meet you at the Marriott at Boca Center for breakfast. Nine thirty a.m. sharp.*

George wondered what questions he should be prepared to ask. Did he need to make a list or just let the conversation flow naturally? In his peripheral vision, he spotted Miss Betsy. She'd dropped a red plastic bone in front of the sofa. With a yelp, she demanded he acknowledge her and toss the bone. He happily obliged.

"Where's Baby Candy Cane?" he called. The little poodle raced across the room to retrieve the toy. With the red bone secured, Miss Betsy charged back, front legs flailing in the air, challenging George to take the bone out of her mouth.

When George's phone rang, he was on all fours in down dog, playfully growling at Miss Betsy. The little poodle was ecstatic, running circles around George, periodically charging at his backside so he had no way to grab the bone from her mouth. George fell into a heap of laughter, rolling onto his back. Miss Betsy swiped at his face, eventually pressing her head against his, the bone an inch from George's open mouth. By the time George reached for the phone, the caller had gone to voicemail.

With a ping, a text arrived from Eleanor: *George, I miss you. We have to talk.*

George doubted there was much to be said. For now, he wanted to enjoy Miss Betsy. Rolling onto his back, he hoisted the little poodle up onto his chest. Miss Betsy relaxed, her body splayed on top of George. Together, they breathed in perfect harmony. George closed his eyes, and for a moment, the world drifted away. He was at peace with life.

Then curiosity got the best of him. His thoughts shifted to Eleanor. He was no longer relaxed.

Did he really want to see her again? So far, it had been an exercise in futility. She'd refused to open up about her life. He essentially knew nothing about her, besides that she'd been married, her husband had died, and she had two sons. George didn't even know her husband's name. Or did he? *She must have told me. And how long were they married?* Odd. He couldn't remember anything.

His thoughts drifted to Benny and Herbie. *No wonder we're friends. We deserve each other. None of us listens to anything the others say.*

George sat up with a start. Miss Betsy growled as if a stranger had entered the room.

Is this the beginning of Alzheimer's? He pressed two fingers to his temple. *Or am I just too self-centered to remember?*

A novel thought came to mind. *Maybe I didn't hear her. Perhaps I should get my hearing checked.*

Eleanor cupped an iced coffee. She shifted nervously as if someone in Starbucks might overhear and actually be interested in their conversation. "George, the reason I've kept quiet about my past is that there really isn't much to tell," she explained.

George wasn't convinced.

"I think every day affords us the ability to start over again," she went on. "It's the only real choice we have."

George sipped his decaf. He had no idea why Eleanor had felt compelled to meet him. Clearly, she wasn't interested in dropping her guard. Nothing had changed since they'd last met.

"But I like you, George. I think we could have a good time together."

George decided to take a risk. "Sylvia spilled the beans."

Eleanor eyes grew wide as saucers. "How could she? She knows nothing about my past."

"It's none of my business, but if you expect to build any sense of intimacy, you really need to let someone into your life."

Eleanor grimaced.

"I'm not going to beg you to tell me your big, dark secrets. God only knows what's gone on in your life to bring you to this moment. Yes, your spouse died. So did mine. But with all your mystery and intrigue, I'm growing concerned that you might have actually murdered him." George smiled at his own cutting wit.

Eleanor looked away.

Had he offended her? Would this be the last time they'd meet?

"Alright," Eleanor said as she rubbed her palms together. "I married my college sweetheart. I put him through law school working as a secretary. Long hours. I wanted to be a doctor. Go to medical school. We agreed that after Joel graduated, I'd do that. Joel had started as a defense attorney, working for the disadvantaged. I was proud of him. He did a lot of pro bono work. Then I became pregnant. Joel became a prosecutor. I became a mommy. Joel took a job as a corporate attorney for a multinational pharmaceutical firm. That's when things changed. Our marriage changed. Joel changed. And still, I thought we were okay."

George leaned in.

"Joel was a sweet man. At the end of the marriage, before he died, was I still in love? I thought I was." Eleanor stared down at her hands. "It's hard to know. What's love anyway? A commitment. A piece of paper. A habit. You see, I wanted Joel to be a certain kind of man. A good man. But what I failed to understand is that sometimes love doesn't last. People change. We shouldn't fight so hard against it. It just happens. It happened quickly to us. Within the first five years. So what becomes of a life when you're married to someone you love, but who no longer seems to love you?"

George couldn't imagine that challenge.

"We had two boys in quick succession. Toby and Steve. Lovely little boys. *Wild*," she said with bold laughter. "They ran me ragged. I was so busy chasing after them. It was during that time that the connection between Joel and I began to slip. At first, I didn't notice. It was so gradual. A strange glance. A distant hello. A forgotten kiss. And before I knew it, we'd grown apart. We were like strangers living in the same house. I should have done something then. What, I'm not sure. But something. Instead, I let it go. It was easier to ignore it. To deny. To pretend…"

"So you fell out of love?" George asked.

"Oh, there's that word." A scowl crossed her lips. "Love. What is that anyway? When you find out, please let me know. Did I love him? Well, I was comfortable with him. We shared a life together. He was still my best friend. Isn't that enough? Isn't that what life is, after all?"

George felt sorry for Eleanor. "I think marriage is more."

Eleanor glared at him. "More? Like when you realize your husband's been unfaithful? When you catch him in the act but decide to look the other way?"

George was mesmerized. "I'm sorry, Eleanor."

"It's better not to think about it." Her eyes moistened.

"He really hurt you."

"You're not listening. It wasn't his fault. There was so little between us. Poor guy. He deserved some attention. I was relieved when he found someone else. It made the whole thing easier. I didn't need to pretend. I could just be."

"Is that what broke up the marriage?"

"Death broke up the marriage," Eleanor answered. "I guess we would have eventually split up. But where was I to go? I'd raised two sons. No career. No way of supporting myself financially. I made the mistake of just *going along*. And then, I began to realize that Joel was considering leaving me. He actually said that one day. Just as matter of fact as I'm sitting across from you. He wanted to leave. He was unhappy.

Unhappy," she laughed. "Who was happy? I wasn't happy. But I wasn't leaving. And then, I met Ruben."

"Ruben?"

"He was the grounds manager for our condo development."

George tried not to register surprise.

"Oh, I know," Eleanor admitted. "It sounds seedy. No pun intended. A lonely woman having a fling with a gardener." Eleanor laughed. "I'd become a stereotype. I couldn't even have an affair without seeming pathetic."

"You're too hard on yourself."

Eleanor looked at George as if seeing him with fresh eyes. "You think so?"

"No one is judging you."

Eleanor tossed her head back. "But you don't understand. I'm judging me." She nervously played with the straw in her drink, twisting it back and forth between her fingers. "My boys found out about it."

"How?" George asked.

She clutched at her throat. "What does it matter?"

"Was it Joel? Did he tell them?"

Eleanor nodded. "He let it slip."

"Slip? That's some slip."

"I guess he was afraid of losing them. So he did what he could to make sure they hated me."

"You could have explained that to the boys."

"They were away at college. Their dad had financially been very generous. Anything I said was viewed negatively. I couldn't undo Joel's effect on them."

"So what did you do?"

"There was nothing to do," Eleanor admitted. "I was the bad parent. The one who created the chaos."

"And the boys never learned the rest of the story."

"Joel died soon after he told them. It was quite sudden. A massive heart attack. The widow-maker."

George was incredulous. "And you've never patched things up."

Eleanor shook her head. "I could never get them to talk with me after the funeral. I'd become persona non grata. As if I killed their father."

George took a deep breath. He couldn't imagine the pain Eleanor had suffered. It all felt like too much to manage. "I'm so sorry. I wish I'd known."

"You know now," Eleanor said. "So what do you say, George? Are we good?"

It was the moment of truth. "Sure," George said.

"Friends?"

"More than friends," George answered.

"But nothing serious," Eleanor emphasized. "You do your thing, I'll do mine. And then, we'll do ours."

George didn't like the sound of the truce.

Dr. Julie Bishop entered the exam room. She was a dead ringer for a 1970s Angie Dickinson. "Your hearing is perfectly fine," she said as she sat on a swivel chair in front of George.

George breathed a sigh of relief. "That's good to know. You'd be surprised how many things I've missed lately. I just assumed it was my hearing."

Dr. Bishop crossed her long legs. "Missed. Like what?"

"Details about my friends' lives. I don't seem to retain much information. I was wondering if maybe I just wasn't hearing them."

"Give me an example," Dr. Bishop prompted.

"Well, my friend Herbie has been married four times. I remember his first wife; she was my sister-in-law. But after that, I lost track of his matrimonial trail."

"Interesting," Dr. Bishop noted in a flat tone. "Did you and your wife socialize with his other wives?"

"Well, no," George said. "It was awkward. Jeanette didn't want to do that. She was totally loyal to her sister. She hated Herbie after the divorce. She wanted me to end the friendship."

"But you didn't," the doctor answered as if she already knew the story.

"How could I? He was my best friend. A best friend doesn't drop a guy because of a second marriage. Or a third." George laughed. "Or even a fourth."

"I suppose not," Dr. Bishop agreed. "Is that the only reason you've been concerned about your hearing?"

"No. You see, a close friend recently died. A golf buddy. And as it turns out, I had no idea what was going on in his life. Completely clueless."

"Then how could he be a close friend?"

"That's what I've been wondering. We golfed together for years. Not every weekend. I didn't live in Florida back then. But I was down often enough. Every two to four weeks. That's a lot of time to spend with someone."

Dr. Bishop removed her eyeglasses. "Some people don't like to talk about themselves. Have you considered he was just a very private person?"

George raised an eyebrow. "I suppose."

"Maybe you're making too much of this," she said as she wet her lips. "I've only spent a little time with you, and I can already tell you're a caring and sympathetic man."

George was flattered. "You think?"

"Your wife is a lucky woman."

George had mentioned Jeanette and now he'd have to clarify. God, he hated the explanation. "I'm a widower."

"How terrible. I'm sorry."

George basked in the sympathy. He was glad he'd shared his feelings. There was something special about Dr. Bishop. A calm serenity. She seemed to intuitively understand George's circumstances. Perhaps she appreciated his struggles. "I see you're not wearing a wedding band. Maybe we might have dinner together."

Dr. Bishop crossed her arms as she glided away from George. "Well, that's forward. I hope I didn't lead you on."

"I'm sorry," George muttered, heat rising in his face. "I just thought…maybe…you might be free."

Dr. Bishop tilted her head as if assessing the situation. "I've never been propositioned in an exam room. Congratulations. You're the first."

George looked down at his hands. "Well, this is awkward."

"It is," Dr. Bishop agreed. "And even if I didn't have a policy that prohibited me from dating patients, I'd pass. Do you want to know why?"

George hesitated. He wasn't sure he needed to know the answer.

"Too many men around here think women are an easy target. Sure, we outnumber you. But this isn't high school, and just having a handsome face doesn't carry the day."

"So you find me attractive."

"It has nothing to do with that, Mr. Elden. You know you're an attractive man."

"Then what's wrong? Tell me the truth."

"To be honest, you don't seem to know who you are. You're going through a phase of self-discovery, struggling to figure out your feelings."

George absorbed the diagnosis. "I guess that would be true of any widower."

"Yes," Dr. Bishop agreed. "But your kind is different."

"I'm a kind?"

"You asked for the truth," Dr. Bishop said, her eyes offering a sympathy that made George uncomfortable. "I'm a professional woman. I have a career. I have friends. And I have no interest in a second marriage. The first time around was plenty for me. But you, well, you seem needy. Without a woman by your side, you think you have no life. I have a life. In fact, a very busy and fulfilling one. Yes, I'd love to be involved with someone special. But I'm not interested in a man who is lost. That's too big a project to take on. So if you'll forgive me, I think I'll pass."

George was dumbfounded. "You figured that all out about me from a hearing test?"

The Flakowitz Bagel Inn was packed. Every seat taken.

"Sounds like you've been a busy boy," Herbie said as he ripped open a packet of Equal. He poured the contents into his coffee.

George didn't think Herbie believed him. "You think I'm making this up, don't you?"

"Not at all. You're a good-looking guy. Single. A commodity in Boca. Why should an attractive lady doctor pass on a date with you?"

"She shut me down cold," George said a bit too loudly.

"You must have really screwed up," Herbie said in a mocking tone. "Life is so hard for you. Poor George. One woman turns you down. And yet, women still flock to you. How do you do it? It must be the jawline. Women love a strong jawline."

George had no idea what Herbie was talking about.

"Or maybe it's your height. Women like six feet. As long as it's above ground."

"I don't think it has anything to do with my looks."

"Oh, come on. You know you're a good-looking guy. You stand straight. You dress well. You have all your teeth."

"That seems like a fairly low bar," George muttered.

"You'd think so, wouldn't you?" Herbie said with a smile. "Face it. Now's your time to howl. Enjoy yourself."

George didn't want to howl. Whatever that was. He didn't want to bounce from woman to woman. He wasn't interested in that kind of experience.

"This is just one of the perks of outliving your wife. If you're smart, you won't blow it and marry again."

George had never felt more misunderstood. "I'm not like you. I'm not a player."

"Right." Herbie sipped his coffee. "You're more like a woman. You have feelings."

George glared at his friend. "Don't be misogynistic. I'm a sensitive guy. It's true. I only want to be with one woman: my wife. And since that's no longer an option, I have to figure things out. But I'm not a teenager. My hormones aren't raging. And I don't want to sleep with every woman who crosses my path. Just a select few."

"Oh, stop bragging," Herbie snapped. "Like everyone really wants to sleep with you. As adorable as I am," Herbie said, his face lit up like a jack-o'-lantern, "I still need to put forth effort to get my fair share of attention. So you must be putting out some sort of hormonal thing. Have you considered that? You're completely hormonal."

George burst into laughter. "You're such an idiot."

"Listen to me," Herbie said as the waitress delivered a plate of scrambled eggs and bacon. "Just think about what you're doing. There are a lot of ladies to choose from. Try to make the right choice."

"You're not hearing me," George said as the waitress placed a bagel and lox platter in front of him.

Herbie pointed a finger. "Choose a woman of means. Like that Angela gal from Willy's memorial thing at Mona's. Someone who can offer you a lifestyle."

George had never considered money an important factor in love. But with Jeanette's medical bills still hanging over his head, and the condo not yet sold, the suggestion seemed reasonable. Yet he was certain there was more to a relationship than financial stability. "I don't need a woman to take care of me." George knew his male pride was talking.

"Of course you do. Everyone does. Who knows how long we'll live? Why would you be with a woman who can't help financially?"

George recoiled. "That's mercenary."

Herbie buttered his toast. "I've been through too many marriages to ever want to marry again. But I wouldn't mind a woman who could carry her own weight."

"So, you'd live with the right woman."

Herbie paused, tilting his head. "I'm too high-maintenance. I like my own space. Besides, we're different. You're the type who gets married."

"Says the guy who married four times."

"Sure. But you *really marry.* When you say 'I do,' they don't need to add 'till death do you part.' You show up to the wedding with a casket strapped to your back."

George sipped his coffee as Herbie attacked the plate of eggs with gusto. In retrospect, life with Jeanette had seemed so easy. They'd settled into a natural rhythm. The tug-of-war at the start of a relationship had long been settled. Boundaries agreed on. Concessions made. It wasn't going to be easy in any new relationship. He'd have to start all over from square one. Adjust to another person's way of life, their view of the world. Jeanette had been the dominant force in the house, raising the children and building their social life. Perhaps it'd been easier since he was busy with a career. That had allowed him plenty of space to be married and still essentially himself. Would a second marriage at this age be different? A match of companionship versus love?

"Herbie, do you think it's different now that we're retired? Do you think being married might be more of a challenge?"

Herbie wiped his face with a napkin. He missed a spot on his chin where a bit of egg had settled. "I guess it depends on the woman. If she wants a playmate, a best friend to hang out with, you better make sure you like her. But if she has her own life, is independent, you better make sure you have something going on."

That made sense. "You know, it's times like these that I realize why we're friends. You can be very wise."

Herbie looked up from his breakfast plate. His scrambled eggs were nearly gone; only a slice of bacon remained. "Thank you. I appreciate that. But here comes the disclaimer: none of us knows what the hell we're doing. The best advice in the world isn't worth squat if you make the wrong choice. And the real challenge is making the choice. I keep screwing it up. To tell you the truth, I wouldn't trust myself to make another major life decision. Oh, I always seem happy-go-lucky, but deep down inside…" Herbie held a thumb to his chest. "I'm terrified. There's only so much rejection any man can stand. And honestly, I think I've had enough for one lifetime."

George was touched by Herbie's candor. "So you've retired from women."

Herbie rubbed his face as if he needed to be fully alert before imparting his answer. "Of course not. But no more serious commitments. I'll continue to have women friends, but I won't be moving in with anyone. Not as long as I can live on my own."

"And when you can't?"

"Well then," Herbie said, eyes lit with an inner glow, "I'll live with you, George. Or better yet, Benny." Herbie let out a laugh. "Could you imagine me living with Benny? At least that big gorilla would be able to carry me to the toilet."

– 21 –

GEORGE'S CONDO SOLD at the end of August to an out-of-town couple from the north shore of Long Island. They'd purchased the unit sight unseen. George remembered Jeanette's reaction to the view. Now, that was someone else's problem.

There'd be a lot of work ahead. But George didn't care. He felt relieved. A weight had been lifted off his shoulders. Soon, he'd be out of the Boca mortgage, the homeowner association fees, the property taxes, and all the other financial impediments, not to mention the golf club dues that came along with the Boca Raton Resort & Club lifestyle.

He was at Starbucks having coffee with the guys when Herbie offered to help with the move. "Just tell me when you need me to come over."

Benny folded back a corner of the newspaper as he checked the sports scores. "Let's do it this weekend."

George broke off a piece of glazed donut and popped it in his mouth. He didn't want anyone to see the place. Certainly not before he had a chance to go through Jeanette's things.

"Thanks, guys, but I've hired a local moving company. They'll come in and pack up. I need to be out in two weeks. It's a pretty fast turnaround."

Herbie's eyes bulged. "Two weeks."

"Those were the terms."

"Where are you going to go?" There was genuine concern in Herbie's voice.

"I have my eye on a building that takes pets and has a pool. I stopped by the other day to check it out. I already put in an application."

Benny looked up. "Do you have anything for charity? I can haul it anywhere you want in my truck."

"You've been dying to make use of that truck," Herbie teased, nodding to George. "And he said he only needed a truck to haul himself around."

"So, this building," Benny asked. "Is it very young?"

"You mean new?" George had no idea when it was built. "I don't know. But it's nice. Clean."

Herbie cleared his throat. "Benny means, are there a lot of young people?"

George had noticed quite a few women who appeared to be Carole's age. "A few."

"That settles it," Herbie insisted. "We're going to be hanging out at your pool."

George had no doubt.

George stood in front of Jeanette's open closet with a large black Hefty bag and Miss Betsy at his feet. He took a deep breath. There remained a hint of Jeanette's favorite scent, Shalimar.

How should he begin?

It had been months since Jeanette had died, and though he'd told Carole he'd taken care of packing up her things, he hadn't touched any of it. Not a blouse, skirt, belt, or shoe. Not her dressing table. Not any of the dresser drawers. Not the bathroom cabinets or toiletries in the shower. Everything remained exactly as Jeanette had left it. There had been something comforting in leaving her possessions in place. He could pretend he wasn't alone. And though the pain of her death still lingered, he knew the time had come to move on. No matter how long he might wait, she wasn't coming back.

He reached for the first garment on the rack. Then, he pulled his hand back. He remembered the day Jeanette had stood in front of his closet in Garden City and directed him to donate his suits. All but the black one. The one he'd ultimately worn to her funeral.

He was flooded with memories. Jeanette on the beach, wiggling her toes in the sand. In bed, welcoming him into her arms. Flashes of their life together danced before his eyes. The love of his life, once again warming his heart. And then, in a cruel instant, she was gone.

Miss Betsy pawed at the garbage bag in his hand.

He had to empty the closet. But how? The closet had become a sacred memorial of Jeanette. A memorial he had no power to disturb.

How could he break the spell?

"Oh, my God," George said as he slowly slid to the floor, leaning up against the closet door. *How am I going to do this? I miss you, baby. I wish you were here. How could you leave me alone? I've never been any good without you.*

Miss Betsy suddenly lurched forward. She snatched one of Jeanette's fluffy pink slippers from the bottom shoe rack. She growled as she violently shook the pink prey.

"Hey," George said as he reached for the slipper, trying to get it back. "That isn't for you." But the little dog refused to let go. George lost his grip as Miss Betsy fled the room with the prized possession.

George was in shock. What to do?

Miss Betsy charged back into the room. The pink slipper was still in her mouth, a bald spot on the instep.

"Now, what did you do?" George pulled the little poodle close. She wiggled, emitting a low growl. Three hard shakes of the slipper and she pulled away, spun, and confronted George, the slipper still firmly in her mouth. She whimpered, inviting George to play.

George leaned forward. He tried to grab her. "Give me that slipper."

Miss Betsy released a low grumble as she raced to the bedroom door, stopping short of the threshold. She turned to see if George was chasing her. In a flash, George was on his feet, laughing with delight as Miss Betsy eluded his grasp and charged into the hall, George close on her heels.

Two hours later, Jeanette's closet was stripped of its contents. All items were neatly folded and tucked into large Hefty bags at the front door. A quick call to Benny and arrangements were made to drop off the bags at Levis Jewish Community Center's Resale Boutique. Jeanette's jewelry box sat on top of the kitchen counter. George would ship the box to Carole.

A bottle of Shalimar remained in the medicine cabinet. Nearby, just in case George needed it.

Eleanor applied lipstick as George entered the master bathroom. "George. Put on a towel," she bellowed, catching George's naked reflection in the mirror.

George stopped in his tracks. "Where's your hair dryer?"

"Over here." Eleanor pointed at the vanity and stepped aside. "Top drawer."

George lifted the dryer from the drawer.

"It's a professional model. Best on the market." She noticed dark hairs popping out of George's ears. Were those hairs always there? She hadn't noticed them before.

George bent over to inspect his five o'clock shadow in the mirror.

Eleanor couldn't avoid seeing his rear end. A patch of hair nestled at the base of his back, trailing down to a brush of fur covering his cheeks.

"You don't have shaving cream, do you?" he asked, buttocks in full view, his bottom not quite as firm as she'd imagined. The cheeks were somewhat droopy.

"Please put something on," she begged.

"I will in a moment." George turned on the hair dryer, blasting his tousled hair. He lifted each arm, blowing warm air into his pits.

"George, I'm getting *depressed.*" It was a Freudian slip. "I mean, *dressed.*"

George ignored her as he turned the dryer on his crotch. "It feels so good," he said, eyes closed, a goofy smile on his face.

"George, really. I like my privacy when dressing. Can't you take that thing into another room?"

George pulled on the cord. "I don't think it'll reach."

Eleanor sighed. "That's because you have to unplug it. Here," she said handing the cord over. "Take it." She'd forgotten what it was like to have a man around.

"Dear God, men are animals," Eleanor later told Sylvia. "There's hair everywhere. In the shower. In the sink. And if he breaks wind one more time, I'm going to kill him."

Sylvia had joined Eleanor at the Boca Raton Resort & Club Hotel bar. She recoiled as if repulsed by the mere thought of a man living in her space. "It sounds dreadful. Are you sure you're not moving too fast? I thought he planned to move into a rental. Don't tell me he's living with you?"

"No, no," Eleanor assured her as she sipped a martini. "He only stays over every now and then. He has this silly dog, Miss Daisy or Betsy, or something like that. He walks her, and then brings her over to spend the night. I awoke one morning and found her in bed staring at me. She bared her teeth! It's disgusting. A dirty animal in the bed. I used to read two books a week. I haven't cracked a book open since George showed up."

Sylvia offered an empathetic murmur. "Don't let him stay over," she suggested, her Manhattan held high. "He'll just take advantage. Tell him you need your privacy. Better yet, why don't you stay at his place? At least that way, you can leave."

Eleanor thought the suggestion absurd. "He's moving soon. There are boxes everywhere. Besides, if I stay at George's place, I can't get up when I want. The whole day will revolve around that silly dog. None of my things are there. And I can't put on makeup in a strange man's bathroom."

"Have you seen where he's moving?"

"He drove me over to take a look it. It's like a twenty-something swinging-singles complex. The pool is *bikini central.* I have two sons older than most of the tenants. How can he live like that?"

"You've don't usually mention your children." Sylvia's voice was deeper.

Eleanor caught herself. She had no intention of sharing secrets with Sylvia. "What's there to say? I just forgot how messy men can be."

"They're horrible creatures."

"Now that I've let him in, I don't know how to put the brakes on. He's always walking around naked."

Sylvia made a face as if she'd just smelled something awful. "That's so wrong. Any man who walks around naked has no class."

"Is that a rule?" Eleanor asked seriously.

"If it isn't, it should be," Sylvia insisted.

"And he's always scratching himself," Eleanor squealed.

Sylvia appeared truly horrified. "When he's naked?"

"Oh, no." Eleanor laughed. "He must be saving that for our one-year anniversary."

"Anniversary?" Sylvia leaned in. "You're really serious about George."

"Oh, I'm just talking. I don't know how I feel. It's too soon."

"But you're thinking long-term. Is that why George is moving into a month-to-month rental?"

Eleanor puckered as if sucking a lemon. "Heavens no. We're not going to be living together."

"Ever?"

Eleanor had to admit that the possibility existed. "Well, who knows? There's something wonderful about having a man around. Even if they are filthy beasts."

Sylvia smiled. "I remember."

Eleanor knew so little about Sylvia's life. She couldn't resist asking. "So, how long has it been?"

"Been?" Sylvia sipped her martini.

"You know." Eleanor rolled her eyes. "Since you lived with a man."

Sylvia bit her lip. "A long time, Eleanor. A very long time. And let me just say, I won't be doing that again. I'm too set in my ways. And life is too short to acclimate to someone new. Hell, I'd get a puppy before that. And you know how long it takes to housebreak a puppy."

"Six months?"

"If they're smart. A man would probably take longer."

Eleanor giggled. "I just wish he wouldn't walk around naked."

"Today it's naked. Tomorrow, he's peeing all over the bathroom floor."

Eleanor winced. She'd already noticed wet spots around the toilet.

Sylvia texted George daily about the two-story Boca property he'd previewed, and though George had initially passed, Sylvia soldiered on, never one to easily concede a potential sale. George, for his part, had no desire to step back into the real estate market. With the move into the new apartment, he'd just started to get a grip on his expenses. And though he hadn't yet paid off Jeanette's medical bills, there was now cash sitting in the bank from the closing on the Boca property. He'd still need to sell some stock to cover a share of the medical bills, but that decision stubbornly remained for another day. For the moment, George luxuriated in his growing financial freedom. Medical bills and credit card balances aside, he was moving in the right direction.

"I'm just not interested," George repeated as they lunched together on the patio of Max's Grille in Mizner Park.

Sylvia had positioned the lunch as a celebration. Her way of thanking George for the listing. It was a lovely afternoon. Perfect weather for September. Mid-eighties. The gentlest of breezes.

Sylvia reached for her napkin, uncurling it and laying it across her lap. "Well, I'm still glad you agreed to meet today. There's something I'd like to talk to you about."

"You might as well give up," George answered. "I won't change my mind. I'm definitely staying in a rental."

"No, not that," Sylvia said as George sipped an iced tea. "We're friends, aren't we?" she innocently asked.

"Sure," George answered, though he didn't consider Sylvia a friend and he wasn't quite sure where the conversation was heading.

"Then let's do as friends do."

George had no idea what Sylvia was talking about. But she'd captured his attention.

"I know you and Eleanor are together."

George gave the napkin in his lap a twist. He'd no interest in talking to Sylvia about his relationship with Eleanor. True, he and Eleanor were together. But things had not progressed as he had hoped. Despite Eleanor opening up about her marriage, she still kept him at arm's length. Dinner once a week. A sleepover now and then. George had even spent a Sunday running errands with her, and still, their relationship was no more than a friendship with benefits. George was unable to crack Eleanor's shell.

"I think Eleanor's wonderful. Really, I do," Sylvia continued. "But George, I'm not sure you're fully aware of Eleanor's backstory."

There it was. Why did Sylvia always have to be so dramatic? "Backstory?" he asked.

"Yes, you know. The messy details that make us all tick."

"You mean how her husband, Joel, cheated on her? How her sons blamed her for Joel's premature death?"

Sylvia straightened up. Her head titled slightly as she took in the information.

Had George revealed more than Sylvia actually knew? Why did she seem so beguiled?

"Why, yes," she said quietly. "So you know."

George furrowed his brow. "Of course I do. She told me all about it."

Sylvia poked the saltshaker, nudging it along the table with the tip of a finger. "Well, I guess then there's nothing more to discuss."

"What do you mean?" George asked. "Is there something she hasn't told me?"

"George, I think I'd be out of line to share anything that Eleanor hasn't directly told you herself."

What more was there? He'd thought he'd heard it all. He'd believed Eleanor. But now, he wasn't sure. "Is there more?" he pressed, certain Sylvia might know.

Sylvia arched her back. “It’s not for me to say,” she answered, baiting George’s distrust. “You can draw your own conclusions. But if that is the type of woman who interests you, George, there’s nothing more I can say.”

“I swear, Sylvia. If there’s something you’re trying to tell me, just spit it out.”

Sylvia offered a coquettish grin. “Why George, I do believe you’re annoyed at me.”

George reached over and grabbed Sylvia’s wrist. “Just say it!”

Sylvia pulled her hand back. “George. I’ve never seen this side of you. It’s practically brutal.”

George struggled to maintain his temper. “I’m sorry. I hope I didn’t hurt you. I just don’t like being played with, Sylvia.”

“I think it’s rather attractive,” Sylvia whispered as she rubbed her wrist. “I hope Eleanor knows what she’s getting herself into.”

George had no idea what Sylvia was getting at.

“Whatever you think of me, George, I don’t hide who I am. And if you ever wanted to give it another shot,” she said, her eyes softening, “I’d do my best to make sure you were happy. Really, I would.”

George was speechless.

“I know how I come off. Hard. Take no prisoners. But I’m not really that way. At my core, I’m like anyone else. I need to love and be loved.”

“Sylvia, please…”

Her posture relaxed out of its usual stiffness. Her head not quite as high. “I treated you badly, George. I shouldn’t have done that. You’re a kind man. A caring man. I didn’t see that at first. But I’ve come to understand it.” She leaned forward, her eyes pleading. “Please don’t look at me as if I’ve just landed from outer space.”

George softened. “I’m sorry.”

"You seem so surprised. I guess that wasn't at all subtle," she said, the color rising in her cheeks. "You know, I've never been very good at subtle. In my world, subtlety doesn't close the sale. But one thing I've learned: when a deal goes south, it's best to walk away. And so, this is my cue."

As Sylvia stood, George noticed her eyes were moist. Was she about to cry?

"I've made my offer, George. And now, I'll leave you. Enjoy your lunch," she said as she turned on her heels and fled.

That night, George picked Eleanor up for dinner. He saw no reason to convey Sylvia's confession. What would be the point? It only reinforced his belief that Sylvia was not Eleanor's friend. He'd first shared that opinion with Eleanor at Willy's memorial gathering, but she had vehemently refuted it. And though Sylvia's proposal had come out of the blue, George thought Sylvia refreshingly vulnerable. Especially in light of Eleanor's resistance to share details about her family history. Had Eleanor not opened up about the difficulties in her marriage to Joel, and the break with her sons, George doubted he would have continued to see her. He'd been touched by her confession. Intrigued where their relationship might lead. He hoped to learn more about Eleanor's family, certain he was at the precipice of something special. A woman with whom he could spend the rest of his life.

At least, he hoped so.

With finances still very much on his mind, George chose Maggiano's Little Italy at Towne Center for dinner. Inexpensive and hearty. George's two favorite adjectives.

George spotted Eleanor by the entrance to the lobby of her building as he drove up. She looked stunning in a white pantsuit. Her aqua blouse was open at the collar to reveal a pearl choker. George wished he'd dressed better. He'd worn his favorite jeans and a short-sleeve pink and yellow Tommy Bahama toucan shirt. He caught Eleanor's expression when he came around to open the car door for her. It was subtle, but unmistakable. She was disappointed in his attire.

"You don't like what I'm wearing, do you?" he asked when he got into the car.

"I think you could have given it a bit more thought."

George bit his lip as a silence settled between them. He liked his clothes. He liked feeling comfortable. Besides, what did it matter what he was wearing? Wasn't his company more important than what he looked like? What was the point of buying expensive new clothes? He'd sold his condo to reduce expenses, not to spend money on things he didn't need. Which brought to mind the still-outstanding medical bills. Why hadn't he taken care of the bills yet? What was holding him back from settling those accounts? He wished he knew the answer.

Eleanor interrupted his mental spinning. "Maybe we should go shopping. It would be nice to see you in a sports coat. Preferably something not made with a *polyester* blend."

The word *polyester* stuck in George's craw. In Eleanor's enunciation, it was an insult. Jeanette had bought all his clothes. He'd relied on her to tell him what he should wear and how to dress. And though he knew Eleanor had no intention of insulting Jeanette, he couldn't help but feel defensive.

"I don't know why you care about this," he said as they merged onto the highway. "I've seen you in your sweats at home lounging about. And though you look wonderful tonight, you're not about clothes. Or things. I know that isn't who you are."

Eleanor shifted. "George, we don't really know each other very well. Yes, I like to be comfortable at home, but when out for the evening, I like to be dressed a certain way. I like a man to wear a sport coat when he picks me up. It's a small thing, but I think it shows good taste and respect."

"I think that's ridiculous. It's putting too much weight on superficial matters."

"You might be right. But these are the things we're going to learn about each other as we spend more time together. And perhaps, one day, you might wear a sport coat."

"And maybe one day, you'll leave your pearls at home."

"Maybe we'll have a blending of ideas."

"It's possible," George agreed.

"All things are possible," Eleanor answered. "As long as we're willing to try."

George liked the sound of that. "I'm willing," he confirmed. "I just wish we had history together. Wouldn't that be nice? I'd know your little peccadillos. You'd know mine."

"It would be nice," Eleanor agreed as traffic slowed to a crawl. "Make the next right, George. We can go the back way."

Indeed, there were many things they needed to learn about each other. One of them: George didn't like being given directions when he was driving.

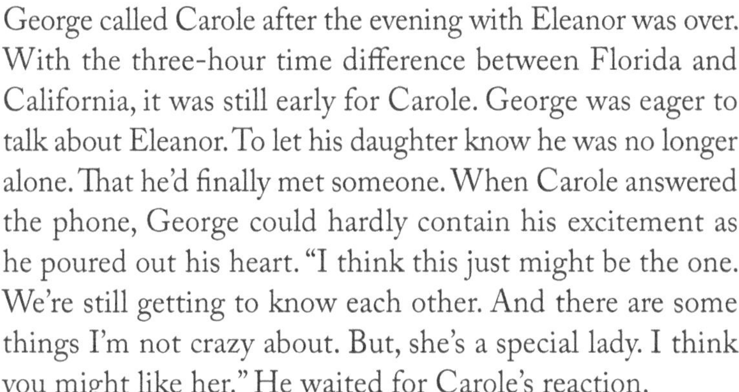

George called Carole after the evening with Eleanor was over. With the three-hour time difference between Florida and California, it was still early for Carole. George was eager to talk about Eleanor. To let his daughter know he was no longer alone. That he'd finally met someone. When Carole answered the phone, George could hardly contain his excitement as he poured out his heart. "I think this just might be the one. We're still getting to know each other. And there are some things I'm not crazy about. But, she's a special lady. I think you might like her." He waited for Carole's reaction.

"Oh," Carole said without enthusiasm. "I guess it was bound to happen. I just didn't think you'd meet someone so quickly."

"Quickly?" George was taken aback.

"Mother died last December. What's that? Nine months. I'm sure there have been plenty of women in your life since December."

The faces passed in front of George like floats in the Macy's Thanksgiving Day Parade: Ava Hendrickson from Tri-County Animal Rescue. Jill Winters from The Golden Funeral Home. Sylvia Haddit, the Realtor. Jordan Archer, the attorney. Valerie Cortland, the insurance agent and dance instructor. Dr. Julie Bishop, the otolaryngologist. And most importantly, Eleanor Rifkin. Some had been intimate relationships. Others, merely cordial. All were the women after Jeanette.

"I didn't call to talk about other women," George clarified, unwilling to cross that boundary with his daughter. "This is different." There was silence on the line as George struggled to determine the next thing to say. "I know you want me to be happy. And being alone is really no life."

Carole paused before answering. "So what would you like me to say?"

"I'm not asking for your approval, Carole."

"Of course not, but if she's important to you, I'd like to meet her. I think that's the very least you can do. Have you thought about coming to the Bay Area to visit?"

"It's a long flight, Carole. And we've only started to go together." He smiled. *Go together. What a quaint expression. Does anyone use that phrase anymore?*

"Have you told her about Peter? Does she know you have children?"

Carole's question sounded like an accusation. And yet, he couldn't deny that he hadn't shared much about the family. "Carole, I don't like your tone."

Carole laughed. "Oh Daddy, you're so transparent. Has anyone ever told you that? I can see right through you. I'm not even there and I can imagine the look on your face. Mother would have been upfront. But not you. There's always something to hide, isn't there?"

"Carole, that isn't true."

"Yes, it is. Face it. You don't like your children. You say you love me, but you don't like me. In fact, I'm not even sure how much you actually love me. I think that whole love thing from you is just a big charade. Your way of appearing like everyone else. Acceptable."

George swallowed. Was Carole right? Was that how he really felt about his children?

"Well don't worry, Daddy. I won't embarrass you by coming to visit and meeting your new lady friend. I wouldn't want to get in the way of whatever manufactured fantasy you've spun about our family. I'll let her see you in only the best light."

The conversation had somehow gotten away from him. "Carole, you're making too much of this."

"No, I think the real problem is that I didn't make more of it from the beginning. I just went along. Whatever you wanted, I did. *Poor dear. You just lost your wife. I mustn't upset Daddy*. Well, I have news for you. I lost my mother, but on the same day, I lost a father too. Only we didn't bury the body. You've hung around, lost, unsure of who you are. One thing is clear. You're not my father. You're someone I don't even know."

"Carole," George warned, "don't say something you'll regret."

Carole's voice quivered. "It's too late for regrets. It is what it is." She hung up.

George stood, phone in hand, wondering what the hell had just happened.

Eleanor reached for George's hand and gave it a squeeze as they walked through Mizner Park on a Friday evening. The entertainment district was packed with people. George had resisted coming. It'd been his special place with Jeanette. She loved to people watch. Somehow, it seemed disloyal to walk through the same space, stare at the same sights, with another woman. A woman who most certainly was not Jeanette.

"George, why the unhappy face?" Eleanor asked as they came upon a 1965 classic red Rolls Royce Silver Cloud parked in front of the valet stand at Ruth's Chris Steak House. Eleanor didn't bother to wait for George to answer. She broke away to peek at the car's interior. "Oh, George." Eleanor's voice boomed. "Did you ever see such a beautiful car? Wouldn't you love to own it?"

"It's a little beyond my means," George muttered as he waited on the sidewalk for Eleanor. He hadn't thought she'd heard him until she glanced over.

"How much do you think a car like this costs?" she asked as if seriously contemplating such an extravagant purchase.

"I guess whatever you want to pay, if you love it."

"But it isn't your thing, is it?" Eleanor clasped his hand and continued their walk.

"I appreciate the car, the nostalgia, but I don't want to spend my precious capital on something like that. It's a gas guzzler. And who needs such fancy transportation? I think it's kind of ostentatious. Showy. A 'Look at me, I'm rich' kind of car."

Eleanor had a quizzical look. "I don't think there's anything wrong, if you have the money to enjoy it."

"I agree," George said. "But why flaunt it like that?"

"Maybe they just love classic cars. Maybe they're using their resources to enrich their lives. Some people work hard for what they have. Why not spend it on the things you enjoy?"

"I suppose," was the best answer George could muster.

"Expensive things enhance your life. It makes waking up a joy."

"I'd rather make a donation to a worthwhile charity."

"Really? And what charity have you given money to in the last year?" Eleanor asked.

George blushed. "I haven't gotten around to it yet."

"It sounds to me," Eleanor said, gently swinging George's hand in hers, "that you're prejudiced against the rich. That's almost as offensive as being prejudiced against the poor."

George was startled. Is that what he'd said? Did he hold a grudge against people who spent their money on over-the-top possessions? "Absolutely not," he insisted, certain it was a matter of values. "I just worked too hard in my life to piss away money on frivolities when there are any number of perfectly beautiful cars to buy that will serve the same purpose."

"You're so practical, George."

George might have normally taken that as a compliment, but coming out of Eleanor's mouth, it felt like an insult. "Well, we just have different ideas about money," he said, hoping to end the conversation.

"Yes. I like money. And I like to spend it. That, of course, is my prerogative. After all, I have no one to leave my money to."

"You have two sons," George reminded her.

Eleanor stopped walking and turned to George. "I don't want to talk about my sons."

George nodded, understanding that it had to be a sensitive subject. "You know, you're not the only one with family problems. My daughter hung up on me last night."

Eleanor seemed surprised. "She did?"

"Carole has very definite feelings about my life and how I'm living it."

"She sounds judgmental."

George suddenly felt protective of Carole. "No, she's a good kid. We just have this…" He searched for the word.

"Struggle. She thinks I could have been a better father. I suppose she's right."

"But she's an adult now," Eleanor pointed out. "She no longer needs a father. She has no right to make you feel bad about your choices."

How in the world had they come to discuss Carole? "Well, she's angry. And my son, Peter. I've avoided his calls. He overwhelms me. At his age, I was already living my life. I had a family. Peter's still so immature. His life is so unsettled."

"Does he have a job?" Eleanor asked.

"Yes. He's a very successful IT guy in Chicago."

"Then it sounds like his life is set."

"Your life is so much more than what you do during the day. I've tried to talk with him, but we just don't connect. Peter wants too much of me. I don't know half the time what to say to him."

Eleanor sighed. "You're better off then."

George caught Eleanor's eye. "What do you mean?"

"You're better off without them, George. I know. Life is too complicated when your adult children behave as if you've disappointed them. I say, move on. Be grateful you're still young enough to have your own life."

George wondered if Eleanor was right. Maybe the challenge he faced with his adult children was more about them than him. Maybe it was time to just let it be. Let them live their own lives and he'd live his. It certainly seemed worth considering.

"So, George," Benny asked between bites of a TooJay's hot dog piled high with sauerkraut. "What's the deal with Angela? Are you two going to be eventually moving in together? And more importantly, when are you meeting Willy's brother? Are we ever going to get reimbursed for Willy's funeral expenses?"

George sidestepped the Angela/Eleanor discussion. "I'm all set with Willy. I mean Wally. We're meeting tomorrow morning at his hotel for breakfast. Nine thirty a.m."

Herbie's hands were wrapped about a double cheeseburger. "Tomorrow? When were you planning to tell us?" He opened his mouth to take a bite.

George was reminded of a hippopotamus he'd once seen at a nature preserve. "I'm telling you now. Besides, I only agreed to meet with him because you guys asked me to. Why me, I'm not even sure anymore."

Benny wiped his mouth with a napkin. "Thanks for doing it, George. I, for one, appreciate it."

Burger juice trickled down Herbie's face. "Aren't you the least bit curious?" he managed to ask as he chewed.

George had to admit, he wasn't. "Frankly, I don't care anymore about why he didn't show at the funeral. I just want to get reimbursed. Does the rest really matter? Isn't it just old news?"

"No," Herbie said. Bits of burger sprayed across the table. "It's an outrage. Imagine your brother not bothering to show at your funeral. It's inconceivable."

George was suddenly grateful he was an only child. "Christ, Herbie. There could be a thousand reasons. And don't talk with your mouth full. It's disgusting."

Benny laughed. "Herbie, where were you raised? In a barn?"

Herbie flashed an annoyed glance. "I challenge you to name three good reasons for missing that funeral," he said to George as he reached for a napkin and wiped his mouth.

George counted on his fingers. "Number one. They hated each other."

Benny nodded. "Possible. But Willy wasn't that kind of guy. How could anyone hate him?"

George held up a second finger. "Two. The guy lives out of town. There's an airline strike. He couldn't make a connection."

"No way," Herbie said. "There wasn't a strike that week. If there had been, we would have known about it."

George ignored Herbie. "Three. His dog got sick. You know how it is when your dog gets sick. It screws up all your plans."

Benny's eyes sparkled. "Dog? You don't know if he has a dog."

Herbie chimed in. "You and that dog of yours. That's not love. That's an obsession."

George sipped his coffee. It was true. He didn't know if Willy's brother had a dog. But still, it seemed a plausible reason. "Well, I didn't say I had the answer. I just said I could name three good reasons."

Benny scratched at his beard. A fleck of something landed on his shirt. "You're crazy, George. Really. A total nutcase."

George looked at his friends and raised his coffee mug as if toasting them. "I must be, with friends like you guys."

Eleanor retreated to the bathroom as George stretched out on the bed. He'd stopped at Eleanor's after lunch, and as usual, things wrapped up in the guest bedroom. He checked the clock. It was four in the afternoon.

He closed his eyes just as Eleanor reemerged.

"George," she whispered.

When he opened his eyes, she was in a white bathrobe, hair wrapped in a towel. She smelled of honey and jasmine, as if she'd showered in a summer field. She nudged him over with a gentle poke, then she squeezed onto the edge of the bed. "George, you like it here, don't you?" she asked, leaning down, her face near his. Her breath was minty fresh. "George, are you awake?"

George smiled. "I am now."

"So tell me what you think."

George shifted. A foot kicked out from under the top sheet. The silky softness of the bed still cradled him in the afterglow of their lovemaking. "It's nice," he muttered, mostly asleep.

"Then you should move in with me," Eleanor announced. "We should live together."

George hadn't anticipated this. For someone who had her walls up, Eleanor's invitation was sudden. Had he misheard her? Was he still asleep? Had it been a dream?

George was unsure what to say.

"George!" Eleanor poked him in the side. "Did you hear me?"

– 22 –

George rushed through the lobby of the Boca Raton Marriott. A car crash on I-95, and the endless traffic lights, had messed with his punctuality after he'd dropped off Miss Betsy at the groomer appointment in Delray. He checked his watch. Twenty minutes late. *Jeez, this is bad.* He looked about the hotel lobby. Wally was nowhere to be found.

"Where is that guy?" George muttered. He imagined Benny and Herbie's reaction. He could already hear them. *What were you thinking, George? How long have you lived in Florida? You should have taken the side streets. You never get on I-95 during rush hour.*

George stopped at the restaurant's hostess stand. "Excuse me, has anyone asked for George Elden? I'm supposed to meet a friend."

The hostess offered a blank stare. George wondered if it was her everyday expression. "Who?" she asked.

"Never mind." George was certain the poor thing had just awoken, alarmed to find herself at work.

"George?" A voice called from a far corner of the lobby. There, sitting with an open newspaper in his lap, was the spitting image of Willy. If George hadn't been at the funeral, he'd have sworn it *was* Willy.

"I'm sorry," George apologized. "I'm never late."

"Not a problem." Wally closed the newspaper and stood up.

George had forgotten Willy was so short. Wally barely came up to George's chest. But the blue eyes were the kicker. So very much like Willy's. For a moment, George forgot the intention of the meeting, where they were, and that this was indeed Willy's twin. The whole thing seemed impossible. Eerily bizarre.

"I thought you'd eventually show," Wally said, breaking the spell. "I hope this meeting will be more civil than the last."

"I can guarantee that," George said, aware that Wally might have forgiven George's lateness, but he wasn't going to overlook the fracas at Morton's. George extended a hand in the direction of the dining room. "Shall we have breakfast?"

"Actually, I've already eaten. I'm an early riser. Besides, that isn't the reason you wanted to meet. To eat breakfast."

"No," George admitted. "Obviously, that's not the reason."

"Then how about we pass on the dining room and grab a cup of coffee instead?"

George watched as Wally poured skim milk into his coffee. Wally had selected a high-top table with metal stools at the rear of the coffee shop. George worried the hard seat might inflame his sciatica.

"I used to take cream in my coffee," Wally explained as he stirred the hot liquid, "but then I decided I was getting a little too big. When I learned about Willy's heart attack, I was sorry I didn't change my diet sooner. But there was a time when I didn't expect to live this long. There aren't many men of my generation still out and about."

George offered a skeptical look. "In Florida, there are lots of men in their sixties, seventies, and eighties. We're at a premium, but we're here!"

Wally nodded. "Not where I live. There's an entire generation of gay men missing. Wiped out by AIDS. The rest of us don't go out much. We tend to stay home. Bars and the internet dating sites are mostly for younger men."

George was dumbfounded. "Gay?"

"Yes," Wally said. "I'm a gay man."

"Oh," George stumbled. "I'm sorry. I didn't know."

Wally narrowed his eyes. "There's no reason to be sorry."

"Well it's just, I had no idea. You'd never know."

Wally looked askance at George. "Is that supposed to be a compliment?"

George sensed he'd said the wrong thing. "I just had no idea."

"Of course you didn't. Willy never talked about me. He was ashamed."

"Was Willy gay, too?"

Wally let out a laugh. "Is that what you think? Because I'm gay, Willy must have been gay."

George didn't know what he thought or why he was saying what he was saying. He'd never given much thought to gay people. "Look. I'm not great with words," George admitted. "If I've offended you, it certainly wasn't my intention. I just—"

"Have never met a gay man."

"Right," George said, relieved Wally understood.

"But you have."

"Have I?"

"Certainly. You've met gay men. Lesbians too. We're your lawyers, doctors, construction workers, barbers. We service your pools, do your gardening, and are your librarians. We're your accountants, nurses, and dentists."

George thought of his accountant, Irving Levine. He'd been too ashamed to discuss his financial situation with Irving. But now with the condo sold, he owed Irving a call. "No. Irving's married with grandchildren. Not gay."

Wally squinted. "What?"

"Irving Levine, my CPA. He's definitely straight."

"I'm just saying, we're everywhere. In plain view. Except, of course, in Hollywood. There are no gay leading men."

"Really?"

"No," Wally said. "I'm being facetious. That seems the only industry where we're still mostly closeted. America isn't quite ready for a gay leading man. Although, there are probably plenty in their midst."

George had no idea about gay movie stars. He'd only seen a few movies since Jeanette had died. Without her to prod him, he'd lost interest in going. He fidgeted with his coffee, gently moving the cup back and forth.

"Am I making you nervous?" Wally focused on George like a hawk. "Don't tell me. You're uncomfortable being with a gay man."

George swallowed. Was he? Or was he just unnerved by how much the two brothers looked alike? "Why would I care about you being gay?"

"I can't imagine," Wally answered. "I'm not a mind reader."

George looked about. Was there anyone he knew around? Anyone to whom he might have to explain this meeting with Wally?

"Are you expecting someone?" Wally asked, still on alert. "Valerie told me it would be just the two of us. If those other guys are coming, I'm leaving. Especially that big guy."

"Sorry," George said. "I was just thinking how easy it'd be to be mistaken for gay. Take Herbie and Benny. We spend so much time together. On the golf course. At lunch. Meeting for breakfast. That certainly doesn't make us gay."

Wally smirked. "Is that what you're concerned about? Whether you and your buddies look gay?"

"No, not at all," George said, slightly rattled. "I'm just saying, it's hard to tell if someone is gay. So when did you know?" he asked, genuinely curious. "How old were you?"

Wally mulled the question over. "Probably the same time you knew you were straight. When did you figure that out?"

George confidently smiled. "I always knew."

Wally's eyes sparked. "You did!"

George recognized sarcasm when he heard it. "Yes," George confirmed. "There's no need to make fun of me."

"Well, good for you," Wally said, arms crossed. "It must be nice to be you."

George exhaled. "Did I say something wrong?"

"You?" Wally replied. "How could you ever say anything wrong?"

George arched a brow. "Okay, I can tell that this conversation isn't going well. I've upset you. I can tell we're…" George searched for the right words. "Not on the same page."

"I wouldn't say that," Wally answered, lifting his head slightly, sticking his chin out. "You're just as I imagined."

"Excuse me?"

"You, my brother. Those other two clowns."

"Hey," George said, a finger pointing at Wally. "Those are my friends. Your brother was my friend."

"Friends," Wally said in a low voice. "Such good friends. You didn't even know Willy had a twin. What else don't you know about Willy? Probably everything about his life."

George was immediately defensive. "If he'd wanted us to know, we'd have known."

"Fair enough. But don't you think being a twin is a detail a friend would know?"

"We were golf buddies," George answered, unsure if that explained anything.

"Is that a different kind of friendship? Friends who enjoy riding in golf carts together?"

George gripped the edge of the table. "I don't know where you're going with this. Do you want me to say we weren't very good friends? Okay. We sucked. You must have been a better friend. After all, you were his twin. We just golfed together. There. Happy? You knew him. We didn't."

"I only wish that were true." There was regret in his voice.

George stared at the man before him. How could someone look so familiar but be a total stranger? It didn't seem possible. "Now, you're confusing me."

"Clearly." Wally sipped his coffee. "It's easy to trip you straight boys up."

George laughed. "Boys."

Wally leaned forward. "Okay, fun and games are over, George. We have a lot to discuss. And I'm not sure you're going to like hearing any of it. In fact, I guarantee you won't."

George was alarmed. "You're not going to tell me about your sex life."

Wally's eyes lit up with amusement. "Are you for real? Now why would I ever do that?"

George blushed. "I don't know. It just sounded like you were building up to something."

"I am," Wally agreed. "But it isn't about my sex life. It's about my brother's life. You two seem to be a lot alike. Maybe, there's a lesson here for you. It'd be nice to think I was helping someone. That Willy's mistakes weren't going to be repeated."

George shifted. "A lesson for me. How could there be? I'm not gay."

"No, you certainly aren't. But you don't have to be gay to come from a family that treats you poorly. There are all sorts of reasons people think they have the right to pass judgment on your life."

George settled back in the chair. "You're one unhappy guy."

Wally nodded. "Now that I agree with. Being in Florida, dealing with Willy's death, and my own health problems, has taken a toll."

"Well, I'm sorry to hear that," George said. But he wasn't sorry. He didn't like Wally. He hoped it didn't show.

"Sorry about what?" Wally pressed. "What exactly are you sorry about?"

"You know," George said, fingers flicking back and forth over the coffee cup.

"No, I don't," Wally continued. "Please, tell me."

"Your health problems," George awkwardly said.

"What are my health problems?" Wally asked, eyes wide with anticipation of George's answer.

"I have no idea," George admitted as he looked down. "How should I know?"

Wally giggled. "You're such an easy target…that's the problem. No wonder you knew nothing about my brother. You don't ask the next question."

George recoiled. "What do you mean?"

"The next question," Wally repeated. "Someone has just told you they're having health problems and instead of inquiring into their health, you let the subject drop. Why would you do that?"

George said the first thought that came to mind. "Some people think it's rude to inquire into matters that are none of their business."

"Yes, I suppose you're right," Wally said, considering. "But I'd bet anything that is exactly how you are with your friends. Maybe that's the reason you know nothing about their lives."

"Hey," George protested. "You don't know me. I didn't agree to meet so you could lecture me."

Wally sipped his coffee. "Okay; maybe you have a point."

George smiled, proud of himself for speaking up.

"That said, you're still a douchebag for not asking the next question."

George weighed his options. "Okay, tell me. What's your terrible health problem? What awful circumstance kept you away from your brother's funeral? And why, for God's sake, have we had to track you down to get reimbursed for the funeral expenses?"

"So," Wally said as if he understood the whole purpose of the meeting for the first time since he'd met George. "It's all about money."

"No," George argued. "Not just the money."

"Oh, yes it is."

"The money would be nice," George repeated. "The cost of the funeral was the responsibility of the executor."

"I agree," Wally said. "But I'm not the executor of the estate."

George's mouth hung open. "But you're the brother."

Wally let out a guffaw.

"You're not the executor?" George asked.

"Nope," Wally shot back. "But I know all about my brother. And the identity of the executor."

George was more confused than ever. "Well, if you're not the executor, why am I sitting here talking to you?"

"Because," Wally said, an impervious look in his eyes, "you want to know why no one from the family attended the funeral. Specifically, me."

George licked his lips. Wally was right. "I do want to hear the story," George admitted.

Wally pressed his palms together as if in prayer. "When we were growing up, my brother and I were very close. Maybe too close. And so when I came out, Willy couldn't tolerate me. What did it mean about him if his twin was gay?"

George took a guess. "Most people would have assumed Willy was also gay."

"Right," Wally agreed. "And so Willy walked away. He decided he didn't have a brother. He wasn't a twin. He just cut me out."

George could see the hurt in Wally's eyes. He wondered how he'd have felt in the same situation. Would he have been able to accept a gay twin?

"But it wasn't just about Willy abandoning me. In fact, it turns out, it wasn't about me at all. It was Willy's pattern. His modus operandi. In Willy's life, when things got tough, he walked away."

George doubted that was true. "We were friends for years," he said as if that fact could wipe out Wally's truth.

Wally clarified. "That's because you were a certain type of friend."

George frowned. "I don't know what that means."

"Had you known Willy, really known him, the friendship wouldn't have lasted."

George twisted his coffee cup. "I don't know about that."

"I do. He did it to me. He did it to his two wives. He did it to his son. There's a long trail of people in his life he lost touch with. By the way, have you ever met my nephew?"

George nodded. "Simon."

"He's a terrific kid. When do you think he last spoke to his dad?"

"You mean before Willy died?"

Wally offered George an incredulous look. "Well, I don't mean after."

George put two and two together. He'd heard Mona's version. Then Simon's. "So, Willy ended the relationship with Simon."

"Yes, Willy ended the relationship," Wally confirmed.

"But why?" George wanted to know.

Wally contorted his face. "When Willy married Mona, Simon was going through a rebellious stage. To put it mildly,

Mona wasn't receptive. A young boy wants his father's attention. His approval. But then, don't we always?"

George couldn't remember his father. The man had died when George was just six years old. Is that why George was such a lousy father? Were there lessons to be learned that he missed out on?

"Willy had no time for Simon. And then, years later, when Willy might have mended the relationship, Simon gave up practicing law."

George thought of the scruffy-faced young man. He'd forgotten he was a lawyer.

"Willy didn't like that turn of events. My brother could be a damn fool. He was adamant that the reason Simon quit was to live off of Willy's money. Imagine that. He thought that brilliant young man was interested in his money."

George thought about his relationship with his own son. "Sons and fathers are complicated."

Wally shrugged. "I have no idea what that means." He ran a palm over the table as if sweeping George's comment away. "If I had a son, I'd never walk away from the relationship."

For a moment, George forgot they were discussing Simon. "It's easy to judge. You don't have kids. How would you know?"

Wally nodded. "You two were friends! That sounds exactly like Willy. 'You're not a parent,' he'd crow. As if that had anything to do with it."

"Well, you're not," George said.

"That's obvious," Wally conceded. "But you don't need to shame me out of having an opinion."

"Shame you? I'm not shaming you."

"Sure you are. You don't like what I'm saying, so you go for the jugular. Like I would have no idea what it's like to be a parent. Like I was raised on a deserted island. I had parents. I grew up in a family. It doesn't take a lot of imagination to understand the blood, sweat, and tears that goes into parenting. I'm sure it's a thankless job at times. But to reject your kid because he's inconvenient. Or he isn't living up to your standards. Or isn't who you hoped he'd be. Well, I don't need to be an expert in family psychology to know that's wrong."

George immediately thought of Peter and Carole. "Some kids are difficult personalities."

"And you think you're the easiest person to get along with? Heck, I just met you and I already feel like smacking some sense into you."

George frowned. He didn't like being directly challenged.

"Your wife must have her work cut out for her," Wally said.

"My wife is dead," George announced, hoping to make Wally feel small.

The expression on Wally's face shifted. He didn't look embarrassed. He looked pained.

Suddenly, George felt small.

"Me and my big mouth," Wally said. "I'm sorry. How long were you married?"

"A long time," George answered, unwilling to reveal too much, afraid that whatever he might say would be used against him.

Wally slumped his shoulders. "It's a hard time in life when you lose that special person with whom you hoped to spend the rest of your life."

George offered a meager "Yes."

"Well, George. That's too bad. You must be lonely."

"I manage," George answered.

Wally's eyes registered a certain understanding. "Oh," was all he said, as if he suspected there was more to the story than George was telling.

"What?" George asked.

"You've met a woman," Wally guessed. "Are you still talking to your children?"

George made a guttural sound.

"I see. You *were* a close friend of my brother! They say birds of a feather flock together. Now, I get it."

"How about we just wrap this up? Write me a check for the funeral and I'll reimburse the other guys."

Wally smiled. "Gosh. You really don't listen, do you? I've already told you. I'm not the executor."

In all the back and forth, it had slipped George's mind. "Right," he affirmed. "But you know the name of the executor."

Wally hesitated. "Have you heard anything I've said today? Does any of it resonate with you?"

"I've heard everything. The sad tale of you and your brother. Too bad about that. And I've heard your criticism of me. Okay. I'm a real stinker. A bad listener. A bad father. I've heard it all and I've been polite. It hasn't been easy, but I've done my best. Now, all I want is the reimbursement for the funeral expenses. And, maybe you can explain why you bothered to personally call me out on all this."

Wally offered a surprised look. "George, I don't know you. I have no idea what kind of father you are. I was telling you about Willy."

"Right," George said, realizing Wally knew nothing about his life or his relationship with his children.

Wally smiled. "I didn't ask to meet you. You asked to meet me."

"Well it's been nice," George said, hoping to gracefully end the conversation. "But I think I've heard just about enough. Before I go, let me just say, Willy wasn't the guy you describe. Had you bothered to attend the funeral, you'd have seen he was beloved. The place was packed. And the same was true for his celebration of life. Mona had a full house. Too bad you weren't there to meet the many people who loved Willy."

There was a pained look in Wally's eyes. "So you think I didn't attend the funeral because I didn't love my brother?"

"Well, you certainly have nothing good to say about him."

Wally shook his head. "You don't understand. I loved Willy. I wasn't the one who put up the roadblocks. I wasn't the one who walked away from my son. That wasn't me. I loved my brother," Wally repeated.

"So where were you that day?" George wanted to know.

Wally paled. "I was in the hospital."

George swallowed. "Did you know Willy had died?"

"Yes, I knew," Wally whispered.

George felt like a heel. "I see," was all he could manage.

"You're right, George. We don't know each other. But I'd bet my soul that you've no intention of asking me why I was in the hospital."

George stared at Wally, uncertain what to say.

Wally shook his head. "Boy, you're really lousy at asking the next question, aren't you? I'll make it easy on you. The day of the funeral, I was in the emergency room at St. Mary's Medical Center. I'd been experiencing intense back pain, nausea, and vomiting. Since then, I've gone through a battery of tests. Turns out, I have pancreatic cancer. I've enrolled in an experimental drug trial. So, I'm here in Florida for the short-term. I'll be checking back into the hospital tomorrow for another overnight stay."

George walked out of the Boca Marriott past the tony shops with their sumptuous window displays of expensive merchandise and fine gifts. The conversation with Wally had struck a chord. And though Wally had not been talking about George, what he'd described of Willy's life resonated.

Had George, too, failed his children?

George's family life passed before him as if he was a spectator seated in a darkened theater. There was Jeanette interacting with Peter and Carole. Birthdays. Graduations.

Holidays. He could hear their voices. The laughter and the moments of family distress. He'd been there. Of that, he was certain. But had he been really present? Actually participated? Or did he just stand on the sidelines and watch the action, never truly part of it?

He'd done his best as a father. He'd provided for the family. His children had been raised in a lovely neighborhood with good schools and lots of friends. They'd gone to summer camps and enjoyed the best of vacations. Jeanette had provided a stable family life. And yet, George could still hear Jeanette's plea. "George, I wish you'd spend more time with Peter. Explore his interests. And Carole needs to know her father. Little girls rely on that special bond."

He'd heard Jeanette, but hadn't accepted the guidance. There was always something else on his mind. Another business deal. Another board meeting. His discomfort with Peter and Carole only intensified as they grew up. He relied on Jeanette to smooth it all over. To fill him in on what he should know of his children's lives. Everything about Carole and Peter had come through the prism of Jeanette's lens. He'd accepted her observations as fact. Allowed her to set the tone. She'd been the glue that held the family of strangers together.

But at what cost?

His phone pinged. Carole had left a voicemail.

He wasn't up to a conversation with Carole. The last one had ended badly. He wasn't in the mood to spar again.

He railed against the inner voice that prompted, *Call her back.*

He stopped in front of the Vertu Fine Art Gallery display window. A framed portrait of a woman wearing a kerchief and holding a blue umbrella in the rain stared back at him. The Alex Katz painting was the spitting image of Jeanette as a young woman. George stared at the picture, waiting for confirmation he'd been a good father. That he'd loved his children. Perhaps all he needed was to reach out and make amends.

"Did I miss your call?" he asked when Carole answered the phone.

"Yes. I was just thinking of you."

It was as if nothing earlier had happened. No angry words. George imagined he was once again the respected father. She, the dutiful daughter.

"What's going on?" George asked, struggling to engage.

"I was wondering if you've moved in with that woman you were talking about the other day."

George suddenly remembered his lunch date with Eleanor. He was supposed to be at her condo by eleven a.m. He checked his watch. He'd lost track of time. It was ten forty. "Oh, honey. I just realized I'm running late."

"So the minute we're on the phone, you have to go?"

George looked off in the distance as a yellow Mustang, top down, sped by. He wished he was in that car. Heading off somewhere. Perhaps a drive down to the Keys. Or maybe north, and across the state to Orlando. "Carole, we're just dating."

"You really like her."

"I do," George said, growing increasingly uncomfortable. He struggled to find something else to talk about. "Have you spoken to Peter lately?"

"No."

"Oh." The tension was palpable.

"Have you spoken to him?" she asked.

It had been weeks since George had heard Peter's voice.

"George," Carole asked, "when did you realize you didn't like Peter?"

George was caught off guard. There it was again. Carole needling him. "What are you talking about?"

"I know you have a problem with Peter. I'm not blind."

"I'm not sure how to answer. It's not that I don't like him," he stammered. "We're just…different."

"It's more than that," Carole pressed.

George squeezed his eyes shut. Why did Carole always make things so hard? Perhaps it was time to turn the tables. Give Carole a taste of her own medicine. "And how about you?" George asked. "When did you decide you didn't like Peter?"

There was a long silence.

"Carole? Are you still there?"

"I was fairly young." Her tone was strained. "Ten years old."

George was surprised. "Ten? What happened when you were ten? Did he hide a favorite doll? Tease you? Older brothers do that."

"That's when he started *touching me*," she answered.

"What?" George was uncertain he'd heard Carole correctly. "I don't understand. Did your mother know?"

"Mom knew," Carole acknowledged.

George reeled. Any illusion of a normal family shattered. "And your mother kept this from me?" He could hear Carole breathing on the other end of the line. "I swear," he said. "This is the first I'm hearing of it. I had absolutely no idea."

"You didn't?" Carole sounded incredulous.

"Of course not," George snapped.

"What do you think you would have done had you known?" Her voice was deeper, more intent.

George struggled to answer. "I just wish you'd told me. That someone had told me."

"It's not always about you, George."

What did Carole mean? "Don't say that. I'm only concerned for you."

"Me?" Carole said, her voice cracking. "When were you ever concerned about me?"

George thought the remark unfair. "I should have known. But I swear to you. I didn't. There's nothing I can say now to make it better. But you should have told me."

"Make it better?" Carole said, her voice haughty. "So now I'm wrong for not telling you. Somehow, this whole thing is my fault and you're the victim?"

George exhaled. It had been a foolish choice of words. Nothing more.

"You should be apologizing for being a lousy parent," Carole quietly said.

George tensed. "Carole, I can't apologize for something I didn't know about. This is your mother's fault. She should have told me."

"You're so predictable, George. I knew I shouldn't have said anything. I knew you'd never own this."

He didn't want to get mad, but he was mad. Mad at Jeanette for keeping a secret; mad at himself for not knowing what was going on under his own roof. "I know Peter has problems. Once, when he was a teenager..." George's voice trailed off.

"It wasn't once."

George bit his lower lip as he suddenly realized the impact of Peter's behavior. Why hadn't he known about it? Had he deliberately looked away? He wished Jeanette were alive. She'd remind him about what he knew. She'd speak up for him. She'd know how to best handle the situation.

"There's no point, George, in rehashing all this," Carole said.

"There is..." George said, voice weak as he suddenly realized Carole was calling him by his first name. "What is this George thing? When did I become George?"

"I think you've always been, George. I just decided it's time to acknowledge it. Let's face facts. You don't care about anyone but yourself. That's how it's always been. And I doubt you ever loved me or Peter."

George's head was spinning. "You've got me all wrong, Carole."

"I don't think so, George. I know perfectly well who you are," she whispered before dropping the call.

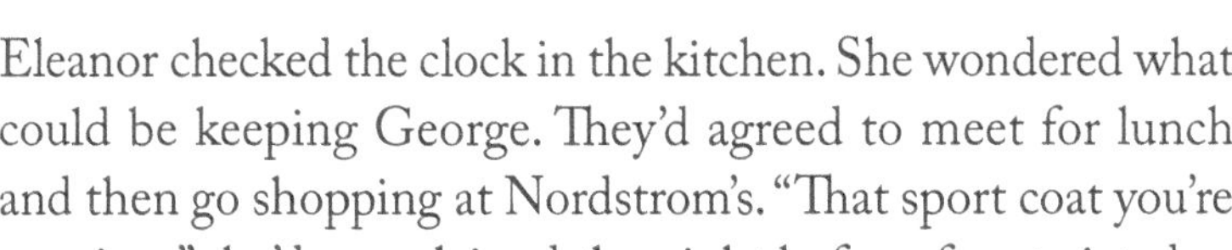

Eleanor checked the clock in the kitchen. She wondered what could be keeping George. They'd agreed to meet for lunch and then go shopping at Nordstrom's. "That sport coat you're wearing," she'd complained the night before, face twisted as if smelling something awful, "has got to go."

Had she been too direct? A bit insensitive?

She grew increasingly impatient. *Where can he be? He said he'd be over by eleven. He should have texted.* And though she certainly could have texted him, she didn't. Instead, she gritted her teeth and wondered why men were so inconsiderate. Joel had often kept her waiting. Was this a pattern of behavior she was willing to put up with again?

Eleanor's phone pinged with a text from Sylvia. She was nearby and wanted to grab lunch. She offered to pick Eleanor up. *Why not?* Eleanor reasoned. *George needs to be taught a lesson.*

"Are you okay?" Sylvia asked as the car exited Eleanor's security gate and turned onto Glades Road.

"I'm so darn mad," Eleanor grumbled from the passenger seat, unable to contain her emotions. "George has me waiting around. He just stood me up for lunch. It's so rude. And this isn't the first time he's kept me waiting."

Sylvia glanced over. "Have you talked to him about it?"

Eleanor hadn't. "He should know better. I shouldn't have to tell him."

"Sweetie, you can't expect a man to read your mind."

"If a man respects a woman, he's concerned about her feelings."

"Yes," Sylvia agreed. "I suppose that rule applies to friends too."

"Absolutely," Eleanor said. "We should all be considerate of each other."

"So, do you think you've been a good friend?"

It was an odd question coming from Sylvia. Their friendship had been mostly cordial. Eleanor hadn't shared her inner self with Sylvia. She'd certainly kept the truth about Joel and her boys hidden. But then, Sylvia had handled the friendship in the same way. Eleanor knew practically nothing about her. They'd been purely social friends. Sylvia camouflaging with a mask of frivolity.

"I don't know if I've been a good friend," Eleanor answered. "You're the only one who can answer that question."

Sylvia pulled into a spot in front of The Cheesecake Factory.

"Oh God." Eleanor cringed. "We're eating here?"

Sylvia turned off the ignition. "You said you didn't care where we had lunch."

Eleanor dropped her shoulders. "Fine."

"No," Sylvia said. "If you want to go somewhere else, just tell me."

Eleanor had no idea where else to go. She wasn't even hungry. Just mad. Mad at George. "This is okay," she relented as she stepped out of the car.

"Things must be really bad between you and George," Sylvia guessed as Eleanor walked ahead. "You're practically raging."

Eleanor pretended not to hear Sylvia as they crossed the restaurant's threshold. To the right, a long glass case of the world's most gorgeous cheesecakes greeted them. Every possible variety. Eleanor thought, *Screw that SkinnyLicious menu. I'm eating cake!*

"Did you hear me?" Sylvia asked as she caught up to Eleanor. "Are you going to end it with George?"

Eleanor gave Sylvia a dismissive look. "Really Sylvia, there are so many more interesting things to talk about than George."

"Eleanor, you brought him up. In fact, that's all you've been talking about since you got into the car."

Eleanor detected an edge in Sylvia's voice. Where was the conversation going? And why did Sylvia seem upset over Eleanor's relationship with George? Was she on a fishing expedition, trying to learn details Eleanor had no intention of sharing? Had Eleanor already shared too much?

"George isn't any man," Sylvia contended as they waited by the hostess stand. "He's different. Sweet. Maybe you should think twice before you make his life too difficult."

Eleanor laughed. "A man is a man. Someone like you should know that by now."

The hostess signaled. She was ready to escort them to a table.

"Actually," Sylvia said as she followed Eleanor, "your affair with George really isn't that unique."

Eleanor stopped. Together they stood amid the buzz of lunchtime chatter. Two women heading for a reckoning. "What exactly are you saying?"

Sylvia waved a hand as if dismissing Eleanor's sudden intensity. "Nothing, dear. Let's just go sit down."

"No," Eleanor said. "Not until you clarify that statement."

Sylvia sighed. "You're not the first Boca matron to discover their man toy is unfaithful."

Eleanor was aghast. She hadn't considered George might be fooling around with other women. What had Sylvia heard? Could it be true?

Sylvia placed a hand on her heart. "I hate to be the one to tell you," she said with all the warmth of an alligator sizing up a goat on the shore. "For months, George has been bed hopping from one lady to the next. It's not surprising he finally landed in your bed. He must have smelled the desperation. And by the way, I know all about your terrible marriage and those sons who want nothing to do with you. I'd only guessed. But a little birdie confirmed the details."

Eleanor tilted her head. Had she heard Sylvia correctly? Was that little birdie named George?

The hostess backtracked, aware she'd lost her party. "Your table's this way," she said, all smiles.

"I don't think so," Eleanor answered, no longer interested in lunch with Sylvia as she headed toward the exit. Outside, she waited for an Uber to take her home.

George called Carole back. But the call went straight to voicemail. He tried again. This time, he left a message. "Carole, you caught me completely off guard. I didn't know what to say. Why didn't anyone tell me? Why?"

His message was impotent. But he had no idea what else to do.

The next call was to Peter.

He needed to hear Peter's voice. Had this really happened? And why hadn't George been told? He had so many questions, all coming back to Jeanette. He'd thought they had a strong marriage. Had he deluded himself? Had his family life been a sham? If so, what else wasn't real?

George's heart pounded when Peter answered the phone. "Peter, I just spoke to Carole and she told me something I'm struggling to understand."

"Hey, Dad. It's good to hear your voice. What did she say? Something about her personal life? I can't wait to hear. As far as I know, she doesn't have one. She's so uptight."

"She told me about her childhood." George felt a certain irony in the statement. Wasn't it his job to share stories about Carole's childhood? The good times. Things she might not remember.

"Not her sad childhood," Peter said. "She was such a lonely kid. Always hanging around me. Mom tried to encourage her to make friends. Remember when she joined that Brownie Troop? She had to drop out after a few weeks. She wasn't able to connect with the other girls."

George didn't remember. He'd always thought Carole was shy and introspective. But that's true of a lot of bright children.

"This is serious," George said. "She told me you touched her when she was a child." The words were a punch to George's gut. "How could you do that to your sister?"

"Oh, no," Peter said. "She isn't peddling that old story. I never touched her."

George was confused. "Why would she make that up?"

"I don't know what's going on in her head."

George took a moment. Could Peter be telling the truth? Why would Carole lie? George had to know for sure. And there was only one way to find out. He'd have to trick Peter.

"You put your mother through hell. All those years she spent worrying about you. How could you?"

Peter took the bait. "She wasn't worried about me. She was scared of Child Protective Services. She was afraid we'd both be removed from the home if she took me to a therapist and they reported the incident. That was her fear. What would people say? How could she have raised a son like me?"

"Oh, Peter," was all George could muster. The horror of the truth washed over him.

"This is as much your fault as mine. I can't tell you why it happened. All I know is, I didn't have a father. You were never around. I had to figure things out on my own. I'm still trying to figure things out. You were never interested in me."

George gasped. "You can't blame this on me. I won't let you."

"But I do," Peter answered, his voice rising with emotion. "You made me who I am. The good and the bad. If I didn't turn out well, just look in a mirror. It's your doing. I'm the product of your indifference," Peter yelled.

George dropped the call.

Eleanor retreated to her terrace with a glass of cabernet sauvignon. She stared out at the ocean, though none of the magnificent beauty of the Florida coast registered. Not the waves breaking on the shore. Not the blue sky overhead. Not the gulls as they gracefully soared, bobbing and weaving, putting on a show of daring athleticism. She was glum, moody, and confused. Was it true what Sylvia had said? Had George strayed? And what had she done to turn him away? Clearly, he'd told Sylvia about Joel and the boys. There was no other way Sylvia would have known.

Her thoughts shifted. *Why do I befriend women who aren't nice to me?*

She took a sip of wine, allowing the liquid to linger on her tongue. High in tannins, the wine left a bitter taste.

She blamed herself. Sylvia might have pushed, but in the end, Eleanor had been receptive to the friendship. Loneliness had forced her to drop her guard. And though there had been red flags, Eleanor had been willing to go along. She'd even enjoyed herself. Now, the sense of betrayal was potent.

Why would a friend tell me about George's dalliances? It seemed especially mean. *And how would she know?*

Eleanor gasped and clasped a hand over her mouth. Had Sylvia also slept with George? Is that what Sylvia's outburst at lunch was about? Was she jealous? And had that all happened before Eleanor met George? And if so, why hadn't Sylvia told her? Warned her?

I would have never dated him had I known she'd slept with him.

Wait. Eleanor's heart lurched. *Were we intimate with George at the same time?*

Eleanor cringed as she remembered the calls from Sylvia following her dates with George. The digging for details.

It's not fair, Eleanor thought as the wine took hold. *Good men are in such short supply. And why do men get so much better looking with age?* The image of a wild bison grazing on the American plains from a PBS documentary flashed in her mind. *If they're walking and have decent breath, they're a catch,* she mused, remembering that George had very good breath. Almost sweet. And he'd been so tender in bed. So caring. Their first time together, when she pulled the curtains and switched off the lights, he asked if he could turn on the nightlight in the bathroom. He'd whispered, "You're beautiful. I'd like to see you."

By the third glass of wine, Eleanor had calmed down. It all was perfectly clear. Sylvia's outburst was about her inability to keep a man. *Poor thing. She's jealous. With all her guise as a seductress, men just don't like her.*

Eleanor was certain she'd stumbled on the truth.

George wandered the apartment. Miss Betsy trailed after him. He couldn't wrap his head around the events of the day.

He'd spent the morning with Wally, learning more about Willy in a few hours than he'd known in their entire friendship. And now, this thing with Carole and Peter. Why had Jeanette kept it from him? George pressed a palm to his forehead, acutely aware that he was living on the edge of his relationships. Present, but out of touch. Isolated in ignorance.

As the sun dipped toward the horizon, the apartment grew dark. George sat on the sofa, feet up on the coffee table, Miss Betsy asleep at his side. His mind drifted to the key moments of life. A proposal to Jeanette, down on one knee. Her exuberance as she accepted. The birth of Peter and the tremendous fear at being a father. Carole's first birthday when she punched the vanilla frosting on her cake and then pressed the white creamy fist into her mouth, screaming with delight. The business meetings. So many business meetings. A symposium of CEOs in Denver during a winter blizzard. Golf outings on Hilton Head. Twice monthly trips to south Florida to review hospital financials. Board meetings differentiated only by the passing seasons. And the windowless airport conference rooms. It had all once been so important. A reason to be away from the family. Now, empty excuses with no lasting value or meaning to his life.

George stepped onto the balcony to get some fresh air. There was a bright, moon overhead. Jeanette had always loved a full moon. She thought it so romantic. But to George, the moon was only a sad reminder of the night Jeanette was taken off the ventilator. The night she died. Then, the moon had ushered in a frightening loss. The end of George's marriage. A terrifying moment that had left George untethered.

Boca by moonlight, George bitterly thought. *Here we are again. Two frenemies. Staring each other down.*

Life hadn't turned out as George had expected. He'd believed in the allure of retirement. A new beginning with the one he loved. If anything, the moon's appearance was a fateful omen. The end of life as he knew it. No wife. No children. No family. George shuddered with a sudden chill. The last day of September had proved a cold and rude awakening.

– 23 –

GEORGE ROLLED ONTO his side. It was eight thirty in the morning and he was still in bed.

He'd slept ten hours, and instead of being rested, he was exhausted. He'd planned on waking up early to take Miss Betsy for a walk along the beach. The cool, bracing ocean air of an early October morning seemed like a good idea until six a.m. arrived. *It's too dark out,* he reasoned as he turned over and went back to sleep, the fog from the night before blanketing him, dampening his spirit, and turning ever thicker in the morning light.

Miss Betsy let out a low grumble. Barely audible to the untrained ear.

George tensed. *She needs to go out.* He lifted himself up on one elbow and turned to his furry companion. Miss Betsy, lying on the next pillow, eyes wide open, followed his every move. There was a heaviness in his body, as if he'd gained weight in the night. He forced himself to sit up, pressing his face into his palms. It wasn't a hangover, but it felt like one. He rotated his shoulders as he got to his feet.

Miss Betsy lifted her head and yawned.

An interminable sadness, like a fine gauze, encased his being as he headed to the shower.

The hot shower didn't help. He was still half-awake. Numb.

"Meet us for lunch," Herbie insisted when George answered Herbie's phone call.

He'd managed a cup of coffee, but had no appetite. Leaning against the counter required considerable energy. "I must be coming down with something," he said, not sure what the heck was going on.

"Not the flu," Herbie said, concern in his voice.

George had no idea. Every breath was an effort. Every step, an impossible demand. Mentally, he'd slowed to a crawl, unable to think clearly enough to read the morning newspaper. "I don't know what it is," he said, lips barely moving. "Maybe I should go back to bed," he whispered.

"I can't hear you, George. Are you still there?"

"I'm here." George slowly slid down to the kitchen floor, his back resting against a cabinet.

"Are you sure it's not the flu?"

George struggled to keep his eyes open. "I don't feel feverish. This is something different. Low energy. Very low energy." A dust bunny wedged into the corner of two cabinets waved at him, its composition one of simplistic beauty. George wished he was that size. So tiny that no one could see him. "What's the point of all of this?" he said to Herbie, acutely aware of the hopelessness of life.

"Whoa," Herbie answered. "That's not the flu, George."

George struggled to breathe. "I told you, I'm not sick."

"You sound depressed."

George heard the diagnosis but didn't respond.

"What did Wally tell you?"

George bit down hard on his lower lip. His mouth had turned to rubber.

"What did he say, George? Anything about reimbursing us for the funeral?"

"The funeral." George had forgotten for the moment about the funeral. "He's not the executor."

"Then who the hell is?"

George thought it a ridiculous question. "Who cares?" he squeaked. "I can't talk anymore. I've got to walk the dog." He lay flat on the kitchen floor, looking up at the ceiling.

"George, you were the one who agreed to meet Wally. We need to know what he told you. You're coming to breakfast."

"I can't," George answered, certain he couldn't get up, let alone drive a car.

"I'm coming to get you," Herbie insisted.

"It's the oddest thing…" George started, but he ran out of energy.

"Not to worry, George. I'll be there soon."

George struggled to dress. The act of putting on a shirt and pants exhausted him. He washed his face again, but it didn't help. *Christ,* he thought as he looked in the mirror. *Snap out of it.*

When the doorbell rang, he considered ignoring it. Any hope of that was dispelled when the doorbell repeatedly chimed. Miss Betsy ran about, her high-pitched yelp bouncing off the walls. George had never heard her make such loud sounds. George covered his ears, suddenly hypersensitive to noise.

"Okay, okay," he muttered. He opened the door, Miss Betsy leaping at his shins.

Herbie leaned against the doorframe, arms crossed. "That took you long enough." He stared at George's face. "What the hell happened to you?"

George shrugged.

"You look like the walking dead. Or one of those wrinkled shar-pei puppies, but not as cute. Jesus, George. Who stole your bicycle?"

George blinked.

Herbie pushed past him. He looked about the living room. "Have you had coffee this morning?"

"Two cups," George answered.

Herbie leaned down and greeted Miss Betsy. "Hi sweetie, remember Uncle Herbie?"

Much to George's surprise, Miss Betsy licked Herbie's hand.

"Have you been outside yet?" he asked the little poodle.

"No," George said. He leaned against the wall for support.

Herbie snatched Miss Betsy up in one hand and held her close to his chest. "Well, we're going to take care of that right now. George, where's the leash?"

George pointed to the hall table.

Herbie attached Miss Betsy's leash. "George, is this about Angela? You know, Benny and I always thought she was wrong for you."

George arched a brow and sarcastically uttered, "I'd never have guessed."

Herbie eyed George as Miss Betsy squirmed in his arms. "Did Angela break up with you?"

George shook his head.

"Then what is it? Your golf game's better. God knows that was off for a long time."

George rolled his eyes. "My golf game. Really?"

"Well, if it's about Willy and the funeral, don't sweat it. We might as well have lent that money to our kids. I've always said, 'If you lend money to your kid, assume it's a gift. You'll probably never get it back.'"

George slumped against the wall and started to slide downward. Herbie grabbed George's arm and pulled him up and over to the sofa. George let out a wail that shook him to the core as he broke down and started to cry.

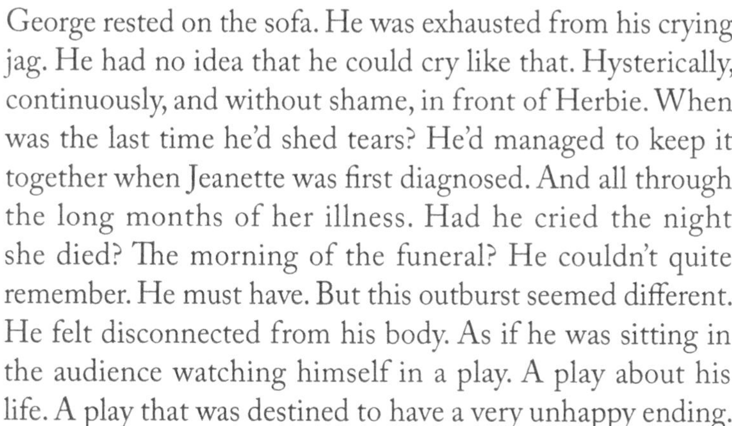

George rested on the sofa. He was exhausted from his crying jag. He had no idea that he could cry like that. Hysterically, continuously, and without shame, in front of Herbie. When was the last time he'd shed tears? He'd managed to keep it together when Jeanette was first diagnosed. And all through the long months of her illness. Had he cried the night she died? The morning of the funeral? He couldn't quite remember. He must have. But this outburst seemed different. He felt disconnected from his body. As if he was sitting in the audience watching himself in a play. A play about his life. A play that was destined to have a very unhappy ending.

When the doorbell rang, Herbie rushed to answer it.

"How is he?" Benny asked.

George covered his ears. He wished Benny would lower his voice. Whisper, if possible.

Benny came into the room and stared at George as if he were a defused bomb. Disarmed, but somehow still threatening. George wondered what Benny must have looked like as a child. How had his parents dealt with Benny's feelings of insecurity over his height? Peter had been a rather frail-looking boy. Small for his age. Perhaps that's why George hadn't taken his issues seriously. Could looks be deceiving? Is that why Peter had crossed the line with his sister? Was he trying to assert himself? Compensate for size? Or had someone touched Peter inappropriately? Where had he learned the behavior? The list of questions was endless. George didn't want to think about it anymore.

But he couldn't stop himself.

Benny knelt down. "Hey buddy. How are you doing?"

George dug deep and mustered the energy to smile. At least, he hoped it was a smile. He remembered that as a boy, Peter had a sweet smile. Innocent. How could his son have done such a terrible thing? Why hadn't they sent him to a therapist? Or did they? George couldn't remember. But Jeanette would've known. She definitely would have managed it all. Did she? Or did they both not see what was happening right in their own home? George was certain he knew the answers to some of the questions. But he was too muddled to truly know.

Benny dwarfed Herbie as they stood nearby, within earshot of George. "I don't understand. How long has he been like this? What's going on?"

Herbie held Miss Betsy close, scratching her head. "I called this morning to ask him to meet us. I wanted to hear about the whole Wally conversation. But he was already in bad shape."

George closed his eyes and relaxed. He felt like dead weight. It was nice to just be. Not to have to speak or explain himself. Or defend his actions. To just sit quietly and listen as Benny and Herbie determined what to do next. For the moment, George was free. Free of worry and doubt. Free to be taken care of.

"Do you think it was something that guy said to set him off?" Benny looked about the apartment as if the clues of George's conversation with Wally might be written on the walls.

"I don't know. We never got that far. George collapsed in tears when I got here. He just cried and cried. I couldn't console him. And now that he's quieted down, he's a freaking train wreck. I've never seen anything like this. I'm worried."

"Maybe he's just having a bad morning."

George released a guttural moan. *Bad morning for a bad father.*

Benny and Herbie eyed him with concern.

George hadn't wanted to admit it, but perhaps Carole was right. He'd never been truly interested in either of his kids. He'd left the parenting to Jeanette. He'd just gone along. She'd always seemed so capable. But maybe, just maybe, Peter was more than even she could manage. He should have been more involved. Why hadn't they taken Peter to a therapist? And what about Carole? Did she have a chance to share her feelings with a professional? Could anything more have been done? Was Peter right? Was Jeanette afraid a therapist would have reported the family to Child Protective Services? Would the kids have been taken away? He wished Jeanette were here. She'd know all the answers. But shouldn't he also know the answers? Or had he blocked such unpleasant memories? He wasn't sure.

Herbie looked askance at Benny. "It's more than a bad morning. He didn't even walk the dog. I did it. And fed her. This is different, Benny. He scared me when I saw him. We should have gone with him yesterday to meet that guy. He's completely…" Herbie lowered his voice as he looked at George on the sofa. "Broken."

Benny leaned in. "Like as in hospitalization?"

"I'm thinking, maybe."

Benny shifted his weight from one foot to the other. "That's major. Are you sure?"

"I'm not sure. That's why I said you better get over here. Our boy is in trouble. We've got to figure something out."

"What makes you think it was what that guy said? It could've been that Angela gal."

Herbie nodded. "Do you think she dumped him? That he's just having a bad reaction? When my fourth wife left, I thought of killing myself."

Benny scrunched up his face. "You didn't."

Herbie nodded. "I know. I appear happy-go-lucky. But I have my demons."

Benny placed a hand on Herbie's shoulder. "It hurts me to think you might have done yourself in. Promise, you'll call me if you ever have those thoughts again."

Herbie looked down, his face beet red.

"Promise me, now," Benny insisted. "We old guys have to look out for each other." He gave Herbie's shoulder a gentle shake.

In unison, both men exhaled.

George mustered his strength to stand up. He'd heard enough. With Herbie and Benny nearby, he knew Miss Betsy would be in good hands. He trudged off to the bedroom. He needed to lie down. He needed to sleep. He needed to escape.

"I thought I heard voices," George said as he wandered into the living room. Benny and Herbie were sitting on the sofa, Miss Betsy tucked between them as they watched ESPN. "How long was I asleep?"

"All morning and some of the afternoon," Herbie said, a concerned look on his face. "We fed and walked Miss Betsy. She's all set. Are you feeling any better?"

George wasn't sure. "Well, I'm awake." He lowered himself into an armchair.

"That's a start," Benny said. "Are you up for telling us what happened?"

George bristled. "I'm not sure I can."

"Because you don't know?" Herbie asked. "Now George, there's no shame in not knowing. That's what psychiatrists are for."

George scowled. "I don't need a psychiatrist."

"Fine," Benny said. "But this morning was not normal, George. Grown men don't fall apart."

George clenched the arm rests of the chair. His eyes filled with tears. "Maybe we should."

"We persevere," Herbie said, his tone dripping with sarcasm. "Why is that?" He directed the question to Benny. "Why do you think we're not supposed to cry? Who made that rule?"

"It's not manly. Unless it's at a sporting event. We can cry when our team wins. We can cry when a famous sports figure dies."

"Right!" Herbie agreed. "What do you think, George?"

Tears trickled down George's cheeks. "I've wasted my life. It's all been a sham."

Herbie nodded. "Of course it has, George. We've all wasted our lives," he said resolutely. "Everyone has."

George stared back. Is what Herbie was saying true? Or was Herbie just humoring him?

"George, life is to be lived and wasted. If you're lucky, you've made some inroads along the way. Done something good for someone. Probably a stranger you'd never realized was even touched by a kindness. But most of us, well, we're just working our way through. Hoping to make it in one piece. Until we don't. And that's life, George. Your only job is to live it. Try to enjoy all the good things that come your way. Like your friendships."

"I don't know." George shook his head. "My children don't want anything to do with me. They're so angry. It's all such a complete mess."

"That sounds about right," Benny said.

George couldn't believe his ears. "What?"

"George, I gave up on my kids long ago. I'm glad they're healthy and well. But they have their own lives. If they want me, they know where I am. The one thing they may not know is that I won't be here forever. So in a way, this is good practice for them. I like that they're independent. That suits me fine."

"But don't you feel guilty?" George wiped a tear away with the back of his hand.

"Why should I?" Benny answered, chest extended. "I did my job. I got them to the starting gate of adulthood. The rest is on them. And my poor daughter lost a child. I can love her. Be there for her. But I can't take that pain away. I truly wish I could. But that would be impossible."

"But I was a lousy parent," George said. "I realize it now. Looking back, I was…disinterested. I don't think I even liked them."

"Did you ever beat them?" Herbie asked. "Did they ever go hungry?"

George shook his head.

"Did they live through their teen years?" Benny asked. "You know, the death rate among teen drivers is why the actuary tables show a declining longevity in life expectancy. That, and opioids."

"You have nothing to feel ashamed about," Herbie said. "Unless, of course, you like feeling as if everything is your fault."

George bit his lip. "But there's more," he said, struggling to find the words. "My son…he abused my daughter when they were children. And I didn't know."

Benny and Herbie froze. George felt a fresh rush of tears as the silence settled in.

Herbie was the first to speak. "I'm sorry to hear that, George."

"Me too," Benny added.

"Maybe it's a good time to speak to a professional," Herbie advised.

George rested his face in his hands. "I don't know."

"I do." Benny withdrew a phone from his pocket. "You can go to the guy I'm seeing. He's amazing. Very insightful."

Herbie nodded. "And if that guy doesn't do the trick, I have another name."

George looked up. "You both see therapists? How come I didn't know that?"

Benny smiled. "You'd have to ask to find out."

George nodded. "You two are good friends."

"I hope so." Herbie said. "We may not have a lot, but we do have each other. And you know what they say. The best way to feel better is to help someone else."

George rubbed his eyes. *Help someone else?* "I've got an idea. Let's go for a drive. Get out of here."

Herbie touched his stomach. "I'm hungry. Do you know, George, there's nothing to eat in your kitchen? Not even a freaking cookie. Or ice cream. What the heck is wrong with you?"

"We went through the cabinets," Benny added. "Sad. Very sad."

George smiled. "Even the mouse ran from my house."

"No kidding," Herbie said. "I say we order pizza."

"No, no, no," George insisted. "Let's go out."

"Are you sure you're up to it?" Herbie asked, wide-eyed. "We don't want to push it."

George stretched his arms overhead. "There's something important I have to do."

Herbie checked his watch. "At three thirty in the afternoon? Is it a woman?"

George pressed his palms together. "Not a woman. I need to go to the hospital."

"I knew it," Herbie said to Benny. "He's still not feeling well."

Benny offered a serious expression. "Do you want us to admit you, George?"

George sighed.

Benny and Herbie exchanged nervous glances. "George, whatever you need, we're here for you."

George nodded. "Then let's get a move on."

The third-floor hallway of St. Mary's Medical Center in West Palm Beach echoed with the footsteps of the three friends. George held up a hand as they stopped to huddle. "Now promise. No acting crazy. This is important."

Benny and Herbie signaled their agreement.

A few more steps, and George was at the door. He gently knocked before pushing the door open. The room was dark. The blinds drawn. George held an index finger to his lips and signaled for the other two to wait as he entered.

The figure in the bed slowly moved. "Who is it?" he asked as he reached for the side table.

George spotted the eyeglasses. He picked them up and placed them in the outstretched hand.

"Thank you," the man said as he struggled to sit up.

"How are you doing?" George asked. He adjusted the blinds allowing for some light into the room.

"Surviving," came the answer as the man's eyes focused on George's face. "What are you doing here?"

"I remembered which hospital you were at and thought you might be alone. It occurred to me that there are some people you might enjoy meeting."

"Oh, I don't think so." The man waved a hand. "I'm not up to it. I can't."

"Well, we won't stay long. I just wanted us to all get together. Actually, you've met them before."

The man's eyes widened. "Oh no, not them."

"I promise you. You're in no danger from us." George stepped to the door. "Come on in, fellas," he motioned. "You remember Willy's brother, Wally?"

Herbie smiled. Benny extended a hand. "Nice to see you again."

Wally nodded cautiously as he took Benny's hand. "You have me at a disadvantage. I really can't get up and leave. Cancer, you know."

"They know," George said. "I filled them in."

"Oh," Wally squeaked. "Then you've come to get that check."

"Check?" George repeated.

"You still think I'm the executor of the estate."

George smiled. "Nothing of the sort. We've forgotten about that."

Herbie started to disagree.

George stared him down, then turned back to Wally. "We know you're all alone here. So we thought, in respect to our friend Willy, maybe, we can help out. Come visit. Check up on you and make sure you're okay."

Wally licked his lips. "That's very nice of you," he said. "But I'm not Willy."

"Oh, we know." George poured a glass of water and passed it to Wally, who took a sip.

"So why would you want to do this? I'm a stranger. I didn't have a relationship with my brother. And, if you don't mind me saying, we don't exactly bat for the same team."

Benny perked up. "You don't like the Marlins?"

Herbie laughed. "I don't think Wally was referring to baseball."

George smiled. "We don't care about that, do we fellas?"

Benny seemed to realize what Wally meant. "No, you can be gay. That has nothing to do with us."

"You're a stranger here and we want to help," George said.

"Well, I appreciate that," Wally said. "But I'm not exactly alone."

"You have a lover?" Benny asked.

Herbie winced. "Benny, I don't think they use that term anymore."

"Actually," Wally disagreed, "some do. But others prefer partner. We're not all married."

Benny smiled. "Neither are we."

George rolled his eyes at the double entendre. "Well, that's fine. We just want you to know whatever you need, we're here. And when you leave, you'll stay with one of us. We'll do our best to look out for you."

Wally held a hand to his chest. "Really, there's no need, but I'm touched. I had no idea my brother had three such wonderful friends. I don't know what to say."

"There's nothing to say," Benny said. "That's what friends are for."

"Right," Herbie said as there was a knock on the door.

Another man stepped into the room. "Gentlemen," the young man said, a small teddy bear in his hand.

"Simon!" Wally called out. "Come over here and give your uncle a hug."

George lifted the coffee mug to his lips. The hospital cafeteria was empty except for two staff members in blue scrubs taking a break. George made a sour face. "Whoa. This coffee has quite a bite."

Benny picked at a piece of lemon meringue pie. "I think we should take this slice directly to the emergency room so they can revive it."

"I told you not to take that," Herbie said. "I could see the moisture gathering under the plastic wrap."

"Well, this isn't bad." Simon ripped open a tiny packet of saltines and crushed them over a bowl of chili con carne. "I don't know what you three are complaining about."

"I guess we're used to better food," George admitted.

"Sure," Simon agreed. "But it's food. Do you know how many Americans are going to bed hungry tonight?"

"Oh, God," Herbie muttered. "I forgot. We're dining with the Dalai Lama from Harvard."

Simon laughed. "Make fun. But the world is a mess and someone has to step up and do something. And since your generation has clearly blown it—"

"Your generation now gets its chance to screw it all up too," Benny interrupted.

Simon slipped a spoon into his bowl of chili. "There's all that negative energy," he said as he mixed the chili. "Maybe with a bit of positivity, we can fix the problems your generation has ignored."

George leaned back in the chair. "God Simon, I hope so. I really do."

Simon pushed the chili aside after taking a taste. "It won't be easy."

"What's wrong?" Herbie asked. "Not what you expected?"

Simon sighed. "Too spicy."

George nodded. "What did I tell you? If you want a good meal, you don't go to a hospital cafeteria."

Simon wiped his mouth with a napkin. "I'll try to keep that in mind."

"So what are your plans?" Benny asked.

"About Uncle Wally?" Simon shrugged. "I don't know yet. I guess I'm going to take it a day at a time."

"Sounds smart," George answered.

"I don't see what other choice there is," Simon said matter-of-factly. "I'm not going to walk away like my dad did. So I guess it's my time to step up."

"Not where you're living," George pointed out. "You can't bring him back to that awful motel."

"I wouldn't do that. I've made arrangements. I just signed a lease last week. A place in Boca."

"I don't mean to be rude," Herbie said, "but you need a down payment to sign a lease. And the last time we checked, you didn't have a pot to piss in."

Simon straightened up. "That's all changed."

"What do you mean?" George asked.

"I guess Uncle Wally didn't tell you," Simon announced, "but I'm now the executor of Dad's estate."

George was shocked. "What?"

Simon nodded. "Uncle Wally was originally designated. I guess that was Dad's way of assuaging his guilt. But since being diagnosed with cancer, Uncle Wally's turned the whole mess over to me."

Benny leaned forward. "So you wound up inheriting Willy's money after all."

"Not directly," Simon said, blushing. "But I have lots of plans for it. Uncle Wally has given me carte blanche. Dad had a foundation. Maybe you three could help me administer it. I'd need a board of directors."

Herbie was at once gleeful. "Terrific! I motion that the first order of business is you write each of us a reimbursement check for the cost of your dad's funeral."

Simon smiled. "You three will get reimbursed as soon as I have a checkbook for the estate in hand. That should take a week or so."

George checked his watch. It was nearly five thirty p.m. "I have to get a move on," he said. "Eleanor is expecting me at seven for dinner. And I have to take care of Miss Betsy."

"Maybe, you should call and cancel," Herbie suggested. "You've had a rough day."

"Oh no. She's not big on that. I stood her up yesterday. She went off on me. She'd never forgive me. You guys stay. I'll Uber."

"George, I thought you'd never get here!" Eleanor rushed back to the kitchen after letting George in. "I've got a pork tenderloin in the oven. I don't want it to dry out."

"I thought you didn't cook," George said as he followed her. The savory aroma of pork stirred his appetite.

Eleanor peeked in the oven before turning to offer George a quizzical look. "I don't. I carried it in from Farm to Fork. The food is always wonderful."

George spotted the open bottle of merlot on the counter. Eleanor's glass, a quarter full, was nearby. "You started without me." He lifted Eleanor's glass and took a sip.

Eleanor took her glass back. "Hey," she said in a teasing voice. "Get your own."

George spotted a wine glass next to the place setting on the counter. "I love eating in the kitchen," he said as he poured a glass of wine. "So relaxed and casual."

Eleanor pulled the pan from the oven. "Perfectly reheated." She rolled a shoulder and lowered the pan, allowing George a peek at the meal. "Cider-brined pork tenderloin with roasted butternut squash and sautéed Swiss chard. Oh, and—" Eleanor pointed to a bowl on the counter. "Cranberry compote."

George settled on a stool at the counter as Eleanor dished the meal onto matching plates.

"George, I don't mean to be one of those women who pries," Eleanor said as she placed a plate before him. "But I'd like to know where you were yesterday at lunchtime. I texted and called, and you didn't call me back. I know we're just casual friends..."

"Is that what we are?" George asked as Eleanor came around the counter and sat next to him.

"It's strange at our age to call it…dating. It sounds so juvenile. So teenage years."

George smiled.

"But we're seeing each other and I'm wondering..." She gently rolled the wine about in the glass and stared straight ahead. "Where do you think this is headed?"

George raised an eyebrow. "I don't want to get married," he confessed, "if that's what you're asking."

Eleanor seemed surprised. "You don't? But do you always want to live alone?"

George pushed the chard with his fork. "I don't like living alone. I'd like to have a partner. But lately, I've had some problems, and to be honest, I need to work them out before I make any changes in my life."

"Oh," Eleanor whispered. "That sounds serious."

George put his fork down and rubbed his palms together. "It is serious," he said as they locked eyes. "You see, my life hasn't exactly worked out the way I imagined."

Eleanor tilted her head. "Well George, whose has?"

"My children. . ." he started, and then changed his mind. He didn't want to go into the details.

"Your children..." she prompted.

A sadness settled in. George didn't like the feeling. "I can't really speak about it. I'm sorry."

Eleanor placed a comforting hand on his knee. "George, how old are they?"

"What does that matter?"

"They're adults." Eleanor removed her hand.

"Certainly."

"Then why, for heaven's sake, are you making plans based on them? They have their own lives."

"Of course they do," George said, his heart beginning to pound. "But right now, we're not talking."

"Is that all?" Eleanor moaned. "We could fill the Whole Foods on Glades Road with all the parents in Boca Raton who aren't talking to their adult children."

"Yes, but my adult children aren't talking to me. That's different."

Eleanor laughed. A strange, bitter laugh. "Sounds like a blessing."

"Oh, come on," George answered. "That's ridiculous."

"It certainly isn't," Eleanor insisted. "Clearly your children are manipulative, mean-spirited, and difficult people."

George furrowed his brow. "Why would you say that? I haven't even told you what happened between us. Why jump to that conclusion?"

"Oh George." Eleanor lifted her head in a superior manner. "Don't you think I know this story? I have two boys who don't talk to me. I know all about these things."

"And how many years has it been since you've seen them?"

Eleanor took a breath. "Long enough to know I'm better off without them."

George wondered if Eleanor was serious. "That's quite a statement coming from a mother."

"I'm not a mother," Eleanor snapped. "I was. But not anymore. They're adults. They don't need a mother."

"You're very independent," George said with a sadness in his voice.

"You're damn right," Eleanor answered, head held high. "I put in my time. Now, it's my turn."

"You talk as if they held you back from living."

Eleanor took another sip of wine. "George, you're not going to make me feel guilty. I'm not going there."

George's ears perked up. That's exactly what he felt when he thought about Carole and Peter. Guilty. Isn't that the feeling he wanted to run away from?

"I deserve to live my life," Eleanor insisted as she swiveled to face George. "I don't need you coming along and telling me I'm a bad person."

The conversation was familiar. Except now, Eleanor had taken on George's role: she was saying the same words he'd said when Wally had described Willy's failed relationship with Simon. In a split moment, George saw it all clearly. "Eleanor, we weren't talking about you. We were talking about me."

Eleanor pulled back. "Of course we were. Can I get you more merlot?" She refilled his glass without waiting for an answer.

They sat in silence as George poked at the meal. He'd lost his appetite.

Eleanor looked away. "I'm sorry if I upset you, George."

"Me too," George answered. "I think I'm going to call that therapist. The guy Benny recommended."

Eleanor faced George. "Oh, George. You don't need a therapist."

"Yes, I do. Someone to talk this through with. Help me sort it out."

Eleanor scoffed. "That's the problem today. No one has any guts. You've a problem, you run off to a therapist. Like that's going to solve anything. It's not going to bring my boys back. They'll never forgive me for having that affair. I always thought that one day, after they married, they'd understand. Joel ignored me. And he fooled around with so many women. There were too many to count. And I put up with all of that, until I didn't. So I had one lousy affair." Eleanor held a finger in the air. "Just one. And Joel had to die. Like I caused his heart attack. And now, I'm persona non grata."

"That's some story," George said. "Joel is dead. Your boys are angry. And you've made yourself the victim."

Eleanor's chest heaved. "The victim! I'm no one's victim."

"But you're the victim in that story," George offered.

Eleanor stared at George. There was a coldness in her eyes. "A victim doesn't leave clues of an affair for her husband to find."

George squinted as if he were in a darkened room and someone had turned on the lights. This was a side of Eleanor he hadn't seen and wasn't sure he liked. "What are you talking about?"

"I decided it was Joel's turn to experience the same pain he'd put me through. So I made sure my infidelity was discovered. Oh, it wasn't hard to do. Not that Joel was paying much attention at that point in our marriage. But I got his attention. Bad heart and all."

"So you knew he had a bad heart."

"Of course, I knew." Eleanor smiled. "And I didn't bother about his follow-up doctor appointments or medications. And when the doctor told him to change his diet, cut out salt, eat low fat, well, I didn't do anything about it," she said proudly. "That was Joel's responsibility. Not mine."

"Because you don't cook."

"That's right. Let him prepare a meal," she said, a thumb pressed to her chest. "I raised those two boys. I did everything in that house. I was damned if I was going to start preparing meals for him. That was his problem."

George was horrified. "I don't think I know you," he said as he rose. "And I don't think I want to."

The next morning, George awoke with a new determination. After a long walk with Miss Betsy, he scheduled an appointment with the therapist Benny had recommended. And though he wasn't exactly sure how therapy worked, he had a sneaking suspicion that if it helped Benny and Herbie, it just might be a good thing for him.

George cringed at the first appointment when the therapist asked what he hoped to get out of their sessions together. He wasn't quite sure how to answer. *I need to find a way forward. To make better choices. To find out who I am and build better relationships.*

The therapist smiled when George voiced these thoughts. George guessed it might have been a good answer.

As the weeks unfolded, George felt a growing sense of clarity. He called his broker. The time had come to clean up the debt from Jeanette's medical bills. He'd held on far too long as a way of staying connected to Jeanette. He'd been blocked.

But no more. He was ready to move on. To release the anger, the frustration, and mostly the worry about his tax situation. George was determined to get his life in order. To wipe the slate clean and step into the future. By the time the youngest tenants in his building emerged in their Halloween costumes, all debts had been paid off and George was free and clear.

At least, financially.

The brisk San Francisco breeze caught George by surprise as he walked north on Powell before turning east on Sutter. He pulled his collar up and shivered. Was he doing the right thing? He wasn't sure as he crossed the street, passing Starbucks, carefully sidestepping the broken pavement that lay before him like a booby trap.

George had decided on the spur of the moment to go. When he'd told Benny and Herbie, they wished him a safe and productive journey.

"George, if that's what it takes, you should definitely do it," Herbie said.

George had been grateful for the encouragement. And glad Herbie had agreed to take care of Miss Betsy.

"And what will you do about Peter?" Benny asked.

George didn't exactly know. Was it up to him to forgive Peter? "He's still my son," George answered, unsure if that was what Benny was asking. "I guess that's a matter I should continue to discuss with my therapist. But for now, I need to go to San Francisco. One step at a time."

"I'm proud of you," Herbie added. "It's very brave."

George didn't feel particularly brave. He'd no idea how things might turn out. Whether he'd make an ass of himself, returning home having gained nothing. But as Benny put it, "Life is a gamble, George. You never know which card to play, which is why I like roulette. You can bet red, black, odd, and even. And sometimes even green. There are lots of ways to get a win."

George thought Benny's observation profound. Lots of choices. He liked that analogy. It made him feel hopeful. Deep down, he sensed Jeanette would be cheering.

He spotted the gallery sign up ahead on the right. Caldwell Snyder. He hoped it wasn't too late. That he hadn't allowed the rift to go on so long that it was irreparable. But mostly, he hoped she'd be willing to forgive him.

Standing in front of the gallery's display window, he gathered his courage. There was an exhibition of Paul Balmer's work, which played on the themes of abstraction and realism. *So appropriate*, George thought as he admired the unique cityscapes with their varying color, light, and perspective. He silently prayed: *Please God, give me this chance to make right what I can. I know nothing will immediately change. I'm realistic. I know there is hard work ahead, but if you'd help me today, I'd be grateful.*

A bell rang when George entered. A man sitting at a desk near the back of the gallery looked up. "Welcome," he called out.

George's heart sank. He'd anticipated seeing Carole. Now he felt like a fool. Had she gone out of town? Was she at the Sausalito gallery? George turned to look at the nearest Balmer painting hanging on the wall, but he couldn't truly see it. He was lost in his failure. Failure to support his daughter. Failure to be the father he should've been. Failure to understand that the world was not set up for his exclusive purview.

And then Carole appeared through a rear doorway. He caught sight of her peripherally and turned to face her.

She stopped when she spotted George. For a moment, they stared: two strangers suddenly recognizing one another.

George held his breath. Would she forgive him? Could he forgive himself? His lips trembled with emotion as Carole approached.

He opened his arms and welcomed his daughter in for a hug.

"Hello, Daddy," she said as she embraced him. "I've missed you."

If you enjoyed reading *Boca by Moonlight:*

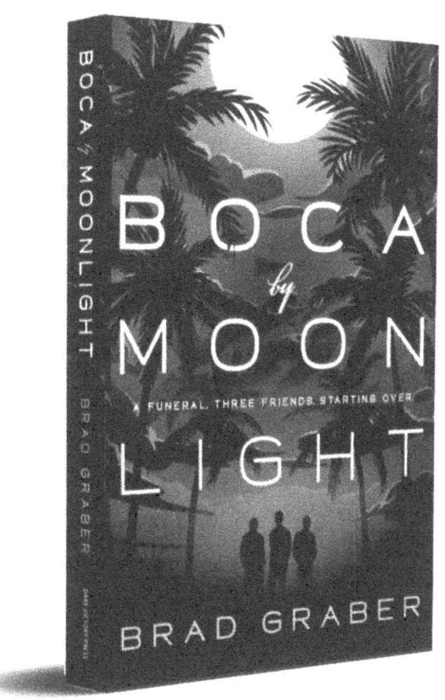

1. Please rate the novel on Amazon and Goodreads.
2. Join Brad Graber's email list at www.bradgraber.com and sign-up for his humor blog: ***There, I Said It!***
3. Recommend the book to your local book club.
4. Invite Brad to be a speaker at your next community event.
5. Send Brad a note at brad@bradgraber.com – he loves to hear from fans.

CHECK OUT BRAD'S OTHER PUBLICATIONS AVAILABLE THROUGH AMAZON, AND ALL FINE RETAILERS IN PAPERBACK, EBOOK, AND AUDIOBOOK FORMATS.

If a stranger knocked on your door, would you welcome them in?

When Dave and Charlie relocate to Phoenix, Daisy shows up at their door after a long illness unaware relatives have sold her home. Charlie assumes the older woman is Dave's aunt from Chicago and happily ushers her into a guest room. **Tales of the City** meets **As Good As It Gets** in this heartwarming page-turner about love, friendship, and the family we choose.

Humorous Observations
on Modern Life!

Ever wonder why a fly is circling the deli? What you can learn from your dog about aging? If Mahjong is the true game of champions? Wonder no more. If you're a fan of the Chicken Soup series, love Erma Bombeck, David Sedaris, and Larry David, you'll enjoy these seventy essays on life, love, and the pursuit of dairy products that don't spoil.